D1759289

HIERARCHIES OF BELONGING

Hierarchies of Belonging

National Identity and Political Culture in Scotland and Quebec

AILSA HENDERSON

McGill-Queen's University Press
Montreal & Kingston • London • Ithaca

ISBN 978-0-7735-3268-7

Legal deposit fourth quarter 2007
Bibliothèque nationale du Québec

Printed in Canada on acid-free paper that is 100% ancient forest free (100% post-consumjer recycled), processed chlorine free

This book has been published with the help of a grant from the Canadian Federation for the Humanities and Social Sciences, through the Aid to Scholarly Publications Programme, using funds provided by the Social Sciences and Humanities Research Council of Canada.

McGill-Queen's University Press acknowledges the support of the Canada Council for the Arts for our publishing program. We also acknowledge the financial support of the Government of Canada through the Book Publishing Industry Development Program (BPIDP) for our publishing activities.

Library and Archives Canada Cataloguing in Publication

Henderson, Ailsa
Hierarchies of belonging : national identity and political culture in Scotland and Quebec / Ailsa Henderson.

Includes bibliographical references and index.
ISBN 978-0-7735-3268-7

1. Nationalism – Québec (Province). 2. Nationalism – Scotland. 3. Political culture – Québec (Province). 4. Political culture – Scotland. 5. Group identity – Québec (Province). 6. Group identity – Scotland. I. Title.

JC311.H387 2007 306.209714 C2007-902380-0

Typeset by Jay Tee Graphics Ltd. in 10.5/13 Sabon

To Barbara Summers Buchan and Annie Bella Henderson,
who both loved to talk about politics

Contents

Tables and Figures

TABLES

FIGURES

Acknowledgments

This book began its life as a PhD dissertation completed while I was a student in the Department of Politics at the University of Edinburgh, and it has benefited tremendously from comments and suggestions provided by supervisors and examiners Alice Brown, Michael Keating, Ged Martin, David McCrone, and Lindsay Paterson. In subsequent trips back to update research, I received continued institutional support and professional advice from colleagues in the Department of Politics, in particular, Fiona Mackay, Andy Thompson, Richard Freeman, Wilfried Sweden, and Annika Bergman, and the Centre of Canadian Studies, its directors Colin Coates and Annis May Timpson, and former administrative assistant Grace Owens. At McGill-Queen's University Press I am indebted to Jonathan Crago, who guided the book from submission to publication, and Elizabeth Hulse, whose editorial suggestions have certainly improved the text.

The intellectual motivations for this work have their roots in the education I received in the Département de science politique at the Université d'Ottawa. I am particularly grateful to François-Pierre Gingras, Serge Denis, and John Trent, who were very patient with the anglophone in their classes doing considerable violence to French grammar, and who unwittingly steered me towards graduate study in political science. During my fieldwork many individuals took time out of busy schedules to meet with me, and their collective insights have greatly influenced this work. In Quebec they include Michael Behiels, David Birnbaum, Lise Bissonnette, André Blais, Pierre Bossett, Geoffrey Chambers, Gretta Chambers, Elisabeth Gidengil, Philippe Gigantes, Keith Henderson, Jack Jedwab,

Jane Jenson, William Johnson, Emmanuel Kattan, Guy Lachapelle, Guy Laforest, Len Macdonald, Andrew Male, Patrice Martin, Matthew Mendelsohn, Val Meredith, Henry Milner, Desmond Morton, Jon Pammett, and Jeffrey Simpson. In Scotland they include Malcolm Chisholm, Anthony Cohen, John Curtice, Margaret Ewing, Henry McLeish, Neil MacCormick, Jan Penrose, Yasir Suleiman, David Tattersoll, Murray Tosh, Gary West, and Iain Whyte. Much of the analysis would not have been possible without opinion data made available by the Canadian Election Study, the British Election Study, and the Scottish Parliamentary Election Study. Additional data were provided by the Economic and Social Research Council, the University of Edinburgh data library, the Queen's University Canadian Opinion Research Archive, Senator Joan Fraser, formerly of the Council for Canadian Unity, Chris Baker at Environics, and Patrick Beauchamp at Ekos. Funding for fieldwork and the opportunity to present conference papers was made available by the Centre of Canadian Studies at the University of Edinburgh, the British Association of Canadian Studies, the Canadian High Commission in London, and the Délégation générale du Québec à Londres.

The transformation of this work from PhD dissertation to book was completed while I held a post-doctoral fellowship in the Department of Political Science at the University of Toronto. I am grateful to SSHRCC and to the department for supplying institutional support and in particular to Neil Nevitte and Graham White, both of whom have provided invaluable encouragement and guidance. The Centre of Canadian Studies at the University of Ottawa and the Intergovernmental Affairs division within the Privy Council kindly gave me the opportunity to present more recent versions of the book's main arguments. Thanks also to my colleagues in the Department of Political Science at Wilfrid Laurier University, who provided a lighthearted and enjoyable environment in which to work.

Away from academic life, many friends in Edinburgh and Toronto have supplied a lively source of distraction. These included Andrew Bennett, Colin Buckie, Anita Haidar, Jason Read, Stephen Roberts, and, in Canada, Chrissy Laing, Shannon McCarthy, Paul and Kimberly Berry, Jamie Doherty, Nick Valetino, Stan Kaethler, Matt Snyder, Jack Hicks, and Jodi Lewchuk. To those hybrid individuals who are both academics and friends, I am grateful for support and helpful comments at both the earlier and later stages of this work.

My frequent running partner Nicola McEwen, who has kindly provided a welcoming home and office while I completed fieldwork, attended conferences, and drafted revisions, has been a constant sounding board for ideas. My transition to Canadian academic life was made far easier than it might have been by Karen Murray, Gerald Kernerman, and John Erk, who were each forced to share an office with me while I revised the manuscript. Thanks also to Melanie Wall, who has supplied years of honest criticism. Each in an inimitable way has helped to improve the book.

A special thank-you to my family: to my Aunt Chris and Uncle Ernie for providing a warm and caring home away from home during the years I lived in Scotland, to my sister Kirsty for her continued friendship, to my supportive parents, whose transatlantic migration initially sparked my interest in identity and belonging, and to Stephen Tierney, my careful critic and strongest advocate, who watched his flat become a marital home inhabited by endless piles of paper with an easy smile, unending patience, and enthusiastic support.

HIERARCHIES OF BELONGING

Introduction

Why do some people feel they belong to a nation and others do not? Under what conditions does nationalism affect people's political attitudes? These questions preoccupy those who try to understand developments in the Balkans, Cyprus, or Northern Ireland. Understanding nationalism, its good and bad sides, can be a first step to understanding sources of conflict. But these questions also affect us closer to home. What does it mean to be a Quebecer? Who can be considered a Canadian? Understanding national identity is part of comprehending belonging, how we feel about ourselves, our neighbours, our nation, our state.

This book contributes to our understanding of national identity and its impact on our political attitudes. It examines three puzzles. First, why is nationalism portrayed in Quebec as ethnic and in Scotland as civic? Second, why, if national identity is so important, does it seem to have so little impact on political attitudes when we measure those attitudes quantitatively? And third, why, in the absence of evidence, are people so convinced that a difference in political attitudes exists? The exploration of these three questions draws us into the building blocks of national identity in Scotland and Quebec, the negotiation of belonging in the nation, and the development of political attitudes. The investigation shows that Scotland and Quebec are more similar than not, but that in each case national identity plays a different role in political debate.

Within two years, electorates in Quebec and Scotland both found themselves voting in referendums that would determine their future levels of self-determination. In Quebec the October 1995 referendum offered the second chance since 1980 to renegotiate the political partnership with the rest of Canada, with the option of full sovereignty should negotiations prove fruitless. The close result, 50.6 to 49.4 per cent for the federalist side, directly reflected a campaign that promised no clear winner and the extent to which the issue of sovereignty divided the population. For Scots, the September 1997 referendum on a devolved parliament provided an opportunity to alter fundamentally the unitary character of the British state and to deliver a much-sought-after measure of autonomy. Scots were asked two questions in the referendum, one on the existence of the parliament and a second on its tax-varying powers. Both questions passed, with 74 per cent support on the first question and 64 per cent on the second, and a tax-varying parliament opened its doors in May 1999. The referendums in Scotland and Quebec were similar, in that they provided a democratic way to achieve greater degrees of self-determination, but they provided differing levels of autonomy, had different levels of turnout, and produced different margins of victory.

Comparisons between Scotland and Quebec became increasingly plentiful when it appeared that, following an expected Labour win in the May 1997 general election, Scotland would acquire its own legislature for the first time in three hundred years (Keating 1996a, 1997; Bateman 1996).[1] Research has explored the impact of nationalism on support for social welfare (McEwen 2006), the normative approaches to national recognition (Tierney 2004), and the nature of the comparison itself (Coates and Henderson 2006). For politicians on either side, each case had its own lessons of success and failure for the other nation. For Scottish nationalists, the electoral strength of the Parti Québécois provided evidence that nationalist parties can govern prudently while at the same time calling for greater autonomy in key areas of jurisdiction. For nationalists in Quebec, radical constitutional change in Scotland offered a striking example of movement noticeably absent in the Canadian arena. For federalists in Canada, devolution in the United Kingdom provided proof of the desirability of federalism and thus the Canadian status quo. For devo-skeptics in the UK, the constitutional mess in Canada was an example of a nation holding a state hostage, spurred on by occasional concessions of greater autonomy. But can all of these conclusions be correct? How well can we really compare Scotland and Quebec? These two nations cannot be all things to all people. Understanding the two cases lies in the recognition of three important points of comparison.

First, Scotland and Quebec do not exist in similar constitutional space. Quebec is a sovereign province in a federal political system. The Scottish Parliament legislates in similar areas of jurisdiction, but sovereignty is formally retained by Westminster and the UK remains a semi-unitary state. In terms of constitutional power, Scotland has more in common with devolution to the Canadian territory Nunavut than with Quebec. Historically, however, the two have followed similar constitutional paths of recognition and accommodation. Canadians know that the Quebec Act in 1774 protected the Catholic Church, the French language, the legal system, and the seigneurial system of land tenure. These institutions thus maintained what would become a Québécois identity. Almost seventy years earlier Scots retained a measure of institutional completeness, to use Breton's phrase, when they negotiated their entry into the United Kingdom in 1707. Faced with the promise of economic prosperity and the implied threat of military invasion, Scottish elites ensured that Scotland would retain a separate Presbyterian church, a separate education system, and a separate legal system. The resulting holy trinity of institutions sustained a sense of Scottish separateness. Broadly speaking, the role of these institutions in Scottish national identity was similar to that of those in Québécois national identity.

Second, much of the appeal in comparing Scotland and Quebec is convenient timing. For the most part, these are democratic, nonviolent nationalist movements in which political parties seek greater autonomy through elections and public referendums. The rise in the 1970s of the separatist Parti Québécois (PQ) mirrors the rise of the Scottish National Party (SNP). The PQ came to power in Quebec in 1976. The SNP attained its greatest ever showing in a British election with 11 seats in 1974. The 1979 referendum in Scotland and the 1980 referendum in Quebec, both unsuccessful, demonstrate that nationalism in Scotland and Quebec has opted for a constitutional path to greater autonomy and has accepted the benefits and setbacks of such an approach. Despite this convenient timing, Scotland and Quebec occupy different stages in their political paths. Thus while it is accurate to draw attention to the similar vibrancy of nationalist movements, autonomist parties, and civic society in Scotland and Quebec, it is an important distinction that Quebec has had its own legislature elected by near-universal suffrage since 1867. Although a cursory examination of the two cases at present would suggest that they possess remarkably similar political settlements, the acquisition of a parliament in Scotland and the process by which it was achieved continues to exert a profound influence on its political culture.

Third, comparisons of nationalism in Scotland and Quebec often pit the two as opposites. Most works focus on the different visions of inclusiveness. If we can distinguish between inclusive and exclusive nationalism, or civic and ethnic nationalism, then Scotland is often seen as civic and Quebec as ethnic. Neither label is entirely accurate. The emphasis on language, on the existence of *pure laine*, or *Québécois de vieille souche*, is taken as evidence that Québécois nationalism is more concerned with the past and thus with ethnic markers of belonging. Arguments that Scotland exhibits the traits of civic nationalism are driven not by the evidence of civic markers but by the absence of ethnic markers such as language or religion. This book takes issue with this definition, arguing that both nations employ ethnic and civic markers in different contexts, and that inclusiveness must be viewed as part of a separate debate. An additional comparison of nationalism acknowledges that each enjoys different recognition as a nation. In Great Britain, Scotland is recognized as a historic nation, along with England and Wales. This is not a new development but viewed without controversy as one of the salient facts of British political life. No one, not even advocates of the unitary character of the UK, would claim that Scotland is not a nation. This is not the case in Canada, where Quebec's status as a distinct society, let alone a nation, is contested by those on opposite sides of the sovereignty debate, even after formal recognition in a 2006 federal motion. Thus even though both received similar institutional protection in the eighteenth century, in one case this is seen as a reflection of nationhood, while in the other nationhood is contested.

THEORETICAL FRAMEWORK

In its examination of Scotland and Quebec, this book analyzes the intersection of two concepts, national identity and political culture, both of which have varied definitions in the social sciences. Examinations of nationalism might focus on the origins of nations, whether they are primordial entities exerting a powerful and long-lasting hold over generations, or whether they are modern creations that serve a specific purpose. Nations and nationalism can be seen as old or new, liberal or conservative, cultural or political.[2] For our purposes, however, there are two relevant debates:

1 the nation as a list of characteristics versus the nation as a shared sociological entity;
2 national identity as a label or tag versus national identity as a process of attachment or belonging.

Theoretical definitions of the nation coalesce around two preferred options, both of which are important when studying Scotland and Quebec. According to the first, the nation is defined as a list of characteristics. Thus a nation exists when a group of people is united by a common language, common territory, common history, and common institutions (Geertz 1963). France is a nation because it has recognized borders, a shared language, a shared history, and a common population. The advantage of such a view is that it deals with various objective facts, making it possible to prove definitively whether a nation exists or not. This is no small feat since proving the existence of a nation is useful from a number of perspectives. Comprehensive Aboriginal land claims, for example, would benefit from proving that a nation with a distinct language, culture, and population occupied a particular territory. This definition ignores, however, that nations might not be homogeneous entities, but might instead have a centre and a periphery. It also pays more attention to whether a nation exists than how it operates.

A second school argues that nations exist as social communities that are willed into existence by their members. Whether created through a "daily plebiscite" or constructed as an "imagined community" (Anderson 1991), the perception of a bond between national members creates the nation. Thus a nation exists if it is perceived to exist by its members. Both of these elements are important when studying Scotland and Quebec. When we meet other Canadians abroad, both a list of characteristics and an invisible bond provide us with a sense of familiarity. We are able to recognize these individuals, perhaps because they have Canadian flags on their backpacks or because we recognize the brand names of clothing. Perhaps we have heard them speaking English with a familiar accent. When we meet, we will be able to discuss recent events, political leaders, and sports successes. At home, however, our daily lives might have little in common. Our sense of allegiance to one another is informed by the *perception* of a shared existence based in part on things that we actually have in common and the intangible things we think we share. If the debate in nationalism studies is about whether nations exist as a list of characteristics or a shared social construct, it is perhaps more useful to view them as both, each informing the other; for in the absence of one, the other would be of little use. For our purposes, both also apply to Scotland and Quebec. Both cases have defined territories, distinct histories, and institutions that sustained a sense of national difference. In each case, there are significant proportions of the electorate who view themselves as different from other Canadians or other Britons. So from this otherwise theoretical debate we can rely on two facts. First, by both possible tests, both Scotland and Quebec qualify as nations. Second, both elements – objective difference and perceived difference – are relevant to nationalism in Scotland and Quebec.

An additional debate concerns national identity. If we were to describe ourselves to others, we might select a number of nouns to serve that purpose: female, Canadian, Cree, francophone, immigrant. When asked in a census to describe our nationality, we might select one option with ease or have difficulty finding something that we feel best fits our own reality. In this act we are treating national identity as a label or tag that we wear, something that describes us to others. Like the first definition of the nation, it deals with objective reality. An individual can prove whether she is female or not, whether he is Canadian or not. As before, proving that we warrant certain labels can be a useful exercise. Belonging to a particular group might offer us certain rights to which we might not otherwise be entitled. Citizenship, our proof of membership in the state, affords us a number of rights and benefits as a result. This process works for ethnicity as well. Proving blood ties is important for status Indians in Canada and for Maori in New Zealand. Often this approach views identity as immutable or unchanging: either we wear the label or we do not.

It is also possible to view national identity as a process. Here our identity affects and is affected by how we go about our daily life. Our identity is not a static list of labels but, rather, is linked to self-perception. This approach views national identity as part of a search for belonging and the need for individuals to feel that they belong to a wider collective group. National identity is thus a process of attachment to a wider collective and a self-determining sense of belonging. This definition draws more on social psychology than does the vision of national identity as a series of unchanging labels. Membership in a social community is seen as a necessity of human nature and the primary good distributed by society (Shils 1982; Walzer 1992), and so the benefits of belonging present themselves forcefully to individuals in search of reassurance. The power of nations stems not from their difference from other communities or social groups but, rather, because they have been able to assert themselves at times as the preferred community of association and self-definition. Likely by sheer size, by influence of institutions, and, most importantly, because the national membership is vague enough that it can become whatever people want it to be, nations and nationalism locate individuals within a people.

Even if we acknowledge that national identity is important, we know little of its operation. How we label our national identity might or might not change throughout our lives. More importantly, what that particular identity means to us, its importance and its content, will likely alter as we age. At one time our national identity will be more important to us than our gender or religion; at others it might become less relevant. What it means to feel Scottish might be different when watching the World Cup than when voting, watching the news, paying taxes, travelling abroad, or walking home from work. While the tag would remain static in each of these circumstances, the impact of that identity and the shared meanings it accesses would vary. Both the tag and the process are relevant to our exploration.

Political culture deals with the collective and with shared meanings. Although the literature reflects a diversity of goals and methods, political culture can be seen as a cultural tool kit that informs individuals about what is usual or normal and thus allows them to participate in political life. If culture integrates us into society, political culture integrates us into the polity. Early works in political culture offered views of national character and sought to describe how Americans, or Germans, or Protestants, act in the civic sphere (Tocqueville 1945; Weber 1958). With the development of social surveys and quantitative social science, a different wave of political-culture works sought to explain the stability of political institutions. Democracy would only be safe, such research argued, if it was supported by the proper blend of political attitudes (Almond and Verba 1963; Pye and Verba 1965; Bluhm 1974). The appropriate balance of efficacy and deference was seen as providing citizens with a sense of security and politicians with the room to govern. Given the importance of the collective culture, one might expect that works on political culture would be littered with references to nationalism and national identity. Such is not the case. First, political culture has all but ignored national identity, treating it most often as a form of state loyalty. Second, on the rare occasions where national identity or nationalism is mentioned, the research focuses on their role as guarantors of democratic stability. They are not linked to self-perception or personal identity but equated with allegiance to the state.

In most literature on political culture, individuals who did not feel themselves part of the nation could not be expected to exhibit the political values and behaviours expressed by other integrated members. Thus if individuals identified with the nation, they necessarily identified with the state. The state was considered to have one integrating culture that would bring citizens into a homogeneous whole. The most explicit reference to the inclusion of national identity in political culture is found in Verba's conclusion to Pye and Verba's *Political Culture and Political Development*. The definition preferred by Verba, of nations as "foci of identification and loyalty," sees nation and state as two sides of the same coin (Verba 1965). Ten years later Bluhm defined nationalism as "the most universally shared aspect of modern political culture" (Bluhm 1974). The presence of rival cultures received attention only as an obstacle to national integration. As Deutsch explains, national integration is seen as the way to overcome attachment to smaller ethnic, cultural, or linguistic groups (Deutsch 1966). That the state could possess more than one nation in anything other than an unhealthy way was ignored by these studies.[3] Giving preference to any identity other than state identity – to religion or gender or ethnicity – was seen as detracting from state loyalty.

Consistent with this view, identity was equated with identification with a larger national group. In such analysis the concept of identity is not presented as a vision of the self but rather as an alignment of the self with others in a larger, bounded, homogeneous polity. For Pye, "[b]eliefs relevant to national identity, for instance, may have a heavy expressive loading in which the major satisfactions derive from the identification itself." In this sense, national identity gives us a collective home. He continues, "The question of national identity is the political culture version of the basic personal problem of self identity" (Pye 1965). In other words, national identity deals with attachment to the collective, just as political culture deals with aggregate attitudes and behaviours. While this statement establishes a link between the two notions of identity, it precludes the possibility that personal identity and national identity are linked; that national identity can influence self-perception.

Putting the literatures on national identity and political culture together, we have reason to suspect that national identity might play a more complex role within political culture than simply serving as a proxy for state loyalty. National identity touches on our attachment to a wider group that might or might not share its boundaries with the state. It also speaks to our own vision of ourselves, our own sense of self-worth. As a result, national identity can be assumed to influence other attitudes we may hold of the collective, including political attitudes. The link between these two concepts stems in part from those two visions of national identity, the tag and the process. In its exploration of this link, this book argues that national identity has a discernable impact on political culture and that this impact is closely linked to the process by which we claim to belong in the nation. Throughout this book political culture is defined as the relationship – both perceived and actual – between a citizen and the state and as the relationship – both perceived and actual – among citizens. This definition is deliberately more expansive than the usual one, which focuses on the dominant attitudes, values, and beliefs exhibited by individuals within a polity; it focuses on more than views of the state. It includes attitudes towards our fellow citizens, our willingness to live near them or interact with them, and the rights we think they should access. It also draws attention to more than our perceptions; it also references the tangible nature of political relationships, to the networks of trust that exist among citizens, and the institutions that govern our interactions with the state.

Whether we can claim to wear the label of a particular identity is more complicated with national membership than with state citizenship, gender, or race, for who is and is not a member of a nation is less clear than who is or is not a member of the state. National identity is, ultimately, a personal – or self-ascribed – decision, although it will be informed by collective consensus. Each nation will promote its own identity, include its own self-defined population, and determine its own goals according to the context in which it operates. Thus what it means to be a member of a nation in Brazil is not necessarily what it takes to consider oneself a member of a nation in Russia or Spain. Each of these is a multinational state, and the perceived rules of membership may vary within the country as well. Unlike citizenship, the requirements of belonging in the nation are murky. There is no definitive list, either of members or of requisite characteristics. What we find, however, is that individuals are often aware of a vague consensus on important elements, what we might define as markers of identity. The process by which we come to recognize these markers of identity is akin to the process of political socialization. We judge whether we belong or not according to cues provided us by leaders in the nation, the media, and even political parties. These cues give us a sense of whether we have credible claims of belonging to the nation. The basis upon which we choose to evaluate our membership provides varied opportunities for inclusion; for although identity is self-ascribed, its validity may not be acknowledged by other members of society. We might feel we belong and others might agree; we might feel we belong and others might disagree. National identity operates as a kind of informal process of negotiation between what we believe and what we think others believe, often without ever really knowing what is in the minds of others. The resulting identity – that which we claim – is what we think we can get away with, given our estimation of the markers of identity.

This process is more visible in societies where nationalism is both a cultural and a political force. In the development of a national political program, nationalist leaders project and encourage a sense of national identity in order to sustain the necessity of the project. The political use of pre-existing markers of cultural identity clarifies the components of that identity, allowing it to be harnessed as a potent political force. The *intentions* of leaders and parties are largely irrelevant, for it is the message, as carried by agents of socialization and construed by citizens, that determines the inclusive nature of the movement. Thus a national identity that is civic in its goals and application does not necessarily make the movement inclusive. Likewise, an inclusive leadership dealing with a population in which hostility and suspicion are common will have little hope of ensuring a consistently inclusive notion of national membership. The values and attitudes held by the population might undermine the efforts of political elites to forge a united identity. Similarly, an exclusive view of national membership in a society where both national identity and autonomy enjoy low political saliency will wreak little damage on the alienated individual psyche. It is this process – the public use of identity and our reaction to it, rather than the label of identity – that affects political culture. The way in which the boundaries of the nation are articulated leads individuals to assess their level of belonging in the nation. The resultant sense of belonging affects other aspects of political culture. Individuals who feel themselves excluded from the nation possess different values and exhibit different political behaviours from those individuals who do not question their membership in the nation.

METHODOLOGY

In its use of political culture and the corollary subjects of political socialization, political attitudes, and political behaviour, this investigation aligns itself with a particular comparative tradition (Almond and Verba 1963, 1989; Almond, Powell, and Mundt 1993; Inglehart 1977, 1990). Rather than presenting an area-studies examination of two separate devolved governments, the book relies on national detail to extract patterns within political culture that transcend national boundaries. It seeks also to provide a sociological understanding of the political relationships among citizens and between individuals and the state in Scotland and Quebec. To this end, it examines how the construction and understanding of national identity in both cases affects traditional measures of political culture. The analysis treats national identity as an independent variable and measures its influence upon the dependent political values, attitudes, and behaviour of two electorates. Numerous studies have analyzed statistical data in an attempt to determine which social characteristics, whether union membership, age, social class, country of birth, language, or religion, affect perceptions of national identity (Adsett and Willmott 1999; Bennie, Brand, and Mitchell 1997; Brown, McCrone, Paterson, and Surridge 1999; Cloutier,

Guay, and Latouche 1992; Mendelsohn 1999, 2003). While these studies are useful, a quantitative and qualitative analysis of the effect of national identity on political attitudes, rather than the other way around, provides for a fuller understanding of how national identity might interact with other social or political variables. The period spanning the establishment and operation of new governmental institutions provides a unique opportunity to measure the prevalence and strength of certain aspects of political culture before new institutions and influences change. Although measures of such culture can provide, at best, brief snapshots of attitudes and behaviour at any given moment in time, an examination of Scotland and Quebec, in the decades following a new parliament and a particularly divisive referendum, allows for a greater understanding of values as affected both by time and by significant events. Periods of heightened political activity, particularly in reference to potential increases in control of political affairs, prompt greater attention to questions of ideal political structures and relationships. Debates concerning how governments, citizens, and society should interact highlight the distance between the ideal future and the present political climate. Traditional measures of political culture such as trust, efficacy, satisfaction, confidence, and levels of participation surface as popular gauges of a healthy democracy. In this context, the book compares the construction of national identity, its promotion, and its influence on political culture in contemporary Scotland and Quebec. The comparative framework employs three methodologies.

The first technique involves a content analysis of the political manifestos of the political parties, government constitutional documents, and final reports of royal commissions and consultative forums, school curricula boards, the Church of Scotland Church and Nation Committee, and the Quebec Order of Catholic Bishops. The analysis highlights the identification of certain pillars of identity, the assumed tenets of nationalist discourse, and the grounds for collective inclusion and exclusion in the nation.

Second, the comparison draws on statistical analyses of electoral studies and opinion polls from the 1997 and 2000/1 elections in Canada and the United Kingdom to measure identity and political attitudes in Scotland and Quebec. Data gathered during an election campaign will capture different moods from data gathered in the middle of a legislative term. Even when data are collected using similar methods and at similar times, the questions themselves might capture different attitudes. Because data collection in Scotland and Quebec employed different sampling methods, different interview techniques, and different questions, sections dealing with quantitative data are separated so that the results for Quebec and Scotland are discussed in isolation. Once the analysis of data has been performed, the two case studies are compared.

Third, the analysis relies on interviews with political actors. Based on a theoretical understanding of the construction of national identity, Scottish and Québécois nationalism, and a preliminary round of interviews with various political actors and academics, fieldwork interviews explored the views of some sixty-five individuals across the spectrum of national membership. These included members of unity groups, sovereignist and nationalist groups, ethnocultural organizations, immigrants, and non-francophones in Quebec, along with Scottish-born residents and those born outside Scotland, in order to provide a range of experiences, from those at the nucleus of political nationalism to those occupying what might be considered the margins of national belonging. It was intended that this selection of individuals would allow for an analysis of the way in which the construction of national identity by various agents of socialization and political actors affects different individuals and groups throughout society.

This book tests a developing theory of integration and belonging through a variety of primary data sources. Party platforms, constitutional documents, and submissions to governmental commissions allow for a reconstruction of the perceived development of each nation's history and identity. Opinion polls and election studies test the acceptance of these constructions within the population. Used to provide a sense of context, primary interviews add depth to the wealth of statistical information available on identity and political attitudes. This hybrid collection of primary sources allows for a greater understanding of the role that key agents of socialization play in the construction of dominant political behaviours.

A final methodological note must address terminology. Throughout the book "nationalist" is used as a general term to refer to all social organizations and political parties that seek to strengthen the culture of Scotland or Quebec or the position of Scotland or Quebec within the host state. If the group advocates a policy of independence, then it is referred to as "separatist" or "sovereignist." If the organization advocates greater self-determination in any form, it is referred to as "autonomist." It is worth noting that there is not a clear-cut division between nationalism and separatism for social movements and political parties in Scotland and Quebec. Indeed, a belief in the existence of the nation and a belief in the need for constitutional change should be seen as two axes along which organizations may move. In other words, a party seeking to endorse greater autonomy in either location need not rely on the rhetoric of nationalism to express its policies. A nationalist organization need not endorse constitutional change. There is a difference between constitutional preference, as explained by the labels "unionist," "autonomist," "separatist," "sovereignist," or "pro-independence," and a nationalist disposition. Levels of nationalism may or may not inform constitutional preferences. The label applied to any organization or political party fits its action at the time. When referring to the entire movement or general consensus for constitutional change in Scotland or Quebec, the label "nationalist" is used as a shorthand for the admittedly diverse views of participants.

OVERVIEW

Perceptions of inclusion and exclusion, as they stem from claims to belonging in the nation, provide the dominant tool for examining political culture in Scotland and Quebec. A secondary level of analysis details how this dynamic affects participation, satisfaction, and the distribution of political attitudes within society. Generated by such agents of socialization as the family, the education system, and the church, political culture establishes the parameters for political attitudes on which all further variants are based. Considered as tools of integration, national identity and political culture share a common purpose and stem from similar civil institutions. By examining how the integration and negotiation affecting national identity influences the political dispositions of citizens, the book explores the potentially integrative role of the polity as a corrective for national exclusion.

Chapter 1 revisits the comparison between Scotland and Quebec and systematically illustrates the similarities and differences between the two and their relationship with the wider state. The chapter argues that while the constituent institutions of political culture might appear informed by a similar Westminster political tradition, the social, economic, and demographic realities of the nations and their host states provide different platforms for nationalist discourse.

Chapter 2 further compares Scotland and Quebec but focuses on variation within the nation, rather than the relationship between nation and state. In so doing, it discusses regionalism and linguistic and religious diversity and illustrates the presence of ingroups and outgroups within the nation. Understanding the context of national identity, both within the larger state and in the nation, provides a useful base on which to later examine public pronouncements about nationalism, self-determination, and inclusiveness. It notes that if national identity is articulated to those "outside" the nation, there are two potential sources for these "outgroups," those external to the nation's geographic boundaries and those internal to its boundaries. The chapter shows that the presence and composition of these outgroups has influenced perceived markers of identity.

Chapter 3 explores the political treatment of national identity at the hands of political actors, both nationalists and non-nationalists. It demonstrates the ways that parties and actors at different points of the nationalist spectrum emphasize a sense of national difference and the logic by which they set the nation apart from the larger state. It turns to the treatment of national identity within discussions of political goals, focusing in particular on the use of history and progress, rights and democracy, and the compatibility of nation and state identities. The chapter argues that political actors in Scotland and Quebec employ similar rhetoric when discussing the nation, but that differences in political context provide uneven incentives for emphasizing the inclusive nature of national membership and have produced misleading interpretations of the civic and ethnic nature of nationalism in each case.

Chapter 4 focuses on the way that individuals understand and describe their own national identities. If chapter 3 provides a view of identity as promoted by political actors, chapter 4 determines whether and how individuals respond to these political messages. The data demonstrate that individuals sometimes hold more exclusive views of national membership than do nationalist political actors, and that they exclude from membership in the nation individuals who nationalist rhetoric suggests might belong. The chapter proposes that self-exclusion, even in the face of relatively inclusive messages of membership, plays a significant role in the identity process. Throughout, the chapter argues that the way we measure identity has much to do with our understanding of its operation.

In chapter 5 I explore political culture in Scotland and Quebec and the extent to which political attitudes and behaviour are different from those in the host state. I examine the conundrum of political difference: the steadfast belief in national difference in the face of data that consistently demonstrate the absence of national subcultures, if we rely on traditional definitions of political culture. A more expansive definition, however, shows that residents of Scotland and Quebec hold different views of the state, policy, and citizenship from those held by other Britons and Canadians.

Chapter 6 focuses exclusively on identity and political culture within the nation. It tracks value differences among national residents, noting the importance of perceived belonging. It argues that while a sense of membership in the nation can predict attitudinal and behaviour variations, the nature of national identity, whether it is shared or held exclusively, is also significant. The chapter identifies individuals who might consider themselves part of the "core" of the nation and those on its periphery, noting that position on this hierarchy, and not just a particular identity label, matters.

1

The Nation and the State

National identity in both Scotland and Quebec rests on how each nation perceives its relationship with the larger state and its sense of distinctiveness. Quebec can thus draw on the fact that it is a French-speaking, largely Catholic political jurisdiction, once a colony of France, which has maintained a level of autonomy since Confederation. Scotland's history as an autonomous state prior to 1707 has justified its administrative accommodation with the United Kingdom and continues to sustain a sense of national difference. Both nations easily identify their markers of difference, one grounded in language and culture, the other in former independence and a history of treatment as a recognized nation, to further the nationalist cause.

The 1995 Quebec sovereignty referendum and the 1997 Scottish devolution referendum demonstrate how two democratically active nationalist movements concerned with national identity have both sought to extend their levels of political autonomy by asking the people to provide a mandate for constitutional change. While it could be argued that the 1997 devolution referendum took place at the behest of the British Labour prime minister, it is unlikely that such an event would have been suggested were it not for the pressure exerted by the coalition of nationalist and autonomist bodies in Scotland that had consistently argued for a devolution of power. The role of the nation in the state, particularly how the nation sets itself apart from the larger state, informs the potential for an inclusive or exclusive form of national identity. Both Scotland and Quebec, for example, have sought and received institutional protection that buttresses distinct demographic profiles. A full understanding of nationalism and national identity in both Scotland and Quebec requires an examination of the position of the nation within the state.

ACCOMMODATING THE NATION

The historical settlement in Scotland and Quebec is relevant both for its impact on institutional development and its perceived role in nationalist rhetoric. In the eighteenth century, institutional protection ensured the distinct nature of key agents of socialization. The Treaty or Acts of Union in 1707 protected the Presbyterian Church of Scotland, the education system, the burgh system of local governmental organization, and Scots law, which was based on the Roman civil code rather than English common law. The Quebec Act of 1774 protected the Catholic Church, the education system, the French language, and the seigneurial system of land tenure. These accommodations were informed by different events and received varying levels of support from elites.

In 1707 Scottish elites freely joined a union with England and Wales. No matter how much pressure was implied in the negotiation, a military defeat of Scotland did not lead the way to the union. Instead, closer ties after the union of the crowns in 1603 and the promise of economic prosperity encouraged elites to support greater political integration. This was a self-determining act. Such was not the case in Quebec, where the territory moved from a colony of France to a colony of Britain as a result of a military conquest. There was, to say the least, an absence of choice in the colonial ruler. So while both were subsumed in a different "other," the circumstances of that change had a different impact on the nation's collective memory. One people was defeated; the other was not.

Both territories immediately became minorities within a larger entity, although in Scotland the entity in which it was subsumed was more proximate than in the case of Quebec. The one million Scots in 1707 joined fifteen million fellow Britons living in England and Wales. Although the francophone, Catholic residents of New France remained a majority in their North American home, they were integrated into a much larger anglophone and Protestant entity across the water. If both became demographic minorities, the gap between the culture of the minority and majority groups was different in Scotland and in Quebec. Scots spoke the same language as their new political partners. Only a small proportion of Highlanders spoke Gaelic, and Scots, although arguably a different dialect, was at least intelligible to the English. Their religions were different, but both were forms of Protestantism. Such was not the case in Quebec, where the inhabitants spoke a different language and where the established church was not Protestant. This comparison is noteworthy, first, because of the difference but, second, because both the language involved, French, and the religion, Catholicism, are not without baggage in British political history. Tudor and Stuart history provides numerous examples of the battles for supremacy between Anglicanism and Catholicism. The conquered people thus not only were different but possessed characteristics that would have been particularly evocative for the English and Scottish political classes.

Accommodation brought varied opportunities for activity within the political, economic, and social life of the state. Scottish elites enjoyed opportunities for representation at Westminster and participation in the British Empire. These advantages encouraged the creation of a new sense of Britishness, a nation and identity built around shared political institutions, military successes, and imperial power. Not all reacted with unchecked glee at the supplanting of one identity with another. Efforts to reinstate a Stuart on the throne in 1715 and 1745 prioritized the distinctly Scottish markers of Highland life. In Quebec there were few opportunities for direct political contact between elites and representatives from the rest of British North America. Only after the union of Canada East (Quebec) and Canada West (Ontario) in 1841 was there an opportunity for direct interaction. Similarly, the successful integration of the Scottish economic elite contrasts with visions of a decapitated social and economic echelon that either left Quebec for France or ceded political control to the new arrivals.[1]

Beyond the initial accommodation, the British state proved itself capable of institutional adaptation in its dealings with the two nations. At the wishes of the British government, the union of present-day Ontario and Quebec in 1841 aimed to assimilate a French and Catholic polity in accordance with the liberal ideals of the day. That assimilation of the French was seen as a means of emancipation has done little for the political capital made of the admittedly paternalistic views of Lord Durham by contemporary nationalists. Assimilation, as called for in Durham's report, has become a symbol of national tragedy and mistreatment experienced at the hands of the British government. Chronologies of Quebec history refer to the period disparagingly, although often laying the blame with England rather than with Britain (Governement du Québec 1979; Bloc Québécois n.d.). Either they were implying that given its history as a colony, Scotland could not be held accountable, or they were conflating England with Britain, as is often done. In either case, difference, linguistic and religious, was seen as something that should be eliminated for the benefit of the individuals involved. This interpretation demonstrates the shifting attention of the British state from the protection of religion to the removal of linguistic barriers. Canadian Confederation in 1867, prompted by political deadlock in the union, economic opportunism, and fear of American military power, ensured a requisite measure of autonomy for Quebec. For Québécois advocates of political change, Confederation would ensure the continued vitality of the French language, the Catholic religion, the culture, and the social structure (Silver 1997; Bonenfant 1967; Martin 1993; Périn 1993). Rather than eliminating difference, Confederation arranged for the removal of distinctly cultural matters from the federal political stage.

British treatment of Scotland was slightly different. In Scotland, initial recognition as a historic nation in the Treaty of Union was eventually followed by a series of exemptions that altered the parallel structure of the union. The creation of the Scottish Office in 1885–86 and the later designation of a Scottish Secretary, for example, provided a separate bureaucracy dedicated solely to the interests of the Scottish population (Mitchell 2004, 2006). The further creation of the Scottish Grand Committee, Scottish Affairs Select Committee, and Scottish Question Time sought to maintain the fundamental character of a unitary state while providing adaptive elements that suited the interests of Scots. These developments should not be taken as proof of British preference for Scottish distinctiveness or a consistent policy of favouritism towards the Scots. Reactions to the Jacobite rebellions in 1715 and 1745 proved that the British government was equally capable of pursuing a policy of assimilation in its own backyard. The banning of the tartan, bagpipes, and Highland games demonstrates a concerted effort to destroy the distinctive markers of Highland life. Nor is such reaction an artifact of history. The twentieth-century treatment of Gaelic and the forced Anglicization of a Highland population demonstrate that the British government has vacillated between cultural assimilation and political accommodation. Two things are worth noting. First, policies of assimilation were aimed more often than not at Highland Scots, a predominantly Catholic population, rather than at Scotland as a whole. Largely because of its homogeneity, a similar distinction was never made in terms of Quebec. Second, as far as political structures were concerned, British governments in the nineteenth century sought at times to accommodate difference, one through its bureaucracy, the other through a separation of jurisdiction that kept Quebec matters out of federal politics. The differing fortunes enjoyed by the distinct populations embedded an institutional ethos that has affected the way Scotland and Quebec interact within their respective states.

THE NATION IN THE STATE

Quebec as a distinct society refers primarily to language and culture rather than to such markers as life expectancy and income, although nationalist programs since the 1960s have made much of the additional economic progress that could be made given greater future autonomy. Over 80 per cent of Quebecers are francophones. Along with New Brunswick and Prince Edward Island, it is one of three provinces with a majority of Catholic residents. These two factors distinguish Quebec within Canada and affect its relationship with the state. Language, certainly, affects the social and political realities of Quebec and plays a central role in nationalist debate.

As the sole unilingual French province in a bilingual federation, Quebec has been able to occupy a position on the national and international stage unrivalled by other provinces. At roughly 25 per cent of the total Canadian population and as home to over 80 per cent of Canada's francophones, Quebec can claim that it exercises a voice as one of the two founding nations in Canada. This view of Confederation, that it was a compact between two founding peoples, still carries tremendous weight in the practical functioning of constitutional negotiations, even if its merits are debated in academic circles.[2] That one of ten provincial governments sees itself as the proxy for a nation and that it has been treated as such by the federal government accounts for a current degree of asymmetry within the Canadian federation.

Canada passed the Official Languages Act in 1969, granting English and French equal status in Canada. The move for such legislation was justified by Liberal prime minister Pierre Trudeau, who argued that the individual rights of citizens necessitated that they be able to receive basic services in either official language regardless of where they lived in Canada. The lack of provision of French services in British Columbia, for example, essentially prevented unilingual francophones from residing outside Quebec. Unilingual anglophones, by virtue of their demographic weight, were thus guaranteed greater mobility within Canada. The inequality of limited mobility for one-quarter of Canada's population can be seen as one of the driving factors of official bilingualism. Trudeau framed this policy not as a sop to nationalism but as an expression of individual rights.

The political and linguistic necessities of bilingual representatives and public servants have, since the late 1960s, ensured the dominant presence of Quebecers in key government roles. With brief exceptions, Canada has been governed since 1968 by a succession of prime ministers from Quebec. The exceptions are Conservatives Joe Clark (June 1979 to March 1980) and Kim Campbell (June to November 1993), Liberal John Turner (June to Sept 1984), and, since January 2006, Conservative Stephen Harper. The first three prime ministers, who are from Alberta, British Columbia, and Ontario respectively, governed for a total of twenty months in more than thirty years. The presence of Quebecers typically extends to between one-quarter and one-third of current cabinet ministers, three of nine Supreme Court justices, one-quarter of the seats in the House of Commons and in the Senate, the head of the armed forces, and 50 per cent of the governors general since the first Canadian held the post in 1952.[3] When Jean Charest replaced Kim Campbell as leader of the Progressive Conservative Party, three of the five official parties were led by MPs representing Quebec seats. For extended periods of time, both the leader of the opposition and the prime minister have represented Quebec seats.

This overrepresentation is not an unchanging characteristic of the Canadian political system. Francophones were underrepresented in the federal civil service and federal Cabinet until the arrival of official bilingualism. In 1971, for example, 18 per cent of federal civil servants spoke French. By the turn of the century that proportion had increased to over one-third (Office of the Commission of Official Languages 1974–97). The transformation of federal political life from a predominantly anglophone workforce to a bilingual one is reminiscent of radical changes attempted upon independence by former colonies, and more recently we can see a similar effort to ensure Inuit staffing of the government of Nunavut bureaucracy. Paradoxically, this rise in political weight coincides with the demographic decline of Quebecers within the Canadian population. The proportion of Quebecers within Canada and the Quebec birth rate have both been declining. At the time of the Conquest, the French birth rate was 55/1,000. It now stands at 10/1,000. In 1867 Quebecers represented 32 per cent of the Canadian population.[4] They now account for 24 per cent of Canadians.

Institutional accommodation in the constitution and twentieth-century policies such as official bilingualism guarantee that Quebec "punches above its weight" in federal politics. This is not unfamiliar territory for students of Canadian foreign policy. Observers of international politics suggest that Canada pursues a similar policy on a global scale, in some cases thanks to its own bilingualism. That the role of Quebec on the national stage remains unchanged in the face of sliding demography has led to expressions of concern from some, usually western-based, politicians and organizations.

As Guy Laforest points out, lists citing the above-average involvement of Quebecers have been employed by some federalists to suggest that Quebec is overrepresented within federal political institutions. Rather than arguing whether this imbalance is of normative benefit to Canada, it is perhaps more useful to point out that it is the necessary result of a bilingual state where one province contains the majority of one linguistic group. In the 2001 census more than 40 per cent of Quebecers reported they spoke both of Canada's two official languages. Only Canada's officially bilingual province, New Brunswick, reports a similar rate of bilingualism, at 34 per cent. By contrast, approximately one-tenth of the populations in Prince Edward Island, Ontario, the Yukon, Nova Scotia, and Manitoba speak both French and English (see table 1.1). The inability of other Canadians to communicate in both official languages makes it more likely that Quebecers will fill key government positions where bilingualism is seen as essential. In short, language ensures that Quebec plays a predominant role in state affairs. The

Table 1.1
Bilingual (English and French) populations in Canadian provinces and territories

	% bilingual	*Bilingual population*
Canada	**17.65**	**5,231,575**
Quebec	**40.81**	**2,907,700**
New Brunswick	34.16	245,870
Prince Edward Island	11.99	15,990
Ontario	11.69	1,319,715
Yukon	10.15	2,895
Nova Scotia	10.06	90,265
Manitoba	9.32	102,840
Northwest Territories	8.44	3,130
British Columbia	6.96	269,365
Alberta	6.90	202,905
Saskatchewan	5.08	49,000
Newfoundland and Labrador	4.11	20,890
Nunavut	3.79	1,010

SOURCE: Statistics Canada, 2001 census.

distinguishing character of national life in Quebec, that it operates in French, has also influenced the political reality of both Quebecers and other Canadians.

Language plays a different role in Scotland. The corollary to French in Scotland is Gaelic, spoken mainly in the northwestern Highlands and Islands. The Gaelic Language Act of 2005 recognizes Gaelic as an official language of Scotland. Unlike francophones in Quebec, Gaelic speakers do not represent a majority of the population. According to the 2001 census there are 58,969 individuals who are able to speak, read, or write Gaelic. This is 10,000 fewer than reported the same in 1991 and represents just over 1 per cent of the Scottish population. The proportion of Scots who speak Gaelic is comparable, for example, to the proportion who report their ethnicity as Indian or Pakistani. By comparison, almost one-quarter of the Welsh population speaks Welsh. The small number of Gaelic speakers in Scotland reflects a concerted policy of Anglicization. Although Gaelic was formally recognized in 1918, its teaching in schools has been limited by a population diminished by years of linguistic neglect. The non-English-speaking population of Scotland has thus traditionally been more concentrated regionally, smaller, and lacked the protection afforded French in Quebec. A spring 2000 Gaelic debate in the Scottish Parliament highlights the efforts of the newly elected politicians to embrace the Gaelic community, although the small proportion of MSPs who could actually participate in the debate underlines the difficulties that the community faces.

Language as a marker of national difference in Scotland also draws on Lowland Scots, a dialect of English with a different vocabulary. One must distinguish between the historical Scots language, spoken by Robert Burns or Walter Scott, and the various regional dialects in use today. Notwithstanding the cultural contributions of Scots authors, poets, and songwriters, the language shows few signs of gaining official status in the Parliament. This is not to say that dialect or accent plays a negligible role in the UK. Until recently, the long-standing practice of the BBC to provide news anchors who used received pronunciation, or the Queen's English, suggested that regional dialects were inferior (J. Miller 1996). This attitude holds as true for the diversity of regional dialects in England as it does for the varied dialects within Scotland. So while there is no official language that distinguishes Scotland from England, Scots sound different from their English neighbours. Within Scotland they also sound different from one another.

What Scotland lacks in sheer linguistic difference, it gains in a full complement of easily identifiable cultural markers, some invented, some authentic, supplementing a sense of history that predates European contact with North America (Broun, Finlay, and Lynch 1998; Trevor-Roper 1983). If, as Seton-Watson argues, each decade of a nation's history lends additional weight to its sense of consciousness and justification for self-determination, a longer history allows for increased confidence in the survival of the nation; it is much easier to predict the continued existence of a nation if it has already existed for hundreds of years (Seton-Watson 1977). For our purposes, this increased confidence could reasonably manifest itself in a decreased vigilance in patrolling the boundaries of national membership.

Most of the easily identified markers of Scottishness stem from the Highland tradition. The marketing of Scotland through its tourist board and the Scottish diaspora both draw on a vibrant material culture that includes tartan, bagpipes, and whisky, activities such as Scottish country dancing and caber tossing, and lore that has room for both Bonnie Prince Charlie and Keir Hardie. Academic research has questioned the authenticity of Scottish tartans, but many of the remaining material markers of Scottishness are linked to those proscribed in the post-Culloden Highlands. Because many of the markers are visual or material, they do not lend themselves to binary opposites in the way that Québécois markers might. While donning a kilt might not imply immediate recognition as a Scot, the notion of "kilting up" is sufficiently well recognized that it is used to describe the process of marketing Scottish versions of English newspapers to a Scottish readership. Clearly, language is more central to notions of difference in Quebec than it is in Scotland, where a material culture conjures the nation more easily than in Quebec. The distinction is an important one but more nuanced than is normally understood. Immigrants from a Spanish-speaking or Arabic-speaking country would, upon arrival in either Quebec or Scotland, have a new language to learn. Anglophones hoping to demonstrate commitment to the nation in Quebec would be expected to acquire French as a language, whereas the same outlay of effort would not be necessary for English or Welsh transplants to Scotland. This is not to say that national membership in Scotland relies on clothing or the acquisition of certain material items, but that expressions of commitment are easier to make and easier to detect than in Quebec. Whether they are meaningful expressions for individuals or perceived as such by others will be discussed later.

If language ensures greater Quebec presence in federal political life and serves as one of the defining markers of difference in any Québécois national identity, the same is not true for Scotland. Although it houses within its borders a domestic population that speaks another language, the demographic weight of that population inhibits special treatment for Scotland as a whole. In short, the type of markers that immediately set Quebec apart from the rest of Canada do little to affect Scotland's role in UK-level politics. Although exerting a smaller power when compared to the overrepresentation of Quebec prime ministers, the presence of Scots within the British cabinet suggests that Scotland is also adept at securing greater political representation than its proportion of the population warrants. It currently boasts just under one-fifth of the UK cabinet ministers and two party leaders, Alex Salmond, leader of the SNP, and Menzies Campbell, leader of the Liberal Democrats. From September 2001 to November 2003 the leader of the Conservative Party, Iain Duncan Smith, was also a Scot, although he represented an English constituency at Westminster.[5]

The overrepresentation of Scottish MPs in the current Labour cabinet has nothing to do with legislation requiring certain characteristics that only Scots possess. Instead, it has more to do with the contemporary alignment of the current government party and Scottish political preferences. Since 1979 Scottish voters have preferred to vote Labour, reflecting in part the support that Labour has shown for devolution in Scotland. Scottish preferences have not always been so stable. In the twentieth century a majority of Scottish seats at Westminster have in turn gone to the Liberal, Conservative, and Labour parties. Towards the end of the nineteenth century until the second election in 1910, the Liberal Party regularly earned large majorities of the seats. Its dominance has not yet been matched by the Labour Party, although it too has won a majority of the Scottish seats since 1959. Relying on voter support, rather than on seats won, is a more accurate gauge of popularity. While the Labour Party has yet to earn a majority of the votes in Scotland, it came close in 1966 and has since 1945 earned between 35 and 49 per cent per cent of the popular vote. The emergence in the 1970s of the Scottish National Party, initially to the right of Labour, introduced the question of national sovereignty. Labour support for some form of home rule could be portrayed as a craven attempt to win the support of Scottish voters or a policy decision grounded in the principles of subsidiarity. In either case, throughout the tenure of Margaret Thatcher and John Major in Downing Street Scots continued to vote overwhelmingly for the Labour Party, which in turn usually promised meaningful constitutional change should it ever be elected to government. What could have been considered lean years in England in terms of securing votes, party members, and seats were positive periods of growth for Scottish Labour. In 1997, when Labour was elected to power, it not only made good on its promises, but also had a number of veteran Scottish politicians in its ranks who soon found themselves in cabinet. Between 1997 and 2005 six Scots served as secretaries of state or higher in the cabinet, and a further fifteen served as ministers of state. Historically, this is the largest proportion of Scots in any British government. It is also worth noting, however, that Labour and Conservative administrations have, since 1963, included no fewer than four Scots as ministers, secretaries of state, or ministers of state.[6]

Thus Scots are in the cabinet because it is a Labour cabinet. In Canada, however, Quebecers tend to be overrepresented in the cabinet, regardless of the party. This was as true for Mulroney's Conservatives as it was for the Chrétien and Martin Liberals. The current

Harper government must be viewed as an exception. In part this overrepresentation stems from the dictates of bilingualism. It also reflects the fact that winning Canadian elections depends very much on the ability to win seats in Quebec. This requirement reflects the proportion of Quebec seats in the House of Commons and the much vaunted homogeneity of Quebec voting patterns, something that recent elections must question. Such is not the case in Scotland, where it is not a necessary electoral feat to win the hearts and minds of Scots before ruling Westminster. In fact, the difference between Scottish political preferences and Westminster governments was seen as a pillar of the nationalist movement in the 1980s and early 1990s. If both Scotland and Quebec are overrepresented in the political life of the state, in Quebec this situation can be attributed to language, while in Scotland it has more to do with the current political climate.

Within the state, the religious profiles of both Scotland and Quebec distinguish them from the larger entity. Quebec is not only French but predominantly Catholic. Although in 2001 the country as a whole reported more Catholics than Protestants (12.9 million compared to 8.7 million), every province except Quebec, New Brunswick, and Prince Edward Island reported a greater number of Protestants. In Canada, Catholics account for 44 per cent of the population, while 83 per cent of the Quebec population is Catholic. Scotland is predominantly Presbyterian, reflecting the dominance of the established Church of Scotland. This religious affiliation distinguishes Scotland from England, where the state church is the Anglican Church of England. The denominations are different, as are their roles in political life. As the established church, the Church of Scotland retains no formal role within the polity. However, as the state church, the Church of England plays a far more significant role in political affairs, linked to the coronation of the sovereign and the presence of lords spiritual in the House of Lords.[7]

Although in a contemporary setting religious differences have very little to do with the integration of the nation within the state, this has not always been the case. Constitutional protection for Quebec stemmed more from intended protection of the church than from the linguistic differences of its inhabitants. This factor is less relevant now in part because of the process of assimilation and in part because of the changing role of religion in social life. In both Scotland and Quebec the number of religiously observant individuals has decreased. In Quebec the arrival of immigrants exacerbates this phenomenon; immigrants to Quebec are integrated into the dominant language, a pattern not necessarily mirrored with religion. While new arrivals may acquire a second, or third, language that they may use at work or at home, they do not acquire a second religion. Although Quebec has drawn immigrants from French-speaking and Catholic countries, the total proportion of Catholics has decreased since 1991. At the same time the proportion of residents indicating they hold no religion has increased. Although in Quebec this constitutes less than 10 per cent of the population, the rate at which the "no religion" group is growing is far faster in Quebec than in the rest of Canada.[8] In Scotland one-fifth indicate they had no religious upbringing, but almost one-third report that they *currently* hold no religion, a transformation that must have occurred between childhood and adulthood. If demographic characteristics form part of the perceived cultural difference between the nation and the state, language and religion distinguish Quebec within Canada, while religion bears the sole responsibility for Scotland in the United Kingdom. In both cases, however, the impact of religion is not clear-cut.

The dominant churches have both been active in political life, making explicit statements about the future of the nation within the state. In Scotland the Church and Nation Committee of the Church of Scotland has involved itself in areas that might be considered the traditional preserve of the church, such as social policy. With its evaluations of party platforms and their impact on Scotland, the committee has also implicated itself in the direction of national politics. Eschewing explicit involvement in politics, the Quebec Order of Catholic Bishops has nonetheless outlined the ways in which provincial jurisdiction over cultural matters, including religion, might better enhance the future prosperity of Quebec as a nation. Whatever their political views, both groups take as given the existence of the nation and the religions they represent as significant pillars within that nation.

THE RISE AND FALL OF THE STATE

The objective markers of difference provide one point of comparison between Scotland and Quebec. The division of power within the state and the extent to which the nation perceives itself on the periphery demonstrate how nationalists are able to argue that greater political autonomy will provide a brighter future for the nation.

Historically, Scotland and Quebec have occupied different positions within the international, or imperial, arena. Quebec began as a colony of France and later, following the conquest of New France, became a British colony. Scotland, in comparison, has simultaneously enjoyed the disadvantages of English imperial attention and, after the union, the economic and political advantages of being an imperial partner.[9] If Quebec began as a colony, Scotland could consider itself both colonized and colonizing. Even before the union with England and Wales, it had tried its hand at erecting a Scottish colony in Panama. The endeavour went poorly, but it contradicts any notion that the Scots were disinterested in imperial power prior to their assimilation in the union.

A less literal application of colonialism has been applied in both Scotland and Quebec. Michael Hechter claims that Britain operates according to a system of internal colonialism, where disadvantaged peripheral regions are exploited for the benefit of an increasingly powerful centre (Hechter 1987).[10] The perception of colonialism is evident also in publications of fringe organizations such as Settler Watch, which argue that English settlers are treating the Scottish countryside as they would a colony. In Canada, Laforest claims that the power exercised by the federal government in the appointment of senators and Supreme Court justices and as holder of the public purse closely mirrors the power of imperial centres over colonies (Laforest 1998). Laforest's contemporary analysis sits among older theories that attribute Canada's political development to its former colonial economic dependence on Britain (Creighton 1956; Innis 1930). Associated with such critiques, differing notions of national confidence and success permeate the contemporary discourse. The use of colonial theories *within* a state reinforce the importance of state activity on perceptions of national self-sufficiency.

On initial examination, the economic fortunes of both Scotland and Quebec appear remarkably similar. Both exist as peripheries to the economic centre of southern England and southern Ontario respectively. Both areas are rich in natural resources but not particularly well off, suffering from above-average unemployment, limited foreign investment, and fluctuating consumer confidence. Equalization payments in Canada and the Barnett formula in Britain ensure that stable funding is guaranteed despite whatever effect such top-up measures might have on perceptions of national self- sufficiency.[11] Economic critiques of the current situation and future prospects as a sovereign state figure in both nationalist discourses. Whether Scotland gains or loses money receives particular attention from both sides of the nationalist divide, each arguing a divergent point of view. Arguments that Quebec might gain money but is generally "held down" by the circumstances of Confederation and a continued fiscal imbalance dominate financial debates within the province. Disputes over natural resources and the receipt of a fair share of public funding provide material for political parties occupying various points along the nationalist spectrum. The first elections to a Scottish Parliament witnessed a series of reports from business groups and think tanks assessing various aspects of the economic situation in Scotland. The most heated debate, and heightened media attention, concerned the predictions of economic well-being for an independent Scotland (SNP Research Dept 1996; SNP Parliamentary Group 1998).[12] In the last two decades the sovereignty debate has focused on the increasing importance of the economic feasibility of independence in Scotland and in Quebec. Political autonomy, predicated in the nineteenth century upon cultural particularity, has given way to arguments about good governance and economic vitality.

In general, the constitutional debate has been much kinder to the Scottish economy than to Quebec. Despite expressions of dissatisfaction from businesses warning that they would relocate should Scotland become independent, the jurisdiction as a whole has not witnessed a deterioration of its economic performance as judged by the outside world. In comparison, New York bond raters such as Standard and Poor's and Moody's have historically been unkind to separatist administrations in Quebec, on occasion ranking the province's bond rating behind that of Newfoundland.[13]

Nationalist arguments for greater autonomy stem from negative assessments of the current economic fortunes of the nation and negative prospects for the nation within the state. This position stems not only from purely financial considerations but also from an assessment of the current international clout of the host state. At the time of Confederation, Canada possessed a political structure that reflected its position as a former colony. Since 1867, however, the development of federalism and the cultural characteristics of the nation distinguish the contemporary state from its colonial master. The passing of the Statute of Westminster in 1931 and the one-week delay in the declaration of war against Germany in 1939 can be considered key steps in the development of a nascent but distinctly Canadian foreign policy. At one time the relationship between the two would have been informed by the roles of imperial power and colony. This position shifted in the twentieth century when the two maintained a close relationship that operated on an increasingly equal footing. Increased equality was achieved because of both the loss of international power wielded by the United Kingdom and an increase in stature acquired by Canada. Financial problems after 1945, the Suez Crisis of 1956, and the process of divesting itself of almost forty colonies in the 1960s and 1970s heralded a significant change in the clout of the UK. Its changed status signifies both a changing world and a transitory position within the international power structure. Its presence initially less commanding on the international stage, Canada had little stature to lose. Participation in international organizations and groups such as the G8, NATO, the Commonwealth, and the United Nations has provided Canada with a stronger international voice despite its middle-power size and wealth. The cultural particularities of bilingualism have also aided a Canadian presence in the diplomatic world. This is not to say that Canada is more influential on the world stage than the UK, but rather that since Confederation its international stature has increased relative to the UK.

The changing fortunes of the larger nation state provide, in the case of Scottish nationalists, an impetus for departure unheralded in more prosperous times. Tying national destiny to a declining hegemonic power provides a prospect of diminishing returns; this was not the promise of security predicted by the architects of the Treaty of Union in 1707. Most often, this argument surfaces as a marriage analogy. The once-fruitful partnership of Scotland and England/Wales is seen by some as no longer advantageous to either partner (Brown, McCrone, and Paterson 1998).

A creeping distance between the two states accompanied their changing fortunes, most evident in the trade relations between Canada and the UK. Where once Canada would have traded more with the UK than with any other country, trade agreements have altered this pattern. At present the two have more economic contact with their continental partners than with each other. The process of continental integration will only drag the two further apart. In Canada this shift stems from the role of the North American Free Trade

Agreement. In the UK, change is driven by its membership in the European Union.

Membership in the European Union embeds the state and its constituent nations within a social, economic, and political infrastructure that is unparalleled in North America. Paradoxically, in a cultural sense the integrative pull of the European continent exerts a much weaker influence on the United Kingdom. Different European languages, cultures, institutions, and histories ensure that the UK is relatively protected from cultural assimilation in continental Europe, if only because there is no homogenizing monolith attempting to assert its influence. Despite the formal economic and political ties binding Britain to Europe, the country has yet to assimilate its political views and its consumer and cultural habits to the continent. Public opinion polls from Angus Reid Group Inc and Europinion "Continuous Tracking" Surveys illustrate this point. In March 2000 Angus Reid gauged perceptions of economic indicators in seventeen countries. UK results distinguish themselves from data gathered in France, Germany, the Netherlands, Spain, and Sweden. When asked about taxes, 51 per cent of UK respondents indicated that they felt tax levels were too high. The average for the other countries was 70 per cent. Similarly, support for public spending was 25 per cent higher in the UK (Angus Reid 2000). In its analysis of attitudes towards the EU, Europinion determined that UK residents are the least interested in Europe about their rights as EU citizens (Europinion 1997), the least convinced their country has benefited from the EU (Europinion 1995), the least convinced the country should integrate more into the EU, the least likely to accept unrestricted immigration from south of the Mediterranean, the most convinced that those suffering human rights abuses should be admitted, and the most convinced the EU should set education and training as a main objective (Europinion 1996). Eurobarometer polls consistently portray the UK as an outlier in Europe (Eurobarometer 2005).

Despite the absence of full-scale supra-national or continental political institutions, Canada is much more a North American country, integrated into more than its continental economy, in a way that Britain has yet to achieve in Europe (Lipset 1990; Nevitte 1996; Inglehart, Nevitte, and Basañez 1996; Surlin 1995; Adams 2003; Boucher 2004). Canadian-content rules aside, Canadians listen to American music, watch American television, and read American magazines, signifying a level of continental exposure unparalleled in the UK. This cultural integration does not necessarily imply a unified political culture, in which Canadian attitudes ape American ones, and the extent to which Canadian values are converging with American views remains a contested issue in academic research. If Canada is more integrated culturally in its continent than the UK is within the EU, the reverse is true for the constituent nations. In Quebec language acts as a barrier to global communication networks operating in English. It insulates Quebec from the cultural influence of the United States in a way that is not the case in English Canada. A community bounded from the rest of the country by its official language exists within a sphere of institutional completeness, allowing for greater control over self-definition (Breton 1964). Some in Quebec feel that the resulting lack of paranoia about American English allows for a sense of continental "Americaineté" absent in English Canada (Lachapelle 1999; Dupont 1995).

The changing fortunes of the two states and their relative levels of continental integration are of obvious importance to the nation. In both cases, nationalists have been more assiduous advocates of continental integration and have been more supportive of greater trade links. They also appear to be much less concerned about their prospects of cultural survival in these new arrangements (Léger and Léger 1990). If Britain is portrayed as an "awkward and reluctant partner" (George 1998) in the European Union, assessments of Scottish participation often demonstrate more support. For separatists in Quebec, the North American Free Trade Agreement and the series of overlapping international organizations of which Canada is a member provide myriad opportunities for economic growth in Quebec and the potential for wider influence. This participation is held up as proof than an independent Quebec would immediately gain access to the same considerations and agreements, an assumption that is vehemently contested by federalists.

Scottish nationalists have not always projected a sense of comfort with the EU. Before 1988 the Scottish National Party did not support the idea of a European Union, claiming that it was no better to be ruled from a different continent than it was to be ruled by London. Institutional accommodation for constituent nations changed the SNP policy from one of isolation to "Independence within Europe." At present, autonomist parties in both Scotland and Quebec are less pessimistic about continental economic and cultural relations than their British and Canadian counterparts.

In both Scotland and Quebec, advocates of greater political autonomy argue that the nation could do better out of existing financial arrangements with the state. In both cases, nationalists are more supportive of international obligations. Quebecers were far more supportive of the Free Trade Agreement than other Canadians, and Scots remain more supportive of the European Union, although such views do not always survive demographic controls. Advocates of greater political autonomy also argue that as independent nations they would be accepted as members of existing trade and political arrangements, to the financial benefit of the nation. This is particularly the case in Scotland, where the UK is portrayed as a partner in decline, standing in the face of progress. Advocates of independence in Scotland and Quebec obviously see in multilateralism an opportunity for the protection of small nations. Varying political preferences between state and nation equally inform perceptions of difference.

NATIONAL POLITICS AND THE STATE

One of the more visible ways in which Scotland and Quebec have distinguished themselves from the larger state is at the ballot box. The push for greater self-determination in both Scotland and Quebec rests in some part on the extent to which voters support different approaches to public policy and back different political parties. The political context in which nationalists argue for greater autonomy underlines political diversity within the state.

Political choice in Quebec is complicated by the presence of different partisan options at the federal and provincial levels (see table 1.2). In federal politics all voters may choose from four political parties. The dominant political party in Canada, in power for much of the twentieth century, has been the Liberal Party, centrist in approach and resolutely federalist. Until 1993 the New Democratic Party was located to the left of the Liberals, and the Progressive Conservatives occupied the right end of the political spectrum. It was an essentially two-party system that had characterized post-Confederation politics in Canada: the Liberals and Conservatives alternating as governments, the NDP later seeking to influence Liberal policy. Other parties existed, often as regionally concentrated

Table 1.2
Voting in Canadian federal elections, 1867–present

	Canada					Quebec				
	Liberals	*Cons/PCs*	*CCF/ NDP*	*Socr/Ref/all*	*BQ*	*Liberal*	*Cons/PCs*	*Socreds*	*BQ*	*Other*
1867	80 (49.0)	**101 (50.0)**				17 (25.2)	**36 (28.5)**			2
1872	97 (49.1)	**103 (49.9)**				27 (32.6)	**26 (31.5)**			12
1874	**133 (53.8)**	73 (45.4)				**34 (34.8)**	17 (17.6)			14
1878	69 (45.1)	**137 (53.2)**				15 (21.7)	**33 (35.0)**			17
1882	71 (46.6)	**139 (53.4)**				12 (21.5)	**38 (37.7)**			15
1887	92 (48.9)	**123 (50.7)**				24 41.7)	**23 (35.6)**			18
1891	92 (46.4)	**123 (52.0)**				**33 (45.9)**	24 (45.4)			8
1896	**118 (45.1)**	88 (46.3)				**49 (53.8)**	16 (45.4)			
1900	**132 (52.0)**	81 (47.4)				**57 (56.3)**	8 (43.6)			
1904	**139 (52.5)**	75 (46.9)				**53 (55.1)**	12 (43.0)			
1908	**133 (50.6)**	85 (47.0)				**52 (53.0)**	12 (39.5)			1
1911	86 (47.8)	**133 (51.2)**				**38 (50.2)**	27 (48.1)			1
1917	82 (40.1)	**153 (57.0)**				**62 (72.7)**	3 (24.7)			
1921	**116 (40.7)**	50 (30.3)[1]				**65 (70.2)**	0 (18.4)			
1925	99 (40.4)	**116 (46.6)**				**59 (59.7)**	4 (34.2)			2
1926	**116 (43.6)**	91 (46.2)				**59 (61.3)**	4 (34.0)			2
1930	91 (43.9)	**137 (49.0)**				**40 (53.2)**	24 (43.7)			1
1935	**171 (44.4)**	39 (29.8)	7 (8.9)	17 (4.1)		**59 (56.0)**	5 (27.5)			1
1940	**178 (54.9)**	39 (30.6)	8 (8.5)	10		**62 (64.4)**	0 (1.1)			3
1945	**125 (41.4)**	67 (27.7)	28 (15.7)	13 (4.1)		**47 (46.5)**	1 (9.7)			17
1949	**190 (50.1)**	41 (29.7)	13 (13.4)	10 (2.4)		**68 (60.4)**	2 (24.5)			3
1953	**171 (50.0)**	51 (31.0)	23 (11.3)	15 (5.4)		**66 (61.0)**	4 (29.4)			5
1957	105 (42.3)	**112 (39.0)**	25 (10.8)	19 (6.6)		**62 (57.6)**	8 (30.6)			5
1958	49 (33.8)	**208 (53.7)**	8 (9.5)			25 (45.6)	**50 (49.6)**			

Table 1.2 continued

	Canada					Quebec				
	Liberals	*Cons/PCs*	*CCF/NDP*	*Socr/Ref/all*	*BQ*	*Liberal*	*Cons/PCs*	*Socreds*	*BQ*	*Other*
1962	99 (37.4)	**116 (37.3)**	19 (13.4)	30 (11.7)		**35 (39.2)**	14 (29.6)	26 (26.0)		
1963	**129 (41.7)**	95 (32.9)	17 (13.1)	24 (13.1)		**47 (45.6)**	8 (19.5)	20 (27.3)		
1965	**131 (39.8)**	97 (32.1)	21 (17.7)	5 (3.62)		**57 (45.6)**	8 (21.2)	9 (17.5)		1
1968	**155 (45.5)**	72 (31.4)	22 (17.0)			**56 (53.6)**	4 (5.4)	14 (16.4)		6
1972	**109 (38.5)**	107 (35.0)	31 (17.7)	15 (7.6)		**56 (49.1)**	2 (17.4)	15 (24.4)		1
1974	**141 (43.2)**	95 (35.4)	16 (15.4)	11 (5.1)		**60 (54.1)**	3 (21.2)	11 (17.1)		
1979	114 (40.1)	**136 (35.9)**	26 (17.9)	6 (4.6)		**67 (61.7)**	2 (13.5)	6 (16.0)		
1980	**147 (44.3)**	103 (32.5)	32 (19.8)			**74 (68.2)**	1 (12.6)			
1984	40 (28.0)	**211 (50.03)**	30 (18.8)			17 (35.4)	**58 (50.2)**			
1988	83 (31.9)	**169 (42.0)**	43 (20.4)			12 (30.3)	**63 (52.7)**			
1993	**177 (41.3)**	2 (16.0)	9 (6.9)	52 (18.7)	54 (13.5)	19 (33.0)	1 (14.0)		**54 (49.0)**	1
1997	**155 (38.5)**	20 (18.8)	21 (11)	60 (19.4)	44 (10.7)	26 (36.7)	5 (22.2)		**44 (37.9)**	
2000	**172 (40.8)**	12 (12.2)	13 (8.5)	66 (25.5)	38 (10.7)	36 (44.2)	1 (5.6)		**38 (39.9)**	
2004	**135 (36.7)**	99 (29.6)	19 (15.7)		54 (12.4)	21 (33.9)	0 (8.8)		**54 (48.9)**	
2006	103 (30.2)	**124 (36.3)**	29 (17.5)		51 (10.5)	13 (20.8)	10 (24.8)		**51 (42.1)**	1

NOTE: Proportions of popular vote in parentheses. Results in bold are for party winning the most seats in each jurisdiction.

1 Progressive Party earned 69 seats and 29 per cent of the popular vote. The Conservatives and Progressives later merged and ran as a single party for the 1940 general election.

protest movements. The two major parties managed to prevent these from becoming effective rivals by dealing with regional and other sectorial interests within the party structure. Rather than constituting one party for religious conservatives, one for the working class, another for francophones, and still another for the west, the parties in Canada sought to accommodate each of these interests, in part through the assiduous courting of regional stars, in part by a loose dedication to policy and ideology. Canadian political scientists have characterized this system of "brokerage" politics as one of aggregate stability and individual level volatility (Clarke, LeDuc, Jenson, and Pammett 1979; Clarke Jenson, LeDuc, and Pammett 1996). Voters, faced with the ever-shifting goals of parties, may realign themselves at every election, but in the aggregate the results do not produce wide swings in partisan support.

For much of post-Confederation politics, Quebec voters helped to determine electoral results by voting as a block. Thus Liberal governments would come to power on the basis of Quebec support, and when Quebecers shifted that loyalty to the Conservatives, it was the Tory party that would govern. Until 1993 a Liberal government had never come to power in Canada without a plurality of the Quebec seats also going to the Liberals. In the eight elections when Quebec voters rewarded the Conservatives with a plurality of the seats, the party went on to win the general election. The Conservatives have not earned a majority without a plurality of the Quebec seats since 1930. Before 1993, Quebec voters were out of step with the rest of Canadians on eight occasions, each time because they backed the Liberals while voters in the rest of the country rewarded the Conservatives with governments. In the conscription election of 1917, for example, 73 per cent of Quebecers backed the Liberals, while 57 per cent of Canadians supported the Conservatives and their Union coalition with western-based Liberals. It was not until 1993, however, that Quebec voters began to deviate consistently from the voting preferences of other Canadians by backing a party that did not stand for seats outside Quebec.

The brokerage system of parties fell apart when the coalition of Ontarian, Quebec, and western interests in Mulroney's Conservative government shattered under the strain of successive and tortured constitutional failures. The formation of the western-based Reform Party in 1988 and the separatist Bloc Québécois in 1990 transformed the system from a two-and-a-half to a five-party system, or a one-party system, as only the Liberals have managed to gain a majority under the new arrangements. These changes clearly altered the choices available to Quebec voters. In elections from 1993 to 2006 Quebecers have showed continued support for the left-of-centre Bloc Québécois, although since the 2000 elections the party has not earned more than half the popular vote in the province. The BQ formed the official opposition in 1993 and was a sizable group within Parliament after 1997. The transformation of the Reform Party into the Alliance and, more recently, the Progressive Conservatives' merger with the Alliance to (re)form the Conservative Party have returned Canada to a system of three-party politics in all but Quebec. Within Quebec, however, the Bloc Québécois continues to win considerable support at the expense of the Liberals, who in turn are no longer able to rely on a divided right to guarantee their tenure in office.

Scots have the same political parties available to them in UK elections as they do in Scottish parliamentary elections (see table 1.3). At the UK level, the Conservative Party is the corollary to the Canadian Liberal Party in terms of electoral dominance. Placed on the right of the political spectrum, the Conservative Party competes for votes with Labour, until recently a socialist option for voters, and the Liberal-Democrats, a centrist party formed from the Liberal Party and the breakaway Social Democrats. The partisan options available to British voters have been more stable than the parties facing Canadians. The main shift occurred in the first two decades of the twentieth century when Labour supplanted the Liberals as the main rivals to the Conservative Party. Since then there have been few partisan additions beyond the creation of the Social/Liberal Democrats and the arrival on the electoral scene of nationalist parties from Scotland and Wales.[14] Since 1945 a greater proportion of Scottish voters have supported the Labour Party, a fact that should not obscure strong prior support for both the Liberal and Conservative parties in Scotland. Indeed, since the Second World War only one party has earned more than 50 per cent of the popular vote in any UK election, an honour earned by the Conservative Party thanks to Scottish voters. At the same time, Scottish voters have been more out of step with other British voters than is the case in Quebec. In the thirty-two elections since 1885, Scottish voters have backed a different party from the one that formed the government fourteen times. Put another way, the Scottish electorate has

Table 1.3
Voting in UK general elections, 1885–present

	UK			Scotland			
	Conservatives	*Labour*	*Liberal/LibDem*	*Conservatives*	*Labour*[b]	*Lib/LibDem*	*SNP*
1885	247 (43.4)		**319 (47.4)**	10		**57**	
1886	**393 (51.4)**		192 (45.1)	12		**39**	
1892	**313 (47.0)**		272 (45.4)	10		**45**	
1895	**411 (49.2)**		177 (45.5)	19		**39**	
1900	**402(50.2)**		183 (45.0)	21		**34**	
1906	156 (43.4)	29 (4.8)	**397 (48.9)**	8	2	**58**	
1910	272 (46.8)	40 (7.0)	**274 (43.0)**	8	2	**59**	
1910	271 (46.6)	42 (6.4)	**272 (44.2)**	7	3	**58**	
1918	**332 (38.5)**[a]	57 (20.8)	127 (12.6)	**32**	7	34	
1922	**344 (38.5)**	142 (29.7)	62 (18.9)	15	**29**	16	
1923	**258 (38.0)**	191 (30.7)	158 (29.7)	16	**34**	23	
1924	**412 (46.8)**	151 (33.3)	40 (17.8)	**37**	26	9	
1929	260 (38.1)	**287 (37.1)**	59 (23.6)	22	**37**	14	
1931	**470 (55.0)**	52 (38.0)	32 (6.5)	**50**	7	8	
1935	**387 (47.8)**	154 (38.0)	21 (6.7)	**37**	24	3	
1945	**393 (48.0)**	197 (36.2)	12 (9.0)	25	**40**	0	
1950	298 (43.4)	**315 (46.1)**	9 (9.1)	26 (37.2)	**37 (46.2)**	2 (6.6)	
1951	**321 (48.0)**	295 (48.8)	6 (2.6)	29 (39.91)	**35 (47.9)**	1 (2.8)	
1955	**345 (49.7)**	277 (46.4)	6 (2.7)	30 (41.5)	**34 (45.6)**	1 (1.9)	
1959	**365 (49.4)**	258 (43.9)	6 (5.9)	25 (39.8)	**38 (46.7)**	1 (4.1)	
1964	304 (43.4)	**317 (44.1)**	9 (11.2)	24 (37.3)	**43 (48.7)**	4 (7.6)	
1966	253 (41.9)	**364 (48.1)**	12 (8.6)	20 (37.6)	**46 (49.9)**	5 (6.8)	
1970	330 (46.4)	**388 (43.1)**	6 (7.5)	23 (38.0)	**44 (44.5)**	3 (5.5)	1 (11.4)
1974	297 (37.9)	**301 (37.2)**	14 (19.3)	21 (32.9)	**40 (36.6)**	3 (7.9)	7 (21.9)

Table 1.3 continued

	UK			Scotland			
	Conservatives	*Labour*	*Liberal/LibDem*	*Conservatives*	*Labour*[b]	*Lib/LibDem*	*SNP*
1974	277 *35.8)	**319 (39.3)**	13 (18.3)	16 (24.7)	**41 (36.3)**	3 (8.3)	11 (30.4)
1979	**339 (43.9)**	269 (36.9)	11 (13.8)	22 (31.4)	**44 (41.5)**	3 (9.0)	2 (17.3)
1983[c]	**397 (42.4)**	209 (27.6)	23 (25.4)	21 (28.3)	**41 (35.1)**	8 (24.5)	2 (11.8)
1987	**376 (42.3)**	229 (30.8)	22 (22.6)	10 (24.0)	**50 (42.4)**	9 (19.2)	3 (14.0)
1992[d]	**336 (41.9)**	271 (34.4)	20 (17.9)	11 (25.7)	**49 (39.0)**	9 (13.1)	3 (21.5)
1997	165 (30.7)	**418 (43.2)**	46 (16.8)	0 (17.5)	**56 (45.6)**	10 (13.0)	6 (22.0)
2001	166 (31.7)	**412 (40.7)**	52 (18.3)	1 (15.6)	**55 (43.3)**	10 (16.3)	5 (20.1)
2005	198 (32.3)	**356 (35.3)**	62 (22.1)	1 (15.8)	**41 (39.5)**	11 (22.6)	6 (17.7)

NOTE: Proportions of popular vote in parentheses. Results in bold are for the party winning the most seats in each jurisdiction.

a Conservative and Liberal totals are for coalition parties. Results also included 50 seats for the non-coalition Conservatives and 36 for the non-coalition Liberals.

b Labour and Labour Party/Co-op added together.

c Totals include results for both Liberals and SDP, running as Alliance.

d Liberals merge with Social Democrats; become Liberal Democrats.

been governed by a party it did not back for 56 of the 120 years between 1885 and 2005.

In both Scotland and Quebec recent electoral results suggest that a significant proportion of voters prefer to back a party that cannot form a government beyond its borders. This pattern must be taken as an expression of a sense of difference, if not overt support for independence. We must not forget, however, that throughout much of the twentieth century Scottish and Québécois voters have backed the same party preferred by a majority of their fellow Britons and Canadians.

STATELESS NATIONS

Comparisons of Scotland and Quebec note that a perceived sense of difference may be informed by a history of institutional accommodation and by demographic distinctions in terms of language, religion, economic activity, and partisan preferences. Part of the reason that the two case studies are interesting, however, lies not in the existence of national boundaries or distinguishing characteristics but how and why such traits have been marshalled by nationalists and those seeking greater self-determination in a political dialogue about the future of the nation. An understanding of the nation and its political culture must acknowledge that at times there have been nationalist campaigns to specifically alter that very political culture.

Debates about national particularity and political autonomy must fall along two axes. First, there is a debate concerning the existence of a nation and the extent to which it is different from the rest of the state. A second debate deals with the right or ability or desire of that entity to separate from the state. The former is grounded in the existence of a distinct population, while the latter deals with political strategy. That Quebec is a French province would typically be mentioned in the first debate. That membership in the United Kingdom has prevented greater economic development in Scotland or that the larger state has pursued foreign policies contrary to national interests would surface more often in the latter debate.

Nationalism in both Scotland and Quebec originally found its political expression in a host of civic organizations that sought to influence politics from the outside. The goals of such groups were diverse and have not always manifested themselves in calls for independence or greater jurisdictional sovereignty. Pressure groups such as the nineteenth-century Scottish Home Rule Association sought to influence existing political parties rather than field candidates in their place. In addition, emerging parties concerned with the national interest were not necessarily separatist in their goals. The Bloc Populaire in Quebec was founded in 1942 not on avowedly *indépendantiste* goals but through a desire to better represent the wishes of Quebecers, informed as they were by the social doctrine of the Catholic Church. Twentieth-century politics in both Scotland and Quebec provide myriad examples of nationalist parties that span a spectrum of separatism, from the Scottish Party to the Mouvement Souveraintè-Association, the Ralliement Nationale, the National Party of Scotland, and Rassemblement pour l'Indépendance Nationale. In the shift from national movements to democratic parties, these bodies received greater attention from both individuals and the media. In a campaign to gain members and voters, they highlighted national particularity and the goal of greater political autonomy, thus bringing what might otherwise represent a narrow cultural movement into the mainstream political discourse. The first conclusion about political nationalism must be that the rise of modern, organized nationalist parties in the twentieth century does not mark the beginning of dissatisfaction with the constitutional solutions reached following the British Conquest and Acts of Union. Resistance to Canadian Confederation and the British state has a long and rich history. The second point worth making, however, is that nationalism in Scotland and Quebec, both political and cultural, has not always suggested an uneasy relationship between a strong sense of national distinctiveness and pride in or attachment to the state. The notion of Scotland as North Britain and the fact that Quebecers preferred until the 1960s to consider themselves *canadiens français* should suggest that believing in the existence of two nations within a single set of boundaries was not the automatic inconsistency we might consider it today.

Single-issue parties, united in their vision of change but representing diverse political and economic platforms, emerged in the 1960s. In Quebec the formation in 1967 of the Parti Québécois ensured the presence of a sovereignist electoral option, campaigning for seats within Quebec. The PQ thus hoped to form a government in Quebec and, in so doing, influence Canadian policy. The same can not be said of the Scottish National Party, which had no option but to campaign for seats in the Westminster Parliament. One useful distinction between nationalist parties in Scotland and Quebec is that in Quebec the nationalist argument and rhetoric was internal to Quebec politics. In Scotland the SNP only campaigned for Scottish seats, but the goal was to bring the nationalist argument directly from the party to Westminster. In Quebec that public role would be performed by representatives of the Quebec government, not by the Parti Québécois itself. The locus was different, which in turn affected who would eventually advocate on behalf of the nation: a sub-state level of government or a political party. Notwithstanding the varied political support for the nationalist parties, this factor would have had an obvious impact on the perceived mandate of the body self-appointed as the voice of the nation. SNP support fluctuated wildly throughout the 1970s, from 11.4 per cent in 1970 to 30.4 per cent in the second election of 1974, but the party has run third or fourth in all but three elections since 1970. Over the same decade PQ support varied between 23 and 40 per cent of the popular vote. Although earning only ten points more of the popular vote, the party was able to form the government in Quebec. This institutional feature of nationalist debate structured the goals of the nationalist parties and the expression of nationalist desire in Scotland and Quebec. In terms of nationalist chronology, both nations witnessed periods of intense activity at the end of the 1970s and the beginning of the 1980s and again in the 1990s.

Public opinion data show increased support for sovereignist options during these periods of heightened activity. During one of these surges in support, the Labour Party in Scotland began advocating some form of devolution for Scotland that would bring democratic accountability to the autonomous Scottish Office. After forming the government in 1974, the Labour Party in 1976 introduced the Scotland and Wales Bill, later splitting it into two to better ensure that opposition to devolution in one nation would not endanger the safe passage of the bill through Parliament. The Labour Party was by no means unified in its support for devolution, as voting on both the 1976 bill and its 1978 counterpart confirms. In an effort to prove that devolution would only occur if Scots wanted it, Labour MP George Cunningham introduced an amendment that established a higher threshold for public support in a public referendum. Forty per cent of the total electorate, rather than 50 per cent plus one of those voting, would have to back devolution in a referendum.

When it was put to a vote in 1979, 52 per cent of those who voted (but only 32 per cent of the electorate) said yes to devolution. The election of a Conservative government in 1979 saw the repeal of the act and moved the locus of institutional change from Westminster to civil society. Faced with an avowedly anti-devolutionist party, despite its previous flirtations with softer forms of institutional change, those seeking reform in Scotland organized coalitions among political parties and civic organizations to campaign for change. Existing organizations such as the Church and Nation Committee of the Church of Scotland and the Scottish Trades Union Congress were vocal advocates of change. Bodies such as the Campaign for a Scottish Assembly and, later, the Scottish Constitutional Convention included members of pro-devolution parties such as Labour and the Liberal Democrats. During this time, the SNP maintained an uneven distance from such bodies. The party joined, for example, the Scottish Constitutional Convention, only to later remove itself under the argument that devolution fell short of its goals. By the late 1990s, however, the party appeared to change its mind, agreeing that any movement towards independence, even a half-measure such as devolution, would be an improvement over the unitary system of government. In this approach the party returned to tactics it had employed in the early 1970s.

Throughout the 1990s the Scottish Constitutional Convention and its Constitutional Commission produced a number of reports describing a future Scottish parliament. Such plans identified the number of seats, the methods of election, and methods to improve the representation of women and to introduce a new legislative culture in post-devolution political life. When Scots eventually went to the polls in 1997, their only understanding of what any Scottish parliament would look like would have been informed by coverage of the deliberations and reports of the Scottish Constitutional Convention.

Public discontent with the Conservatives in England likely ensured the arrival of devolution in Scotland and in Wales. Throughout the 1980s and 1990s Scottish voters continued to provide a plurality of the vote to the Labour Party. The nadir of the Conservative Party arrived in 1997, when not one Conservative was elected in Scotland. Scottish dissatisfaction likely had little impact on English voting preferences. While Scottish support for Labour during its lean years in England probably ensured continued party commitment to devolution, and while civic activity on devolution ensured voters had a clearer vision of what devolution might mean in 1997 than they had had in 1979, the Scottish Parliament owes its existence to the election of a Labour government, a feat made possible by the converted partisan preferences of English voters.

Originally, the Labour Party had promised immediate action on devolution in the event of its election. Concern about democratic support for devolution led the party to advocate a two-question referendum, the first on the very existence of the Parliament and the second on its tax-varying powers. Both questions passed in September 1997. Advocates noted that had the elevated threshold of 1979 been reintroduced, both questions would still have passed. The No side trailed throughout the campaign. It is possible that the suspension of campaigning following the death of Princess Diana hampered its efforts, but it likely made little difference to the final results. The chronology of devolution will be well known to students of Scottish politics. First elections were held in February 1999, and the Parliament opened its doors on 1 April.

Attempts by nationalists to secure greater measures of sovereignty for Quebec are, in an international setting, quite similar. Here, too, democratically elected political parties offered referendums to the electorate. The referendums also occurred at similar times, in 1980 and 1995. Their organization was different. The Scottish referendums were initiated by Westminster, whereas the 1980 and 1995 Quebec referendums were organized by provincial authorities, with federal authorities backing the No side in each contest. In terms of results, the most obvious difference is that the second referendum in Scotland ensured a greater measure of self- determination, while in Quebec the close result brought no additional power to the National Assembly. Campaigns for change in Quebec were also met with opposition different in scale and tenor from that in Scotland and were involved in larger pan-Canadian projects of constitutional engineering that guaranteed the involvement of those outside its borders.

The presence of a provincial legislature in Quebec provides not only a second debating chamber for nationalist aspirations, which in itself is a significant resource, but also an attainable goal for nationalist political parties. The election of the separatist Parti Québécois in 1976 presented an interesting conundrum to sovereignists. By holding the mantle of power, the PQ could no longer have separation as its main goal, but rather the creation of legislation and the administration of a Quebec public service. If one can distinguish between separatist or nationalist groups that campaign as political parties and those that seek to exert influence from the outside, as civic organizations, one can further differentiate between parties competing for the chance to form a government, such as the Parti Québécois, and parties that by their locus or tactics hold no such goal, such as the pre-devolution SNP. Since the first election of the PQ, the goals for those seeking greater sovereignty have thus been twofold: first, to convince voters of the theoretical importance of independence and, second, by evidence of good governance, to suggest that such a goal is possible and desirable.

Within its first mandate the PQ called a referendum on sovereignty-association. The referendum question itself was a bit convoluted, and varied public understandings of how sovereignty-association differed from both federalism and full independence cannot have helped those seeking to enact change. The No side won the referendum, with 60 per cent support of voters. Using the phrase "Mon non est québécois," the No side argued that voting no was not somehow a denial of Quebec national identity. Opposition to sovereignty-association not only involved francophone politicians active within the provincial arena but also relied on those holding seats in the Canadian House of Commons. In this regard, opposition was similar to that in Scotland, where politicians of various parties representing Scottish seats in the UK Parliament opposed devolution. The absence of a Scottish debating chamber necessitated the involvement of Westminster-based Scottish politicians in 1979 and 1997, but in the 1980 Quebec referendum the involvement of MPs served to pit the provincial level of government against the larger state. This is not to say that all within the Quebec National Assembly backed sovereignty-association or that the Canadian House of Commons did not contain Liberal or Conservative representatives who were sympathetic to sovereignists, but that the campaign focused on the oppositionalism between the pro-change crowd in Quebec City and the anti-independence cohort of Quebec politicians in Ottawa.

Following the referendum, and possessing a clear mandate, Prime Minister Pierre Elliott Trudeau began a campaign of constitutional reform that affected Quebec's role in the federation. It also ensured that greater sovereignty for Quebec became a Canadian issue, rather than something debated purely within the borders of one province. The patriation of the constitution, its first major overhaul since the Statute of Westminster in 1931, introduced two features that continue to affect the context of political nationalism in Canada. First, it established a domestic constitutional amending formula that made further changes to the constitution subject to a tortuous process of approval among the provinces. Second, it introduced a Charter of Rights and Freedoms that sought to protect individual rights while protecting rights for certain collective groups as well. Quebec's displeasure at the absence of a constitutional veto has prompted several trips back to the bargaining table. Prime Minister Brian Mulroney's efforts to bring Quebec into the fold appeared moderately successful in 1987, but the resulting Meech Lake Accord could not wind its way through the amending formula that had been established and ultimately failed in 1990. The fate of the Charlottetown Accord was similar but delivered at the hands of the electorate, rather than political elites. Fundamental to both agreements was some form of recognition for Quebec as a distinct society, a phrase that falls far short of the national label used to describe Scotland since 1707.

Armed with proof that the Canadian federation had been insufficiently adaptive to its needs, the Parti Québécois government of Jacques Parizeau offered Quebecers the opportunity to determine Quebec's place in Canada. In 1995 Quebecers went to the polls on a question that promised the option of independence should negotiations for an undefined partnership prove futile. The result, 51 to 49 for the federalist side, was followed by a period of self-examination about the meaning of national identity and, later, relative silence.

Those opposed to greater self-determination in Scotland and Quebec reacted in two ways to the calls of nationalists, one rhetorical, the other rule-based. The best example of rule-based opposition to self-determination can be seen in the attempts of those in government to ensure that the democratic process truly reflects the wishes of the electorate by elevating the bar of democratic success. This approach subjects decisions about self-determination to a higher bar than that used to determine elections, and thus beyond that which ensures the tenure of most governments in office. In 1979, in the face of internal opposition to devolution, it was a Labour amendment that introduced the 40 per cent rule for support in the Scottish referendum. In Canada, federalist reaction to the 1995 referendum prompted a reference case to the Supreme Court. Asked to determine whether there was anything in international or federal law that would allow the unilateral secession of Quebec, the court indicated that unilateral secession was not necessarily legal, but that if a clear majority of Quebecers voted on a clear question for separation, the federal government would have a duty to negotiate. Faced with this response, the federal Liberal government then set out in its Clarity Act to define the meaning of a clear question and the necessity of a clear majority. That there has been such concern for the proper representation of the democratic will from parties then enjoying governing majorities thanks to only a minority of public support must have seemed to nationalists in Quebec an odd display of concern for democratic wishes. Rhetorical opposition has focused on the dangers of nationalism itself, on the grim economic circumstances following any degree of independence, and on the advantages of an adaptive status quo ante. Each of these surfaces in discussions of political nationalism in chapter 3.

CONCLUSION

This chapter has pointed to the ways in which Scotland and Quebec distinguish themselves from the United Kingdom and Canada. It has noted that on measures of social demography, Quebec is more distinct from the rest of the country than Scotland is in the UK, where religion appears to be the single largest demographic distinction. We have also seen that the two nations have enjoyed different patterns of institutional accommodation. While both owe part of their continued national identity to the institutional protection afforded the education system, the church, and the legal system following integration within a larger whole, that accommodation was grounded in different visions of the polity. We could expect a decreased vigilance in patrolling the boundaries of the nation from Scots who have three hundred years of history and formal recognition as a nation on their side. The discussion also speaks to how individuals might express commitment to the nation, noting the difference between demographic variations, on the one hand, and a more easily accessible, vibrant material culture, on the other. Taken together, these considerations suggest that nationalist life in Scotland has had a slightly easier time than in Quebec.

The chapter has also pointed to differences in political context that structured political debate and to the political preferences, both partisan and otherwise, that distinguish the nation within the state. We should be cautious, though, of assuming that all within the nation share the same views and exhibit the same behaviours. That each nation houses within it a considerable diversity of opinion and variations in terms of language, religion, and ethnicity forms the focus of chapter 2.

2

Inside the Nation

Examining the characteristics that distinguish the nation from the larger state provides us with a sense of the salient markers of nationhood. If we subscribe to the first definition of a nation, that it is a bounded territory with a population that shares a history and culture, then establishing the existence of a separate language or religion or identifying patterns of institutional accommodation is useful to understanding the external boundaries of the nation. If we rely on the second definition of a nation, that it is a sociological construct willed into being by its imagined community, then we must acknowledge that it is a living organism, not just a list of characteristics. Here the nation is not a homogeneous entity but houses regional, economic, ethnic, linguistic, and partisan divisions. If a nation lives in the interaction of its members, then understanding diversity within the nation is as important as understanding its external boundaries.

It is helpful if we assume that a nation has two potential boundaries. The first perimeter is a physical border around the geographic domain of the nation. In the case of former independent states, the existence of such borders can be an artifact of history, or nations can be the product of more modern political developments. Those in possession of geographic borders have a more convenient position from which to achieve statehood, though history is certainly full of examples of the violability of such borders. Scotland and Quebec have these types of borders. Scotland as a political jurisdiction retains borders set before the Treaty of Union in 1707, although historians will note that the current borders are north of Hadrian's Wall, a previous incarnation of the Celtic-Saxon/Roman divide. Quebec, never an independent state, owes its current borders to land acquired since Confederation in 1867. Contemporary Quebec is thus not only far larger than the province that entered Canada but larger still than the colony of New France, upon which it is based.

In addition, a nation can have sociological boundaries drawn around the population of the nation. These types of boundaries assume heightened importance in the absence of physical borders, as a national population tries to sustain itself through its culture, language, religion, or history. While physical borders are visible and usually recognized, sociological boundaries are often invisible and thus more subject to dispute. The boundary around the nation depends on how one defines members in the nation: who is included and who is excluded. Usually there is no list of national members, although progress on referendums or land claims may from time to time produce de facto lists from voter enumeration or records of beneficiaries. The social boundary is in part a product of group consensus and individual hypothesis. Individuals are given clues about their ability to claim membership by all around them, by those in positions of political authority, by those presumed to speak for the nation, and by their peers. The most inclusive definition of membership in the nation would automatically make the social boundary and the physical border of a nation coterminous. Rhetoric to this effect is common in multicultural, immigrant societies such as Canada and Australia, and it is evident too, as we will soon see, in Scotland and Quebec. At the same time, however, definitions and discussions of who is and is not a true Scot or a *vrai Québécois* suggest that there is room for uncertainty. The key points on which the nation distinguishes itself from the larger state are the starting positions for key markers of identity. If the nation is relatively homogeneous in the way that it distinguishes itself from the state, then defining the characteristics of the nation and its membership is a relatively easy task. Heterogeneity within the physical borders of the nation, however, raises questions about inclusion in the nation.

Let us assume, for the moment, a very restrictive definition of national membership. If, for example, Scotland distinguishes itself from the United Kingdom as a whole by its Presbyterian church and by ancestry, or if Quebec distinguishes itself by language and religion, then let us include only these types of individuals – descendants of Highland and Lowland Scots and Québécois *de vieille souche* – in the nation. In this ethnic definition of the nation we automatically exclude those without ancestral links to the political nation. Understanding who is excluded by such a definition – their characteristics, their number, their level of social and political organization, their position within debates about nationalism and self-determination – will help us to understand the potential for inclusion and exclusion within constructions of the nation.

We know that Quebec is predominantly a French and Catholic province, but its population is not uniformly of one religion or language. In demographic terms, the province is more Catholic than it is French. That over 80 per cent of the population belongs to one religion and that this population is also overwhelmingly French reinforces a sense of difference. It also diminishes the potential for intercommunity conflict given the disproportionate size of the majority community. But Quebec also houses sizable anglophone, allophone, and Aboriginal populations, groups that themselves exhibit religious and ethnic diversity. Four key points are worth noting.

First, Quebec houses diverse Aboriginal populations. Over 10,000 Inuit live in communities along the Hudson and Ungava coasts, in Nunavik. Cree and Innu occupy the west and east of the northern portion of the territory. In addition, there are over 15,000 Mohawk, most of whom live in Kahnawake and Akwesasne, the latter straddling Ontario, Quebec, and the Canada–US border. The relationship between the Aboriginal populations and the majority francophone population has not always been easy. In 1990 Mohawk near Oka barricaded themselves to protest the expansion of a golf course onto a former burial ground. The standoff lasted seventy-eight days and resulted in the death of one police officer. The barricade was certainly the most publicized evidence of discord between indigenous peoples in Quebec and francophone authorities. At the same time, however, it is worth noting that similar events have occurred in New Brunswick, Ontario, and British Columbia and in each case have been prompted by similar grievances over land use and rights for indigenous peoples. It would thus be difficult to argue that the standoff in Oka was more likely because of the perceived existence of a Québécois nation. This is not to say that the indigenous population is supportive of nationalism or uniform in its views. In 1995, prior to the referendum on self-determination in Quebec, Cree held their own referendum and voted overwhelmingly to stay in Canada. The relationship between indigenous peoples and sovereignist administrations in Quebec is further complicated by progress made on land claims. Inuit in Nunavik have recently signed a land claim agreement, just as the James Bay Cree signed one thirty years ago. Arguments for Quebec separatism are grounded in a logic familiar to those calling for the self-government of Aboriginal peoples, something to which nationalists have demonstrated varied if increasing support.

Second, Quebec houses a large anglophone population, concentrated since the nineteenth century in Montreal. The dominance of anglophone merchants in the largest city once not only established an unofficial boundary between the city and the rest of the province but also physically divided Montreal. An anglophone business class has now given way to a bilingual workforce. Its community, diminishing in size before the election of the separatist Parti Québécois in 1976 and the referendum on sovereignty-association in 1980, was further affected by increased out-migration during this period. The anglophone community houses differing visions of separatism and nationalism. Two of the most vociferous opponents of separatism stem from this community. The Equality Party, an English-rights political party that at the height of its success won four seats in the 1989 elections to the National Assembly, has articulated the most vigilant position. Its civic counterpart is Alliance Quebec, an anglophone pressure group that decries the use of language legislation. The province also contains allophone communities that in turn possess differing approaches to linguistic integration, nationalism, and separatism. The allophone community in Quebec is not of one mind on the nationalist question. Certain organizations have campaigned for sovereignty, while others have suggested that independence would deny these communities fundamental rights. The views of the Fédération des Groupes Ethniques du Québec, for example, are not shared by the Conseil des Minorités Ethniques. Much of this difference in outlook depends on the extent to which members of these linguistic communities have integrated into a francophone milieu. Language legislation has resulted in a siege mentality among some anglophones and allophones, while for others it has aided their social and economic integration and prosperity, something that the original framers of the legislation had in mind.

Third, linguistic differences and immigration have ensured religious diversity within the province. Historically, the principal religious cleavage in Quebec would have involved Protestants and

Catholics, a gulf reinforced by linguistic divisions between these two populations. By the twentieth century, however, the province was home to a vibrant Jewish community and, more recently, a Muslim community. As with language, much of this diversity exists in Montreal. The relationship between the minority religious communities and the state, whether nationalist or not, has not always been easy. Public examples of anti-Semitism have received continued attention in academic and journalistic works, most noteworthy of which were various comments by novelist and essayist Mordecai Richler. The position of the oft-quoted Abbé Lionel Groulx in contemporary Quebec society tends to polarize the active religious organizations if not their members. The campaign by B'nai Brith to remove from a subway stop the name of a man who openly advocated intolerance has met with frustration, not least from former Quebec Liberal leader and *Le Devoir* editor Claude Ryan. The nationalist *Le Devoir*, never with a circulation much above 17,000 in the period before the Second World War, in the 1930s and 1940s provided additional examples of anti-Semitism. Throughout the early part of the twentieth century anti-Semitism in Quebec manifested itself as an opposition to immigration. Within the anglophone community, McGill University, founded in 1821 from the estate of Scottish merchant James McGill, enforced quotas for Jewish students until the end of the Second World War. The Faculty of Arts at McGill set higher entry standards for Jewish students – 750 instead of 600 on entrance requirements – and the Faculties of Law and Medicine both employed quotas for Jewish students (Frost 1984). More recently, the Muslim population, again concentrated in Montreal, has encountered difficulties with cultural intolerance. Young Muslim girls, for example, have been prevented on occasion from wearing the hijab in public schools. Quebec and Quebecers, however, by no means have a monopoly on such behaviour, as visible-minority populations living in other provinces and territories will attest.

While greater homogeneity of religious belief in Quebec mitigates the potential size of any religious minority and thus minimizes the potential for intercommunity conflict, evidence of past and present religious intolerance, permitted both by the state and by citizens, highlights the significance of religion as a relevant cleavage (Young 1999, 2006). This cleavage is of political salience in part because of the reputed opposition of religious-minority voters to separatism.

Scotland, on the one hand, is a far more homogeneous jurisdiction than Quebec. While historical visions of the nation may ground Quebec in a French and Catholic population, we know that almost one-fifth of the contemporary population does not belong to one of these groups. If we similarly ground Scotland in a Presbyterian, English- or Gaelic-speaking public that reports its ethnic origin as Scottish, we can immediately note the far smaller presence of outsiders. At the same time, because the nation in Scotland was never grounded in the characteristics of a people but in its institutions, there is immediately room for more heterogeneity *within* the nation. This is not to suggest that the boundaries of national membership are guarded with more or less vigilance than in Quebec, but merely that the linguistic, ethnic, and religious diversity long present within the geographic borders of one nation is not present in the other.

Scotland's visible-minority population, at approximately 1 per cent, is much smaller than the English proportion of 7 per cent. Glasgow holds the highest share, at a little over 3 per cent, incomparable to more diverse urban centres in the UK such as London and Leeds. The rest of Scotland is notably homogeneous on measures of ethnicity, something that limits the potential for inter-group tension. This consideration should not detract from research highlighting persistent racism experienced by minority communities, as works describing the integration of Italian and Chinese populations in Scotland's more homogeneous towns such as Edinburgh can attest.

The relative lack of a substantial ethnic minority population in Scotland reduces potential objects of racism, although two points are worth considering. First, sectarianism on Scotland's west coast detracts from whatever intolerance-free image Scotland might desire (McCrone 1992; Harvie 1998). Irish migration to the west of Scotland provided a population distinct by markers of religion and prompted, at the time, a strong anti-Irish movement. While it would be churlish to compare the sectarian violence in Northern Ireland to the relationship between Protestants and Catholics in Scotland, the west coast of the nation has witnessed its share of sectarian difficulties (Bennie, Brand, and Mitchell 1997; Devine 1998, 2000). A declining church attendance, credited with removing much of the doctrinal salience of religion, has not vitiated discrimination and violence. In Scotland as a whole, however, the relationship between religious community and political power has more often determined voting behaviour rather than interpersonal friendships, and the extent to which it affects daily life decreases as one moves east or north. Second, discrimination cases launched by English employees in Scotland who feel they have been passed over for promotion are often held up, not for lack of evidence, but because of a lack of clarity over whether the English represent a distinct race. That intolerance in these cases is not directed towards a distinct race of people should not detract from the fact that prejudice is no less present in Scotland than it is in Quebec. How prevalent it is, or is felt to be, will obviously have an impact on the extent to which individuals of different religions and countries of origin feel they belong in the nation.

Scotland also lacks the spectrum of intercommunity antagonism among linguistic groups, in part because of size and in part because language has not been considered a central element of national identity in Scotland. If Quebec can be characterized by the diversity of its urban centres and the homogeneity of its smaller communities, Scotland is a comparatively homogeneous entity. The value and importance of the different linguistic groups in Scotland should not be confused with the fact that they represent a very small proportion of the population. That they do so has an obvious impact on the way that the boundaries of the nation are articulated and to whom they are articulated.

When markers of identity are mobilized by nationalists or by other organized interests within society such as the media or political parties, there are two key pillars of identity: the extent to which the nation is different from the state and the existence of differences within the geographic boundaries of the nation. Within Quebec the demographic majority group, by language and religion, is both large and relatively uniform. There is little to divide it except partisan views or economic reality. Any sense of difference comes from those outside this group. Anglophone, allophone, Aboriginal, visible-minority, and various religious communities all provide variation within Quebec's demography. Within Scotland there is comparatively little variation in terms of ethnicity. There is neither a sizable indigenous population seeking different relationships with the state, nor has immigration resulted in an overwhelmingly multicultural metropolis in Scotland. If diversity within Quebec comes from non-ancestral groups, diversity in Scotland, if we again remain within a very restricted definition of the nation, is located within

Table 2.1
Linguistic, ethnic, and religious diversity within Quebec and Scotland

	Quebec	*Scotland*
Population	7,125,580	5,062,011
Non-dominant language	1,266,460 (17.77)	126,814 (2.5)[1]
Visible minority	497,975 (6.99)	101,677 (2.01)
Aboriginal ethnicity	188,315 (2.64)	na
Non-dominant religion	1,185,865 (16.64)	1,243,239 (24.56)

SOURCES: Statistics Canada census 2001; 2001 Scottish census.
NOTE: Proportions in parentheses.
1 Language data for Scotland uses country of birth as a proxy. The census in Scotland does not ask about mother tongue other than to probe knowledge of Gaelic.

the "ethnic" nation. There is both more religious variation and greater linguistic variation among those who would consider themselves, without question, to be Scots. The only "outsiders" in such a situation are English "newcomers" and a growing visible- minority population predominantly in the west of the country.

Table 2.1 shows that Quebec houses within its borders a larger proportion of those considered distinct from an ethnic definition of the nation. Almost one-fifth of the population reports its language of use as non-French, and 10 per cent of the population would not fit a restricted ethnic definition of the nation. In Scotland, however, the near absence of a visible minority or non-English-speaking population is accompanied by a larger proportion of individuals who do not consider themselves members of the Church of Scotland. And yet diversity concerns more than ethnic, linguistic, or religious divisions that might challenge definitions of national membership.

The economic realities in Scotland and Quebec provide still further examples of regionalism within the nation, although these have tended to be mobilized less frequently by nationalists. Perceptions of difference in Scotland are compounded by the geographic and economic dictates of regional location. Although small by Canadian standards, Scotland's geography encompasses a variety of landscapes, some resource-rich, others less so. Scotland comprises the northern third of the British mainland, numerous islands on its west coast, and the Orkney and Shetland Islands to its north. The Shetland Islands are closer to Norway than they are to Edinburgh, which remains an expensive flight away. A flight from Lerwick to Edinburgh costs approximately the same as one from Glasgow to

Toronto. The distribution of economic resources and wealth, from the more prosperous central belt and oil-rich Aberdeen to the economically depressed Highlands and Islands, is linked to geography and the related factor of economic activity. Residents in the low-density Highlands and Islands, where the majority of Scotland's Gaelic speakers reside, are harder hit by a variety of policy decisions formed in the south. Increases in petrol prices, for example, disproportionately affect those in the Highlands. For consistently underperforming areas, economic disparity, when added to geographical distance, potentially increases perceptions of dislocation. Economic imbalance is tied also to the felt presence of southern English residents integrating themselves into rural economies (Jedrej and Nuttall 1995). Frustration with the pattern of land sales and composition of the rural population has led to the creation of a small number of nationalist grassroots organizations intent on monitoring the incursion of English landowners and incoming residents into the Scottish countryside (Scottish Watch 1993, 1994).

The divisions between Highland and Lowland Scotland have their roots in historical tradition. The religious and linguistic composition of these two areas further compounds contemporary economic reality. Even within the Lowland central belt, however, the relationship between power and economic performance accounts for the rivalry between Edinburgh and Glasgow, Scotland's two largest cities. This form of regionalism manifests itself in the form of popular-culture competitions between the two cities, from magazine reports on which city produces a better quality of life to television commercials advertising the frequent rail links between the two cities. Economic disparity and the perception that, as the seat of Parliament, Edinburgh gets a better deal point to a more serious perception of dislocation in Glasgow. In 1998 the latter city was declared a jobless black spot worthy of additional funding under new Labour's New Deal (Scotland Office 2000), and unemployment, though halved since then, remains high. Economic inequality often compounds existing demographic diversity. Unemployment rates among Scotland's Pakistani and South Asian population, for example, is 12 per cent, five points higher than the rate for non-visible-minority Scots.

Furthermore, despite the annual two-week relocation of the Parliament that allowed the Church of Scotland to hold its General Assembly in its own building, Glasgow has not met with great success in its efforts to house elements of the political system. In his analysis of London's financial success, Rosie argues that the presence of British institutions provides capital residents – and only capital residents – with a steady source of employment. In Scotland, Edinburgh, not Glasgow, houses the majority of "national" institutions, including the Royal Museum of Scotland, the National Gallery, the National Portrait Gallery, the Scottish Agricultural Museum, the Scottish Mining Museum, the Scottish Museums Council, and the Scottish Vintage Bus Museum, in addition to the Scotland Office, the Scottish Arts Council, the Scottish Charities Office, the Scottish Higher Education Funding Council, the Scottish Law Commission, and various consulates for foreign countries (Rosie 2000). Even though the distance between them is small by Canadian standards, the varied economic realities of the two cities reinforce a sense of difference, something compounded by their different religious and ethnic profiles. This perception of regionalism within Scotland is an important fact in itself. If the nation is a living organism, it is relevant that some members of the organism see themselves operating in conditions unrecognizable to other members. Perception alone could establish a sense of distance within the nation that would strike a chord were it not borne out by very real economic disparities among the regions. As it stands, the differing economic fortunes of Highland and Lowland, east and west, ensure that the daily lives of individuals are remarkably varied within the nation.

As in Scotland, almost 80 per cent of Quebec's population lives in the southern portion of the province. In Quebec this includes the fertile St Lawrence Lowlands next to the river. Initially encompassing land on either side of the St Lawrence River, the provincial boundaries were extended in 1912 to include all land up to the Ungava Peninsula. Also as in Scotland, most Quebecers live in two cities, Montreal and Quebec City, the smaller provincial capital. Until 2004 Montreal was Canada's second largest city, a spot now held by Vancouver. Any sense of difference between Montreal and Quebec City stems from the presence of a multicultural and multilingual population that distinguishes Montreal from the rest of the province. By measures of ethnicity, mother tongue, and language use, Montreal's heterogeneity stands in stark contrast to the provincial capital, let alone other smaller cities within the province. Although Quebec as a province hosts a visible-minority population comparable in proportion to Manitoba – 7 and 8 per cent respectively – the proportion of Montreal residents belonging to visible-minority groups is 14 per cent. The visible-minority populations of the other cities in Quebec vary from 0.6 per cent in Saguenay to 2.6 per cent in Sherbrooke. The numbers are equally striking when we look at the immigrant population in the urban centres of Quebec. Almost one-fifth of Montrealers were not born in Canada. By contrast, four of the remaining five largest towns in the province contain immigrant communities that represent less than 5 per cent of the population.

Levels of economic activity vary throughout Quebec. The nationalist Lac Saint-Jean/Saguenay region recorded an unemployment rate for 2003 of 11.3, while the jobless rate in Trois-Rivières stood at 10.5. By 2005 these figures had dropped to 9.8 and 7.4 respectively. Both rates not only are higher than the capital's rate but rival rates of joblessness in St John's, the capital of perennially depressed Newfoundland. The cities of Quebec, including Montreal, have four of the nine highest urban unemployment rates in Canada.[1]

Also as in Scotland, the concentrated population affects the location of industry and employment prospects. Inaugurated in 1959, the St Lawrence Seaway was considered the main entry point to the North American continent and linked the Atlantic Ocean to the Great Lakes. Proximity to the seaway thus brought prosperity. The north of the province, by contrast, is sparsely populated; the five northernmost federal constituencies occupy 1,133,243 kilometres.[2] This area represents just over 10 per cent of the total Canadian land mass and almost three-quarters of Quebec's territory. Approximately 370,000 individuals live in these five constituencies. Thus an area almost five times larger than the UK and fifteen times larger than Scotland houses the population of Edinburgh. The concentration of population and economic and political resources obviously undermines the perceived national homogeneity in both Scotland and Quebec.

Table 2.2 explores the distribution of visible-minority and foreign-born populations in the largest cities in Scotland and Quebec. In addition, it uses unemployment as a single proxy for economic health. In the four largest cities in Scotland, unemployment varies from 5 per cent in the capital to double that in Glasgow. Although proportions of foreign-born and immigrant populations vary slightly, it is worth noting that levels in general are far lower than they are in

Table 2.2
Economic and ethnic diversity by metropolitan centres, Scotland and Quebec

	Pop	*Unemp't*	*Visible-minority population*	*Foreign-born population*[1]	*Yes vote 79/80*[2]	*Yes vote 97/95*	
Glasgow	635,409	11.0	5.5	4.8	54.0	83.6	75.0
Edinburgh	445,026	5.0	4.1	7.6	51.0	71.9	62.0
Dundee	154,674	10.0	3.7	4.5	49.5	76.0	65.5
Aberdeen	207,974	5.0	2.9	5.9	48.3	71.8	60.3
SCOTLAND	**5,062,011**	**7.0**	**2.0**	**3.4**	**51.6**	**74.3**	**63.5**
Montreal	3,507,200	9.5	13.6	16.4	33.3	34.8	
Quebec	696,400	6.8	1.7	2.2	47.0	53.5	
Sherbrooke	157,000	7.4	2.6	3.8	43.2	53.3	
Saguenay-LSJ	157,800	11.3	0.6	0.7	56.3	68.9	
Trois-Rivières	140,100	10.4	0.9	1.3	41.0	55.6	
QUEBEC	**7,125,580**	**9.1**	**7.0**	**9.9**			

SOURCES: Statistics Canada 2001 census; Scotland's Census 2001.
1 Immigration figures for Scotland do not include residents born in the Republic of Ireland.
2 The 1979 referendum results were calculated at a regional level. These represent the figures for the Strathclyde, Lothian, Tayside, and Grampian regions respectively. The 1980 referendum results were aggregated from constituencies. Saguenay–Lac Saint-Jean includes the 1980 constituencies Chicoutimi, Dubuc, Jonquière, Lac Saint–Jean, and Roberval, Quebec includes the 1980 constituencies Charlesbourg, Charlevoix, Chauveau, Jean-Talon, Limoilou, Louis-Hébert, Montmorency, Portneuf, Taschereau and Vanier. Montreal includes the 1980 constituencies Anjou, Bourassa, Bouget, Crémazie, D'Arcy McGee, Dorion, Bouin, Jacques-Cartier, Jeanne-Mance, L'Acadie, Lafontaine, Laurier, Maisonneuve, Marguerite-Bourgeoys, Mercier, Mont-Royal, Notre-Dame-de Grâce, Outremont, Robert Baldwin, Rosemont, Sainte-Anne, Saint-Henri, Saint-Jacques, Saint-Laurent, Saint-Louis, Sainte-Marie, Sauvé, Verdun, Viau, and Westmount.

Quebec, something that can be expected given the aggregate results discussed earlier. Although aggregate results of ethnic diversity are higher in Quebec, four of the five largest cities have foreign-born and visible-minority populations indistinguishable from the rates present in Scotland. Even if we think of Quebec as a relatively heterogeneous nation in terms of ethnicity, its capital, Quebec City, has a smaller proportion of foreign-born residents than Edinburgh, the capital of the far more homogeneous Scotland. The table serves to illustrate, then, that within these nations, their urban centres can produce different demographic backdrops for nationalist debate, and that in some respects urban centres in Quebec have more in common with large cities in Scotland than they do with the metropolis. According to the numbers listed here, Sherbrooke looks more like Dundee than Montreal.

POLITICS IN THE NATION

The previous chapter emphasized the ways in which voters in Scotland and Quebec distinguish themselves from other Britons and Canadians, but it is also worth noting that not all within the boundaries of the polity share the same partisan preferences; nor do they wish for the same constitutional settlement. Sovereignists in Quebec and Scotland may have campaigned for increased self-determination, but this was not a uniform preference, or even the dominant one at times. Significant portions of residents in Scotland and Quebec have consistently backed parties other than those espousing nationalist or sovereignist programs, have shied away from supporting greater self-determination, and in some cases have not considered themselves to be "Scottish" or "Québécois." Sometimes their preference is informed by demographic characteristics, such as language or religion. Understanding the extent of support for and opposition to nationalist projects of institutional change helps to better illustrate the interactions among national members. We can approach such views both in an organized or collective sense and through an examination of individuals.

Partisan divisions within Scotland and Quebec for Canadian and UK elections help us to understand the aggregate preferences of the nation but also demonstrate that at each election a significant proportion of individuals voted contrary to the tide of public opinion. While the Labour Party was earning a plurality of the votes and seats in Scotland, the Conservative Party continued to earn more than a third of the popular vote for much of the postwar period. Labour's apparent hegemonic status in Scotland has had more to do with the way the electoral system transforms votes to seats, and the comparative electoral failure to earn similar proportions of either in England, than any absence of rival partisan preferences. In Quebec, close elections were not uncommon, despite what the distribution of seats might suggest. To say that Scottish voters have tended to prefer the Labour Party and Quebec voters have tended to prefer the Liberals in federal elections must not take away from the existence of a substantial proportion of the electorate that does not support these options. Although it came close in 1966, Labour has not won a majority of the vote in Scotland in the postwar period. In the same span of time, however, the Liberals in Quebec have earned at least half of the popular vote in six elections, capturing in 1980 over two-thirds. Although Labour in Scotland has fared comparatively better than the Liberals in Quebec, we must acknowledge that between one-half and one-third of the electorate has in each case preferred to vote contrary to the majority. In addition, the nationalist parties have not carried a majority of electoral support in Canadian and UK contests, although here the Bloc Québécois has been a more dominant force on the electoral stage than has the SNP. Since 1993 the BQ has earned between one-third and one-half of the popular vote. The SNP, by contrast, has bounced between just over 10 per cent and just over one-third. All this suggests that a significant proportion of the electorate has shied away from backing what might be considered national trends in voting behaviour, just as a similar proportion has avoided the nationalist partisan option.

Territorial politics within the nation provide an additional opportunity to view the diversity of partisan views. Obviously, the occasion to make such observations is limited in Scotland, given the absence of a parliament until recently. That partisan politics operates in local elections, however, helps us to understand the distribution of partisanship within the nation. From 1974 to 1994 local elections in Scotland were divided between regional council elections, covering nine regions of the mainland, island council elections for the Western Isles and Shetland and Orkney Islands, and district elections, which were more akin to those for municipal governments in Canada. As of 1994, the local council system was reorganized into thirty-two authorities. If we examine the voting patterns for the local elections, then, we acquire an approximate sense of how voting in any Scottish assembly might have unfolded. Obviously, there are concerns with such an approach. Local, rather than national, issues would have dominated such elections. A party adept at making connections at the local level would not necessarily handle policy for an entire polity particularly well. But because the regional and district councils were responsible for the delivery of services that would have been governed by policy in any Scottish assembly, services such as housing and education, we may feel relatively comfortable with such an approach.

Three conclusions emerge from the regional and district voting data (see tables 2.3 and 2.4). First, there are significant variations in support across Scottish regions. The island councils, for example, were dominated for twenty years by Independents, rather than by Labour or the Liberals. In the first election in 1974 Independents

Table 2.3
Voting in regional council elections, Scotland, 1974–94

	Labour	*Independent*	*SNP*	*Liberal*	*Other*
1974	172 (36.6)	114 (11.8)	18 (12.0)	11 (4.9)	.5 (7.6)
1978	117 (38.8)	89 (4.8)	18 (20.4)	6 (2.2)	6 (4.2)
1982	186 (37.6)	87 (5.1)	23 (13.43)	21 (18.2)	1 (0.1)
1986	223 (43.8)	79 (4.8)	36 (18.2)	33 (15.0)	2 (1.2)
1990	233 (51.8)	73 (5.4)	42 (26.4)	40* (10.5)	5 (3.5)
1994	220 (41.1)	65 (4.7)	73 (26.7)	61* (12.2)	3 (1.5)

NOTE: Data are based on ward-level data found in Denver 1994; UKDA Study 3301. Results are seat won, with popular vote in parentheses.

* Includes Liberal Democrats, voters for Liberals now included as "other." Results do not include voting for unitary island councils, where Independents captured in excess of 85 per cent of the popular vote in every election, 1974–94.

Table 2.4
Voting in district council elections, Scotland, 1974–95

	Labour	*Conserva-tive*	*Independent*	*SNP*	*Liberal*[1]	*Other*
1974	428	241	345	62	17	23
1977	299	277	318	170	31	22
1982	494	229	289	54	40	21
1986	545	189	267	59	1	92
1990	554	163	227	110	84	20
1994	468	204	228	150	94	14
			After council reorganization			
1995	613 (43.6)	82 (11.5)	155 (7.7)	181 (26.1)	121 (9.8)	7 (1.4)

NOTE: Data are based on ward-level data found in Denver 1994; UKDA Study 3301. Results are seat won, with popular vote in parentheses.

1 Results are for Liberal Democrats as of 1990.

received 100 per cent of the popular vote, and by 1994 they were still garnering 90 per cent of voter preferences. In the mainland regional and district councils, however, Labour clearly dominated. Thus the mainland partisan competitions had far more in common with Westminster elections. Indeed, for much of the period, the support received by the Labour Party in local elections was almost identical to the proportion of votes received in Westminster competitions. The same level of support was also garnered by the Conservatives. Third, Liberal, or LibDem, and SNP support in local elections, whether at the regional or the district level, appears to emphasize Westminster electoral success. Clearly, the two were not, however, benefiting equally for partisan divisions. From 1978 to 1983, for example, the Liberal Party saw a dramatic increase in its share of the popular vote, doubling its support upon its reincarnation as the Liberal Democrats. The SNP, by contrast, saw its support halve over the same period, from 20.4 per cent in the first regional election in 1974 to 11.8 in the federal election in 1983. Over the next decade, the fortunes of each party reversed, so that SNP support gradually climbed again and Liberal Democrat support fell. For both parties the trend is obvious, and in each instance in the opposite direction. Local and district voting in Scotland does not appear to highlight different voting preferences from those present at the state level. Stable Labour and Conservative support in Westminster mirrors stable support in local elections. The declining and rising fortunes of the SNP and Liberal Democrats merely highlight trends evident at Westminster. The same cannot be said of provincial voting in Quebec.

Provincial voting patterns in Quebec provide more robust findings. Voting in National Assembly elections (see table 2.5) contributes more to our understanding of national identity and political culture; if self-determination is a goal for a significant proportion of the population in Quebec, then the National Assembly would be considered the forerunner to any independent parliament. Even among those not calling for greater self-determination, the body that creates policy for the nation could be considered the focal point of its political culture. Partisanship in Quebec, however; does not operate as it does in Scotland. For example, all parties contesting seats in Quebec can be described as nationalist. Distinguishing among them requires one to examine their support for separatism and their position on the left-right spectrum. These two spectra overlap, but not perfectly; nor have the parties been static on these spectra. The Parti Québécois is at present both the most supportive of constitutional change and the most left-wing or social democratic in its policies. As a result, voters in Quebec might choose the PQ for its social democracy or for its position on the national question, or both. The other main option available to voters is the Parti Libérale du Québec (PLQ). Similar in colour scheme and economic outlook to its Canadian counterpart, the PLQ since the 1960s has advocated a range of constitutional options that fall short of independence but promise more than unreformed federalism. In time for the 1994 election these two were joined by the Action Démo-

Table 2.5
Voting in Quebec National Assembly elections, 1867–2007

	PLQ	*Con/UN*		*PQ*	*Others*
1867	12 (35.5)	**51 (53.5)**			1 (11.1) (1 riding vacant)
1871	19 (39.4)	**46 (51.7)**			
1875	19 (38.6)	**43 (50.7)**			3 (10.7)
1878	31 (47.5)	**32 (49.5)**			2 (3.0)
1881	15 (39.0)	**49 (50.4)**			1 (10.7)
1886	**33 (39.6)**	26 (46.2)			6 (14.2)
1890	**43 (44.3)**	23 (45.1)			7 (10.63)
1892	21 (43.7)	**51 (52.4)**			1 (3.9)
1897	**51 (53.3)**	23 (43.8)			
1900	**67 (53.2)**	7 (41.9)			
1904	**67 (55.4)**	7 (26.7)			
1908	**57 (53.5)**	14 (39.9)			3 (6.6)
1912	**63 (53.5)**	16 (43.0)			2 (3.45)
1916	**75 (60.6)**	6 (35.1)			
1919	**74 (51.9)**	5 (17.0)			2 (31.1)
1923	**64 (51.5)**	20 (39.3)			1 (9.2)
1927	**74 (59.3)**	9 (34.3)			2 (6.4)
1931	**79 (54.9)**	11 (43.5)			
1935	**47 (46.5)**	17 (18.9)			25 (29.4)
1936	14 (39.4)	**76 (56.9)**			
1939	**70 (54.1)**	15 (39.2)			1 (2.3)
1944	37 (39.4)	**48 (38.0)**			6 (22.7)
1948	8 (36.2)	**82 (51.2)**			2 (3.3)
1952	23 (45.8)	**68 (50.5)**			1 (3.7)
1956	20 (44.9)	**72 (51.8)**	UN		1 (3.3)
1960	**51 (51.4)**	43 (46.6)			1 (2.0)
1962	**63 (56.4)**	31 (42.2)			1 (1.5)
1966	50 (47.3)	**56 (40.2)**			2 (3.1)
1970	**72 (45.4)**	17 (19.7)		7 (23.1)	12 (11.2)
1973	**102 (54.7)**			6 (30.2)	2 (9.92)
1976	26 (33.8)	11 (18.2)		**71 (41.4)**	2 (5.4)
1981	42 (46.1)			**80 (49.3)**	
1985	**99 (56.0)**			23 (38.7)	
1989	**92 (50.0)**			29 (40.2)	4 (3.7)
1994	47 (44.4)	1 (6.46)		**77 (44.8)**	
1998	48 (43.6)	1 (11.8)	ADQ	**76 (42.9)**	
2003	**76 (46.0)**	4 (18.2)		45 (33.2)	
2007	**48 (33.1)**	41 (30.8)		36 (28.3)	

NOTE: Proportion of popular vote in parentheses. Results in bold are for party winning the most seats.

cratique du Québec (ADQ), a broadly federalist party that offers an economic platform more in common with conservative options.

Given support for the Liberal Party federally, one might expect a string of provincial Liberal governments since 1867. This has clearly not been the case. Provincial politics has been characterized

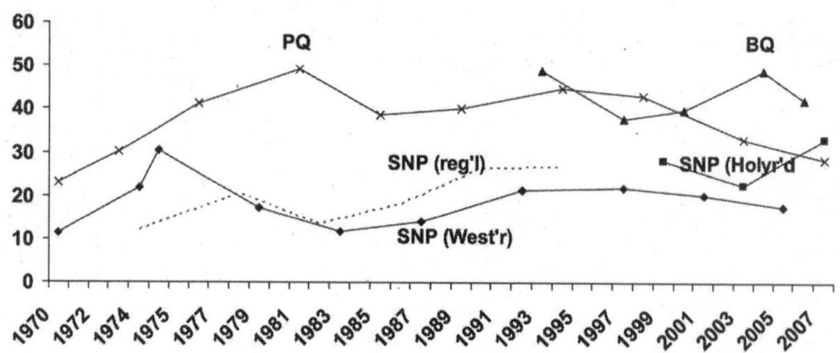

Fig. 2.1 Support for autonomist parties in Scotland and Quebec, 1970–2007

by the presence of conservative voting options for Quebecers, whether as the Conservative Party, the Union Nationale, or the more moderate and recent ADQ. Politics in the 1970s and 1980s were distinct, first, in their relative absence of a viable conservative option for voters. The second distinguishing characteristic of this period was the presence of a sovereignist party. In some respects the PQ has served as had the Conservative and UN parties: as a viable alternative to Liberal governments. Recently, Quebec voters have turfed out governments after no more than two terms, a process that began in 1960 with the election of the Liberal Party. Before then, governments could count on more stable support. The Union Nationale formed a government for fifteen years, and the Liberal Party was in power from 1867 to 1936.

As can be seen with the federal results, provincial partisan support has not been one-sided. While the option of two main rivals increased the likelihood that one would earn a majority of support, significant proportions backed the losing candidates, even when the distribution of seats offered landslide majority governments. In 1931, for example, 79 of the 90 seats went to the Liberals, even though 43.5 per cent of voters had backed the Conservatives. Since the second election in which it contested seats, the Parti Québécois has earned more than one-third of the popular vote, on par with support for the Bloc Québécois. This is more than the SNP has earned in the first three elections of the Scottish Parliament.

Graphing support for the nationalist parties in Scotland and Quebec, we see clear peaks in support: one in 1974 for the SNP and in

Table 2.6
Voting in Scottish Parliament elections, 1999–2007

	Labour[1]	*SNP*	*Conservatives*	*LibDems*[1]	*Other*
1999	56 (38.8, 33.6)	35 (28.7, 27.3)	18 (15.6, 15.4)	17 (14.2, 12.4)	3 (1.8, 6.8)
2003	50 (34.9, 29.3)	28 (23.8, 20.9)	18 (16.5, 15.5)	17 (15.1, 11.8)	17 (7.7, 16.5)
2007	46 (32.1, 29.2)	47 (32.9, 31.0)	17 (16.6, 13.9)	16 (16.2, 11.3)	3 (2.1, 14.6)

NOTE: Proportions of constituency votes and regional list votes in parentheses.
[1] Coalition partners, 1999–2007.

1981 for the Parti Québécois (see fig. 2.1). Both saw their support swell in the early to mid-1990s, but levels have not changed dramatically since. The 2004 strong showing for the Bloc Québécois could have stemmed from frustration with the federal Liberal Party, rather than increased support for independence. Disappointment with the Labour–LibDem administration in Edinburgh likely also explains the 2007 surge in support for the Scottish National Party.

In some respects, the options facing Scottish voters in devolved elections have much more in common with the choices available during British general elections (see table 2.6). This is not the case in Quebec, despite parallels one might draw between the PLQ, PQ, and ADQ to the Liberals, Bloc Québécois, and Conservative parties. The Labour Party, Liberal Democrats, Scottish National Party, and Conservatives all contest seats at both the UK and devolved levels, and the extent to which they are autonomous versions of the British party or are subsumed in the larger whole varies from party to party. While Scotland may be portrayed as a Labour stronghold, even the Conservatives, the party assumed to have preferences anathema to the wishes of typical Scottish voters, holds just shy of 20 seats in the 129-seat legislature. These parties have been joined by a number of other smaller parties, such as the Greens and Scottish Socialist Party, which because of the first-past-the-post electoral system employed in Westminster elections, could not hope to gain seats easily. The Additional Member System (AMS) in the Scottish Parliament ensures that the varied preferences of Scottish voters are better reflected in the composition of the legislature. This is not the case in Quebec, where demographic trends require Liberal support to increase dramatically before the party is rewarded with seats in the National Assembly. AMS also all but guarantees Labour coalition governments in perpetuity.

Comparing sub-state voting in Scotland and Quebec, one finds that both the autonomist parties have placed themselves on the left of the political spectrum, a choice not always made by nationalist parties. Indeed, even within Scotland the SNP began as a nationalist alternative to the Conservatives, earning itself the nickname "tartan Tories." Both currently advocate internationalist policies and are more supportive of the EU and NAFTA than their partisan counterparts, although the SNP is a later convert to this position than the PQ. Perhaps most important, both have advocated a variety of constitutional options since their incarnations, from greater self-determination to independence, sovereignty-association to undefined partnership. Given that they were formed by an amalgam of interest groups and parties on the left and the right and representing a diverse range of constitutional preferences, this position is not surprising. In addition, the tactics by which greater self-determination might be acquired have also occupied members of the party. These have included a parliamentary approach and what might be considered a consultative approach: for some within each of the parties, gaining support in elections provides a mandate to negotiate constitutional change; for others, it provides the opportunity to hold a referendum, which would result in a mandate to negotiate should a majority of voters express their support. It is worth noting that there is not only diversity within the nation but also diversity within the nationalist movement on its ideological moorings, its goals, and its tactics.

Public support for the varied constitutional options can help to give a sense of dominant preferences within the nation (see fig. 2.2). In the last thirty years, independence has been supported in both Scotland and Quebec by smaller proportions than have softer constitutional options such as devolution or sovereignty-association. In Quebec, for example, support for independence peaked at 50 per cent in 1990 but for most of the period hovered between one-quarter and one-third of the population. Sovereignty-association – and more recently, sovereignty partnership – has consistently polled above 50 per cent, reaching as high as 67 per cent in the early 1990s. In Scotland, devolution polled consistently above 45 per cent, reaching its lowest levels of support in the years following the 1997 devolution referendum. Interestingly, support for devolution was declining as the 1979 referendum approached, but it spiked sharply afterwards and again in the years before the second referendum. We do not see similar differences in support either before or after the two referendums in Quebec. We see marked increases in support for both inde-

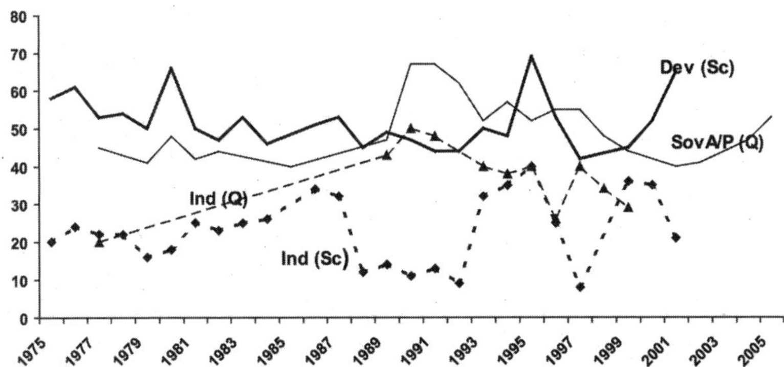

Fig. 2.2 Support for constitutional options in Scotland and Quebec, 1975–2005

SOURCES: Data are from Cloutier et al. 1992; Pinard 1997; System Three; CROP 1996–2005.

pendence and sovereignty, however, during the ratification efforts of the Meech Lake and Charlottetown accords.

We know that just as Scotland and Quebec possess characteristics that distinguish them from the larger state, so too do they possess within themselves considerable demographic, economic, and political variation. It is worth probing further the relationship between demographic and economic differences and varying support for nationalist parties and greater self-determination. Are members of all linguistic groups equally supportive of the PQ or sovereignty-association? Is religion a relevant predictor of devolution or support for the SNP? Part of the salience of diversity within a nation depends on the way in which it exacerbates or masks political cleavages within the nation. Understanding the relationship between demographic and political diversity will help us to better understand perceptions of national identity, inclusion, and exclusion. This analysis in turn will enable us to examine the impact of national identity on political culture.

DIVERSITY AND NATIONALISM

We began this chapter by adopting a relatively exclusive definition of national membership. This was of analytic utility as it helps us to better understand diversity within the borders of a nation. It certainly should not be seen as an unexamined pronouncement about membership in the nation. And yet individuals within both Scotland and Quebec might at times question their membership in the nation because of just such a definition. The concern that the Québécois nation includes only French Catholic residents descendant from the original settlers of the province is clearly a key issue in the nationalist debate. The implicit assumption of such charges is that Quebec is a white nation, inhospitable to newcomers. Charges of exclusion are not limited to one linguistic group or religion and have not been helped by the intolerant views held by individuals who have aligned themselves with the nationalist cause. More than historical artifact and not purely of recent provenance, exclusion within Quebec nationalism has been aimed at a series of overlapping groups such as anglophones, visible minorities, the Jewish community, and the Muslim community by diverse individuals and organizations. Polling data also demonstrate that the last three groups have been subject to exclusion outside Quebec's borders, and still further data point to similar experiences for francophones outside Quebec. Separatist efforts to prove that Quebec offers an inclusive nation to which all willing participants may feel they belong rely on repeated statements by both the Parti Québécois and the Bloc Québécois and on the party membership of individuals from the anglophone and visible-minority communities. Public pronouncements about inclusive membership have not, however, eradicated the inherent suspicion with which some individuals view the Quebec national project. The issue, perhaps, is not how many individuals support independence or the PQ or see themselves as Québécois but, rather, who holds such views.

In the UK, England contains more residents born in Scotland than Scotland contains migrants from south of its borders. English migration to Scotland is an issue less because of the number of individuals involved and more because of the perception of class. Never more than fringe organizations, Settler Watch and Scotland Watch have long decried the admittedly small number of English landowners in the Highlands of Scotland. The English community is not particularly tight-knit, but evidence of anti-English discrimination has prompted some to suggest that English residents are as likely to find themselves victims of racism and harassment as visible minorities. By analyzing the social demographic factors that can account for support for various political parties or for sovereignty itself, we can provide a clearer picture of diversity within the nation. The election studies for Canadian and British elections include questions about support for constitutional options and parties supported in the past federal and provincial, or sub-state elections.

In both Scotland and Quebec, those from non-dominant groups, whether linguistic, ethnic, or religious, have charged that nationalism as a political project does not leave room for their membership in the nation. Such criticisms are often grounded in the lived experiences of individuals who feel they have faced discrimination from the state, from organizations, or from individuals. At the same time, nationalist political parties and their leaders and spokespeople have made repeated public pronouncements that the only condition of membership in the nation is residence within its borders and have suggested that the only precondition necessary for membership in the sovereignist cause is a fundamental belief in the importance of greater self-determination for the nation. In the face of this contradiction, it is worth noting two things. First, individuals who feel they do not belong because their lack of membership in the nation has been made clear to them, by the actions or behaviours of others, are clearly not imagining things. Even if they are, their perception forms the basis for a subjective national identity. Second, the inclusive messages provided by the leadership of nationalist and sovereignist political parties clearly coexist with more exclusive visions of the nation held by members of their own parties. Nationalism in Scotland and in Quebec contains figures who have articulated explicitly racist and intolerant views about "incomers" and "ethnic voters" and true members of the nationalist cause. There is not only evidence of such views from the past but also more recent examples. The task of those who belong to non-dominant groups is to determine whether the views of others determine their own perceptions of belonging. The eventual decisions made by such individuals help us to better understand the relationship between the nation and the state, between national identity and political culture.

Given levels of demographic diversity within these two nations, we might expect support for sovereignty, or for sovereignist parties, to be distributed unevenly. The results certainly suggest that this is the case. For each nation we can focus on four dichotomies: whether individuals are members of the dominant linguistic group, whether they are members of the dominant religion, whether they are immi-

Table 2.7
Support for sovereignty among demographic groups in Quebec

	Bloc Québécois	*Parti Québécois*	*Quebec sovereignty*
French	.488	.594	.423
Non-French	.308	.135	.194
Catholic	.476	.552	.400
Non-Catholic	.381	.344	.328
Immigrant	.427	.343	.311
Canadian-born	.466	.543	.398
Cosmopolitan centre	.433	.447	.353
Not cosmopolitan centre	.468	.550	.426

NOTE: Results are mean scores of support for the BQ, PQ and Quebec sovereignty respectively. Results in bold indicate T test scores that are statistically significant at the .05 level.

grants, and whether they live in a cosmopolitan setting. If we focus on these four dichotomies, we find that there are indeed differences in levels of support for sovereignty and sovereignist parties in Quebec but not in Scotland.

The 2000 Canadian Election Study asks respondents how they feel about the Bloc Québécois and the Parti Québécois and how they feel about sovereignty. If we convert both of these scales so that they run from 0 to 1, where 1 implies maximum support, we can examine the mean responses for each question. Table 2.7 shows that francophones and non-francophones possess statistically different levels of attachment to sovereignty as a political goal and to the main sovereignist parties contesting elections. In addition, religion appears to be a significant predictor of support for sovereignty. Catholics are far more likely to be supportive of the BQ and its policies. If we look at cosmopolitanism and immigration, however, we find that while Canadian-born Quebecers and those outside large metropolitan centres such as Montreal are far more likely to support sovereignty as a political ideal, they do not hold the BQ in higher esteem than immigrants or Montreal residents. Interestingly, support for the Parti Québécois is more in line with support for sovereignty as a concept than it is with the political goals of the BQ. For all four groups there are significant differences in levels of affinity for the PQ.

When we analyze similar data for Scotland, we do not find similar differences in attitudes. There are no statistically significant differences between voters in Scotland's largest city, Glasgow, and those in the rest of the nation. Although the British Election Study does not gather data on immigrant status, it does ask about visible-minority status. Unfortunately, the numbers of non-white residents and of non-English speakers are so small – less than 15 in both cases – that comparisons to other respondents is not possible. These figures confirm points raised earlier: that the geographic boundaries of Scotland contain a far more homogeneous population in terms of ethnicity and language than that found in Quebec. There are, however, significant differences between Presbyterians and non-Presbyterians in terms of support for independence. Presbyterians were far less likely to support independence than were non- Presbyterians. An investigation of support for independence suggests that those who do not belong to any organized religion are most supportive of independence, followed closely by Catholic respondents. In Quebec those belonging to the dominant religion are most supportive of independence. In Scotland, however, those in a similar position are least likely to support further constitutional change.

The relative weight of demographic predictors is not particularly surprising. If we know that nationalism is grounded in particular traits, then those who hold such traits might be supportive of its political goals. And so if pillars of national identity in Quebec have focused on demographic traits and in Scotland they have focused on institutions, then we might expect that demography would be more likely to produce political cleavages in one nation and less likely in the other. These data provoke, however, far more questions than they answer: to what extent do political parties acknowledge these cleavages and employ them in their political rhetoric? how does identity play a role in these decisions? to what extent is this evidence of ethnic nationalism in Quebec? The following chapters answer these questions.

CONCLUSION

Clearly, the markers of difference that distinguish Scotland and Quebec from their larger states also serve to distinguish citizens within the boundaries of the nation. In the case of internal diversity and demographic similarity, it is the sociological importance of the distinction that guarantees its salience and influence. The different constitutional structures in Scotland and Quebec have dictated that nationalist political parties assert themselves and pursue their goals differently. The early recognition of administrative autonomy in Scotland has provided a generally accepted recognition of national status. The institutional accommodation available to Scotland and Wales, particularly in the form of a secretary of state, was not available for equally diverse regions in England (MacCormick 1998). Despite the presence of a provincial government and its role as the de facto representative of French Canada, recognition of Quebec's nationhood has been much less accepted by the rest of Canada. The consensus that exists among British parties operating in Scotland pre-empts the need for discussions about particularity that drive much of the debate between Quebec and the rest of Canada. National status for Quebec is thus contested in a way that it is not in Scotland. Its recognition was central to constitutional negotiations in the 1980s and 1990s, and reluctance among federalist parties to acknowledge Quebec's status as a nation has encouraged autonomist parties to reassert the objective and subjective markers of nationhood. Its continued salience is evident in the desire of contenders for the leadership of the Liberal Party to declare Quebec a nation. The apparent appeal of such a declaration was later exploited by Prime Minister Stephen Harper, whose government in November 2006 introduced a motion declaring that "the Quebecois form a nation within a united Canada." The nuances of the motion and its potential impact on political debate will be discussed in subsequent chapters. For now, the lack of recognition has affected the way in which Quebec nationalists have constructed the boundaries and membership of the nation. That there is still much convincing to be done by Quebec suggests that full acknowledgment of Quebec's distinct society could move the debate away from social characteristics and closer to the value-driven debate in Scotland.

Scotland and Quebec exist not only as sociological constructs but as bounded polities. Nationalism in both cases has employed that which distinguishes the nation from the state and has identified potential cleavages within the nation that serve as fodder for political argument. We are interested in Scotland and Quebec not just because they are nations but because of the interaction between national identity and political culture. It is worth noting that just as not all citizens share the same language or religion, so not all citizens share the same political views.

In this way anglophones, for example, have sometimes doubted whether the Quebec nation has room for them within its boundaries. This is an example of those not possessing what is seen to be a pillar of national identity failing to align themselves with a nationalist or sovereignist party, political option, or identity. In other cases, individuals might not lack an identified trait or characteristic, but might still feel outside the nation. Literature on national identity does not enunciate a list of desirable characteristics for national membership, and it certainly does not suggest that one must be of a particular race to be Scottish or Québécois, but visible-minority voters and allophones have publicly questioned whether they belong. If we want to understand the boundaries of the nation, we have to understand both the charges made against inclusion and the ways in which nationalists enunciate the characteristics of the nation and its membership.

3

The Political Use of National Identity

Research on the development of political attitudes grounds our personal beliefs, visions of society, and participation in agents of childhood socialization such as the family, religious environment, and education system. The media, political parties, and the governments they form can colour our perceptions as adults, socializing us into a wider culture. Often it is state institutions that exert a dominant role, largely because the state has a monopoly on the institutions that structure our daily lives, whether through education, law, or the government. In stateless nations, the absence of a state does not leave individuals without agents of socialization. Instead, national institutions are left to fill the gap. For some authors, the very absence of a state infrastructure, which could provide objective markers of difference to citizens, encourages a level of vigilance in the protection of a national identity. Civil society, as the guarantor of that identity, would thus assume a heightened importance in such situations. Those looking to examine the discourse on national markers of identity might consider political party documents and government accords that deal explicitly with issues of national identity or the political future of the nation. The intended audience of many of these documents is the national electorate.

In his exposition of banal nationalism, Michael Billig highlighted the subtle ways in which public debate forms people's perceptions about the nation. In "commonplace discussions about politics, foreigners and royal families," nations assert an "everyday ideology" of national identity (Billig 1995a). The salient features of national identity, the markers of belonging, can be discerned either by their explicit enunciation or by more nuanced displays. In other words, if we want to know who is included in a nation, we can look for statements about membership and inclusion and national boundaries: X is a member, but Y is not; our nation is founded on such shared characteristics as *a*, *b*, and *c*. We can also look for less explicit statements about the important pillars of identity. These surface in debates about the nation and political autonomy. Examples of both explicit and implicit treatment may be found in Scotland and Quebec. Nationalist publicity in both nations highlights markers of belonging in its attempts to establish a sense of national difference. If greater political autonomy is desired by many nationalists, part of the justification for any separate treatment is that the current situation does not serve a particular population and that the population, by virtue of certain characteristics, warrants such treatment. In so doing, nationalists articulate the boundaries of the nation and the criteria for national membership.

The chronicling of national characteristics in party manifestos and constitutional documents, often used to establish comparisons between the nation and the rest of the country, identifies the relevant markers of belonging. By emphasizing certain markers or characteristics over others, we can start to see how perceptions of the nation and national identity might take shape. Cues about nationhood, for example, might give us a sense of whether we have a credible claim of belonging to the nation. If having Scottish ancestry is important to claiming Scottish national identity, then we might doubt our own belonging in the nation if this is something we do not possess. Similarly, if fluency in French is seen as an important marker of membership in the Québécois nation, we might feel confident that we belong if French is our mother tongue.

Scottish identity is not, however, an essentialized, reified object bestowed upon residents at the border. Equally, there is no Québécois identity kit that awaits new arrivals. There are, though, common identity markers that Scots or Québécois may draw on to animate their national membership. These markers are rooted firmly in institutions of daily life and the values that those institutions are supposed to inculcate. The resulting national identity is a product of social and historical forces manipulated, wittingly and unwittingly, by a political and cultural elite and the population within the physical borders of the nation. These produce common images and perceptions of the nation and its members for both an international and a domestic market.[1] This approach sees nations as living, breathing organisms, existing because of the support of their members. According to such a construction, it is individuals who ultimately determine their own level of belonging in the nation. They may base their judgment in part on cues from agents of national socialization.

Given previous descriptions of Scotland and Quebec, we might have a preconceived idea about the potential markers of identity. If the two cases distinguish themselves from the rest of their respective countries by language, religion, political preference, and institutions, we might expect that these elements would play a central role in the sociological boundaries of the nation. Similarly, we already know that these two nations contain populations exhibiting diverse religions, languages, ethnicities, and political views. We can watch for the treatment of the elements that unite the populations in Scotland and Quebec and the issues or characteristics that divide them.

Scottish national identity draws on the existence of a separate people who were incorporated into the larger United Kingdom. It thus draws on the shared history of a people that enjoyed independence and on the institutions that distinguished it following its loss of independence. In public debate much less is made of the links between contemporary Scottish national identity and an independent Scotland. Instead, the roots of contemporary Scottish national identity are linked to the trinity of post-union Scottish institutions that sustained a sense of separateness after the Treaty of Union in 1707. Interestingly, much of the dialogue suggests that the nation of modern Scotland exists *because of* the treaty rather than despite it. The image of an egalitarian nation, communitarian and meritocratic in ethos, where members get ahead by hard work rather than by connections, is linked in public documents to the existence of the church, education, and legal system, institutions that predated and survived the eighteenth-century union.

Each of the four political parties operating in Britain chronicles the characteristics it believes to best highlight Scottish distinctiveness and emphasizes the importance of post-union institutions. As the sole party explicitly linking nationalism to independence, the SNP and its members not surprising provide frequent references to the pillars of Scottish national identity. Often, these imbue modern Scotland with the legacy of its past: "Scottish society has a historical base of its own which has framed much of the Scottish character and approach" (SNP 1987). "The Scots ... have also inherited and retained ways of life and thought and expression which are unique to Scotland" (SNP 1983). The consistent message, through manifestos and speeches of the 1980s and 1990s, is that Scotland is unique, not only from England and Wales but in the world, "an ancient European nation in our own right" (Salmond 1995b). Or, as Allan Macartney put it, "Few people around the world would doubt Scotland's identity as a nation. Scots are recognized as such all over the world ... Scotland is, without question, one of Europe's most ancient nations. Her borders have been stable since the early middle ages and her political independence was preserved into the modern era" (Macartney 1997, 2).

That a nationalist party sees Scotland as distinct is not particularly surprising. How it sees the nation as distinct, however, can tell us more about the boundaries of the nation. "Scotland's institutions in the law, religion, education, administration and in sport still have their distinctive national characteristics despite persistent erosion by the Westminster Parliament" (Macartney 1997, 2). "Scotland prides herself on a history of invention and enterprise ... [and] is synonymous with educational excellence and technological advance" (SNP Parliamentary Group 1998, 1, 9). Education is seen as particularly important pillar. Once "the envy of Europe" (SNP 1983), the Scottish education system is credited with a legacy of literacy and seen as evidence of contact with an intellectual tradition in Europe. Another institution protected in the Acts of Union, the legal system, also receives attention. Long "viewed with pride and rightly so" (SNP 1999, 31), the legal system is portrayed as a philosophy rather than a trade (W. Ewing 2002, 2).

References to a distinct national character are employed by more than just the SNP. Each of the other three main parties in Scotland has, for example, underlined the importance of the Scottish education and legal systems. Even the Conservative and Unionist Party affirms the existence of a "clear Scottish identity" (SCUA 1992). Conservative leader John Major, the 1992 manifesto adds, "believes that the growing successes of Scotland are down to the qualities of the people of Scotland" (SCUA 1992, 51). The qualities themselves lie undefined, but constant references to a discrete Scottish voice within the document suggests that Scottish distinctiveness is unquestioned. Later documents refer to the Scots as "the world's greatest instinctive entrepreneurs," a nation of "patriots, entrepreneurs and innovators" with "an internationalist outlook ... by culture and history" (SCUA 1997). The Liberal Democrats agree, noting that "Scotland has a proud tradition as inventors and entrepreneurs," "proud traditions in university education," "once led the world in medicine," and has a "tradition of enterprise and innovation" (SLD 1999). Never to be outdone, Labour also notes that "Scotland has a proud educational tradition ... a history of enterprise and innovation" (SLP 2003).

The Presbyterian Church of Scotland, charged with infusing in Scottish identity a sense of egalitarianism because of Calvinism and the democratic structure of the church itself, receives far less attention from political parties. Created by John Knox, the General Assembly of the established church offered opportunities for members to debate and vote on issues related to doctrine, practice, and national life. That process has continued today in the activities of the Church and Nation Committee, which itself discusses the nation and national membership in its publications.

Although each of the main parties emphasizes the importance of post-union institutions, the SNP has been the most explicit in its attempts to link these institutions with Scottish distinctiveness. It refers to such institutions with far greater frequency than the other parties, but the tone is certainly not out of step with its partisan counterparts. The institutional pillars of Scottish society are perceived as important in themselves, but also for how they socialize a population. The education system is believed to foster egalitarianism in its role as the great social leveller. Formal education and its importance is associated with positive movements in Scotland's historical development. The Scottish Enlightenment, that period in the eighteenth century when Edinburgh thinkers such as Adam Smith, David Hume, and William Robertson articulated ideas that made Scotland the intellectual vanguard of Europe, is portrayed as the result of distinctly Scottish traits, highlighting the importance of education in Scottish life. Paradoxically, that period which now so defines Scottish distinctiveness was at the time witness to a desired integration of Scotland within the cultural, social, and intellectual world of Britain. In "North Britain," Scottish patriotism and dedication to the British state went hand in hand (Calder 1994; Colley 1994; Daiches, Jones, and Jones 1986; Devine and Mitchison 1988; M. Lynch 1992).

This is not to say that the education system *has* produced a meritocratic society or that the democratic structure of the Church of Scotland *has* produced an egalitarian nation, but rather that there is a pervasive *belief* that the current nation – communitarian, egalitarian, meritocratic Scotland – owes its existence to these institutions. If nations and nationalism rely on common myths to explain their existence, then this is one of the larger myths of Scottish national identity – first, that the Scots are egalitarian and, second, that it is a result of their institutions that they have developed this way. Thus by doctrine and by structure, the church, education, and the legal system feed a myth of "lad o' pairts" communitarianism credited with influencing everything from approaches to culture to voting patterns (Product 2000; Brown, McCrone, and Paterson 1998). Or, as SNP MSP George Reid puts it, "the whole Scottish tradition [is] a tradition built on the commonweal of the Celts, the moral responsibility of the Calvinists, the social concern of the Catholics, the humanity of the Labour movement and the civic nationalism of today" (Reid 1995, 5). In part, the institutions reinforce a sense of distinctness because they are institutions with which individuals will have the most frequent contact as a result of their mere existence. They are also perceived to be important because of *how* they are different from similar institutions in England.

While in Scotland political parties of all stripes recognize the existence of a nation, in Quebec national status is contested. All mainstream political parties argue that Quebec is distinct, and even smaller parties and federalist organizations affirm that Quebec is unlike other provinces. What distinguishes these two sides, however, is the extent to which "distinctness" implies nationhood. The Parti Québécois has been explicit in its belief that Quebec satisfies the characteristics of a nation. Such pronouncements fulfill almost perfectly the requirements for nationhood as established by Geertz: "the political action of the Parti Québécois is founded on the existence of the people of Quebec; a distinct people; a people occupying a clearly identified territory; a people with the right to self determination" (PQ 1987, 5).[2] Statements such as "la langue française est au coeur de notre identité" (PQ 1990, 6) and "the educational system is the cradle of society ... the sense of belonging to Quebec society [is] shaped within it" (PQ 1994a, 15) further reinforce the message. This view is not limited to the sovereignist PQ. "Le Québec est une nation ... Il possède une identité propre et unique, une culture, une langue et des traditions" (ADQ 2004, 2). In 1980 the Quebec Liberal Party came close to labelling Quebec a nation but shied away, noting that "Quebec forms within the Canadian federation a society which is distinct in terms of its languages, its culture, its institutions and its way of life ... Quebec society has all the characteristics of a distinct national community" (PLQ 1980, 13)

Grounding its analysis in the same distinctions of language, culture, and institutions, the Parti Libérale du Québec has usually argued for the recognition of a distinct society and not a nation. In post-1995 speeches in Alberta and Ontario, PLQ leader Daniel Johnson defended the efforts of parties within Quebec to ensure that province was recognized as a distinct society by citing many of the traits emphasized by the PQ and ADQ (Johnson 1996, 1997). The language of nationhood was absent from such speeches, but avoidance of this factor could have been due to the intended audience rather than the views of the PLQ. In documents from the same period the party refers, for example, to Quebec's "identité nationale" (PLQ 1997). This differentiation, between a distinct society and a nation, is an interesting one. In Scotland parties of all political stripes affirm without fanfare the existence of a Scottish nation. In Quebec, however, the label of nationhood is used with precision. It is as if, for the Liberal Party in Quebec, the avowed preference for political federalism precludes the possibility of recognizing a constituent nation within Canada, a stance that would no doubt strike devolution advocates in the UK as surprising. In Scotland quasi-federalism makes sense *because* of the existence of separate nations. In Quebec it seems that the Quebec Liberals believe an admission of Quebec's nationhood might *undermine* arguments for federalism.

This perception changed following a federal Conservative motion declaring the Quebecois a nation. In February 2007 former federal Progressive Conservative leader and Quebec Liberal premier Jean Charest declared, "Yes, Quebec is a nation. Quebec is a force for change within Canada and a Liberal government represents this locomotive of change for Canadian federalism" (Séguin 2007). The statement is consistent with earlier views of the PLQ, in that it emphasizes the party as main locus of activity, as the province write small. It obviously contains a far more explicit recognition of national status, something that the party had been dancing around for decades. The 2007 electoral program of the party likewise acknowledges the existence of "notre nation et ... son identité unique" (PLQ 2007). Although the federal motion lacks constitutional status, it appears to have allowed the main federalist party operating within Quebec to end the perceived oppositionalism between recognition of national status and support for federalism, something that brings the debate closer to that which usually occurs in Scotland.

The extent to which national membership is portrayed as inclusive or exclusive relies in part on the identified pillars of its identity. Language, of course, provides a key distinction. "We Quebecers ... are undoubtedly North Americans, of French roots and culture," Parizeau explained to a New York Forum on International Business (Parizeau 1991, 11). In its policy paper on the constitutional situation the Liberal Party agrees that "la langue française exprime ce qu'il y a de plus profond et de plus distinctif dans l'identité québécoise" (PLQ 1997, 4). The creation of a distinct identity predates the creation of a francophone province within Canada at Confederation in 1867. The arrival of French settlers in the 1600s and the British Conquest in 1759–60 provide two developmental phases for an identity with an ever-present attention to the "other." Although the Quebec Act of 1774 guaranteed the continued prosperity of the French education system, the Catholic Church, and a seigneurial system of land tenure, the development of a distinctly Québécois identity, as opposed to a French Canadian one, lies in the increasing involvement of the Quebec government in the social welfare of its citizens. With the Quiet Revolution of the 1960s, the linguistic and cultural vitality of French Canadians became a formal priority of a proactive and interventionist provincial Liberal government. While linguistic and religious differences prompted extra constitutional powers in the Constitution Act of 1867, and in turn informed a francophone vision of Canada that relied on the partnership of two founding peoples, it was only in the latter half of the twentieth century that provincial borders began to dictate identity labels. As the 1994 PQ platform notes, "Canadiens du XVIIe siècle, Canadiens français du XIXe siècle et maintenant Québécois, rarement a-t-on vu un peuple chercher aussi longuement son identité" (PQ 1994b, 1).

It was religion rather than language that remained the most important pillar of identity until the 1960s. Following the Conquest, the absence left by a departed political and social elite was filled by a church convinced of its providential mission in North America (Dufour 1989). Language at this time merely provided the cultural buffer that sustained a Catholic presence within Canada. The desire of the institution to maintain a culture served to construct an exclusive national identity. Despite declining attendance, the church remains a powerful pillar. Over 80 per cent of Quebecers are Catholic, and the institution, through its annual statements, often underlines the role of the church in contemporary political debate.[3]

The Yes pamphlet for the 1980 referendum argues that by language and culture, Quebecers are distinct from other Canadians and, furthermore, that not only does this difference convey upon Quebec the status of proxy nation for French Canada but that any constitutional settlement offering less than full equality between the two "peoples" is an injustice to Quebecers (Directeur général des élections du Québec 1980a). In part, the No side agrees, claiming that Quebec possesses a French culture and "spirit" that distinguishes it from English Canada (Directeur général des élections du Québec 1980b). The major difference between the two is that while the Yes side argues that the difference predated Confederation, the No side contends that difference developed as a result of post–1867 constitutional accommodation.

Statements of political parties from within Scotland and Quebec consistently illustrate the importance of key institutions in the generation of a national identity. Documents from the larger state are less consistent. In Scotland political parties based in London have affirmed the presence of a Scottish nation, while in Canada support for a distinct people in Quebec depends on the political stripe of those in government. Federalists and sovereignists alike note that Quebec is different. For federalists, however, this recognition has not necessarily implied the existence of a Québécois nation within a Canadian nation. The 1997 Liberal red book, the collection of policy proposals for the governing party in the first election after the 1995 referendum, noted, "Canada's French fact is concentrated in Quebec, with its distinctive character stemming from, among other things, a French-speaking majority, a unique culture, and a tradition of civil law. It is an essential part of Canadian identity" (Liberal Party of Canada 1997, 22). Although citing the same pillars of national identity mentioned by sovereignists and nationalists opting for less drastic constitutional change, the federalist Liberals emphasized that Quebec is distinct but that Canada is the one nation within the state.

The Conservative motion that recognized the Quebecois as a nation within a united Canada attempted to distinguish two key points. First, its phrasing appears to suggest that Quebec is a nation only so long as it remains within Canada, but that it is not an independent nation. This argument in itself is meaningless, for national recognition cannot be contingent on the absence of sovereignty for the nation. The second distinction offers national recognition to the people of Quebec – "les Quebecois" – but not to the geographic entity itself. This was no doubt another attempt to undermine future claims to self-determination. The result, however, is a motion that is far more exclusive in its definition of national membership that anything offered by sovereignist parties in Quebec. In documents written in French, "les Quebecois" refers to all residents of the province. In a motion otherwise written in English, "les Quebecois" extends national membership to francophones. The motion is thus consistent with what we might remember of Mulroney's Conservative governments, sympathetic to the concerns of Quebecers, willing to recognize distinctiveness, and unafraid of the consequences of such recognition. Its appearance on the federal scene, born of a desire to undermine attention to a Liberal leadership contest and a soon-to-appear Bloc Quebecois motion, seems less thought out, more extreme, and yet less meaningful than anything offered by previous Conservative administrations.

If Scottish national identity is seen as civic and inclusive, this perception could stem in part from the attention to institutions when the boundaries for the nation are discussed. All children, regardless of ethnicity or religion, pass through a Scottish education system that, whatever its actual influence on attitudes and behaviours, is credited with propping up a distinct national identity. It is a universal institution to which all are exposed. At the same time, though, the inclusiveness of national membership has received explicit attention from political parties. For its part, the SNP has gone out of its way to include all within Scotland's borders. By grounding a discussion of national membership in formal citizenship, it moves the debate to what might already be more inclusive grounds. Since its inception, the party has argued that all resident within Scotland, regardless of birth or origin, would be granted citizenship in an independent Scotland. In the early 1990s the party moved beyond qualifications for citizenship and began emphasizing that diversity was "a source of enrichment for Scottish society" (SNP 1992). It was not until 1995, however, that statements of inclusion assumed a far greater role in conference speeches by SNP MPs and that membership in the nation, rather than citizenship in a future Scottish state, or membership in present "society" was on offer: "We cannot adopt for a new nation any symbols or structures that even inadvertently exclude any section of Scottish society. We must find a means to express Scottishness as an inclusive, not exclusive statement of identity" (Salmond 1995b, 2). Later that year Salmond further emphasized: "No one should be asked to sacrifice their identity to be part of Scottish society ... In the same way no minority group should be asked to give up their culture or badges of identity to be fully accepted as Scots. There will be no cricket tests in a free Scotland. We see diversity as a strength not a weakness of Scotland and our ambition is to see the cause of Scotland argued with English, French, Irish, Indian, Pakistani, Chinese and every other accent in the rich tapestry of what we should be proud to call, in the words of Willie McIlvanney, 'the mongrel nation of Scotland'" (Salmond 1995a, 5).

As a nationalist party, the SNP is a target for those who claim that nationalism by its very nature is an excluding force. For this reason, it is not surprising that the party has gone out of its way to communicate an inclusive construction of the nation. The other parties in Scotland, even when relying on nationalist arguments for the existence of a parliament, have shied away from labelling themselves nationalists. As a result, there is far less attention to the language of nationalism, including membership in the nation. Although explicitly addressing issues of inclusion, the Liberal Democrats focus on the polity itself, arguing that all Scottish citizens feel excluded by Westminster politics (SLD 1997). The Conservatives emphasize the importance of recognizing diversity, but for them diversity seems to mean including rural voters, not just urban residents: "Unlike Labour, I recognize that diversity is one of our defining characteristics and greatest strengths as a nation. They have imposed their urban values on everyone" (McLetchie 2003, 4). Labour agues Scotland should be welcoming to "people from different cultures, nationalities and backgrounds" (SLP 2003).

Devolution provides a clear turning point in Scottish political rhetoric. Until 1997 one party, the Conservatives, remained opposed to devolution and grounded its opposition to such change in the negative impact of nationalism: providing a parliament to a people because they claim to be different serves only to emphasize that which distinguishes Britons from one another, rather than what unites them. For much of the 1980s and 1990s the Conservative

Party adopted a rhetoric that emphasized the exclusive nature of nationalism as practised explicitly by the SNP and implicitly by Labour and the Liberal Democrats. This is not to say that the Conservatives denied the existence of a Scottish nation or Scottish national identity. Speeches and manifestos from the party take for granted Scotland's status as a nation, although they credit the union with its continued development: "The development of a clear Scottish identity has been enhanced by the Union" (SCUA 1992, 49). Since 1997 the Conservative Party's rhetoric has remained largely unchanged. In 1998, for example, British party leader William Hague referred to the "corrosive poison" peddled by the SNP (Hague 1998, 1). Such arguments have been joined, however, by the voices of the Labour and Liberal Democrat parties, who view further institutional reform as a sop to nationalism. Where once these two parties advocated institutional change on the basis of national difference, they now emphasize the exclusive and dangerous nature of nationalism. Labour warns of the "upheaval" associated with the SNP's plans (SLP 2003). In this, the post–1997 rhetoric of the Labour and Conservative parties remains remarkably similar, stressing the exclusive nature of nationalism that the SNP tries so hard to dispel. In short, within Scotland all parties advocate the existence of a Scottish nation. Before 1997, three parties – the SNP, Labour, and the Liberal Democrats – believed that national difference warranted separate treatment in the form of an assembly or parliament. After devolution, three parties – the Tories, Labour, and the Liberal Democrats – have argued that national difference is a dangerous basis upon which to seek changes to political arrangements. Both before and after devolution, the unionist parties avoided an explicit definition of national membership or the inclusive nature of Scottish national identity. If we want to know who belongs to the Scottish nation, we have only the views of the SNP to guide us.

The increasing presence of a dialogue of inclusiveness in Scotland is matched in Quebec. Until the early 1990s there were occasional but infrequent references to membership within the nation: "A new inward-looking Quebec would not be worth creating nor worth experiencing. Whether a new Quebec exists or not will depend on the degree to which it opens up to all corners of the earth while assuming the small but equitable place it deserves in the world" (Bernard 1983, 4). It is worth emphasizing that, if infrequent, the rhetoric from the Parti Québécois and its members has in official pronouncements been consistent. When not addressing membership explicitly, PQ documents provide evidence of the value of diversity within the nationalist cause. The 1984 issue of the party's magazine *Défis québécois* highlights the election of Greek-born Nadia Assimopoulos as vice-president of the PQ and the growing appeal of separatism within the allophone community. Statements about inclusion have become far more common since the early 1990s. In 1991, for example, the PQ addressed the issue of national membership by holding a conference and later participating in a "dialogue" with the anglophone community in Quebec. The result was a report in 1993 from the PQ Task Force on the Status of the English-Speaking Community in a Sovereign Quebec. Recognizing that anglophone Quebecers might feel considerable anxiety when faced with the prospect of sovereignty, the report acknowledges the historic role of the anglophone community, the asset that the community would provide to a sovereign Quebec, and the role that anglophones could continue to play in Quebec as long as they choose to remain within the territory. The document stops short of offering membership in the nation, although it does not deny such inclusion. It views as beneficial for the anglophone community "that English-speaking Quebecers feel just as comfortable in Quebec as members of the Francophone majority" (PQ 1993, 25)

In its promotional material the Liberal Party notes that the party itself is open to "toutes les Québécoises et tous les Québécois, sans distinction d'origine, de langue, de culture ou de situation économique" (PLQ n.d.) Indeed, the PLQ argues that it is the only party which has successfully integrated members from different corners of society. In its literature it emphasizes, not the inclusive nature of Quebec, however, but rather the inclusive nature of the Liberal Party. The ADQ, by contrast, has adopted a position far closer to the Parti Québécois. In the 2004 clarification of its constitutional position the party affirms that "tous ceux et celles qui vivent au Québec sont des Québécois, sans exception" (ADQ 2004, 3).

More than just the political parties explore the existence of a nation and its inclusiveness. Resolutely agnostic on the issue of independence (Assemblée des évêques du Québec 1995), the Catholic Church in Quebec is explicit in its recognition of collective membership. Asking if those of French ethnic origin are Québécois, the bishops argue, "Incontestablement! L'histoire, le sang, la terre, l'enracinement, les institutions, les traditions, l'attachement, un projet national, le nombre, un État, tout concourt à former chez lui un très riche faisceau d'appartenances qui lui permet de dire: ici, je suis bien chez moi!" (Assemblée des évêques du Québec 1977). It continues to note that anglophones and Aboriginal Canadians resident in Quebec also feel a sense of belonging to the territory. For the bishops, the boundaries of any French and Catholic nation extend beyond the borders of Quebec: "La communauté canadienne-française constitue un groupe linguistique et culturel enraciné depuis plus de quatre siècles en terre canadienne où il a trouvé comme un berceau de vie, de travail, de souffrance et de rêve" (Assemblée des évêques du Québec 1977). In 1979 the bishops were more explicit, stating that they preferred to refer to "le peuple québécois" rather than the Québécois nation. The boundaries around this grouping were firmly drawn by language: "Les francophones du Québec constituent sûrement un peuple par leur langue, leur personnalité, leurs traditions, leur génie propre, leur sentiment de solidarité et leur 'vouloir-vivre collectif'"(Assemblée des évêques du Québec 1979). By 1995 the bishops had also incorporated the theme of diversity within their statements, although they sought to distinguish between the Quebec population, which included "la communauté anglophone [et] ... de nombreux groupes ethno-culturels" and a francophone "peuple québécois" (Assemblée des évêques du Québec 1995). A similar distinction is found in documents from the government of Quebec.

The Quebec draft agreement on the constitution noted that former prime minister Brian Mulroney had argued the constitution must re-establish the bond of trust between Quebecers and the federal government and therefore must acknowledge the distinct character of the Québécois (Gouvernement du Quebec 1985). The draft agreement notes that recognition of the existence of a people of Quebec is a prerequisite to the agreement and participation of Quebec. Furthermore, it argues that the agreement must be between the people of Quebec and the population of the rest of Canada. Thus it draws a firm distinction between a population – an aggregate of individuals – and a people in possession of a language, culture, and history. Reflecting upon the wrongs caused by the repatriation of the constitution without the consent of Quebec, the draft agreement argues that Canadian institutions must reflect the particular needs of the Québécois people, influenced as they are by a distinct language, culture, and society.

The above exploration of how the nation is discussed by political actors suggests that content and context play a role in our understandings of the nation. The *content* of what is articulated is relevant in identifying the distinguishing features of a national identity. In their emphasis of certain characteristics, agents of socialization project a sense of the nation's boundaries. If Catholicism is salient to Québécois identity, then the boundaries around the nation can be drawn around a Catholic population. The intended *audience* of what is articulated is also relevant. A national identity, and thus the boundaries of the nation, can be identified to those outside the geographic borders of the nation. A sense of Scottish national identity can thus be articulated to an English population living outside Scotland. It can also be articulated to those within the geographic boundaries of the nation. Thus individuals who might not be considered, or might not consider themselves, members of the nation play witness to a debate about the salient features of identity. We know that the potential audiences are not the same in Scotland and Quebec. A more heterogeneous population in Quebec would thus not only be more attuned to perceived exclusion in the dominant construction of the nation, but could also expect greater attention from political actors to the inclusive nature of Québécois national identity. The more homogeneous Scotland is less attuned to potential exclusion in the way identity is constructed; nor does it warrant the same dialogue of inclusive membership from those hoping to temper or contradict perceptions of exclusion.

The *context* of the articulation is also relevant. Context can affect how national identity is framed, the perceived importance of national pillars, and the perceived salience of national identity among the public. In this sense, it can affect the impact of the content on the audience. For our purposes, two differences in context are worth highlighting. First, within the United Kingdom Scotland is recognized as a nation, while within Canada Quebec has not been. This previously discussed feature affects the goals of nationalists in both cases, as for one group the demand for differential treatment, concessions, or greater respect depends on a prior debate about existence. That Scotland is assumed to be a nation removes the obligation for nationalists to enunciate the many and varied ways in which Scotland and Scots distinguish themselves within the UK. In Quebec, however, this is not the case. Quebec politicians re-emphasize the pillars that distinguish Quebecers from other Canadians, not because of a backwards obsession with history, but because national status has never been recognized.[4]

In part this is a tricky argument. On the one hand, Canada is perceived as a compact of two founding peoples, English and French. In this sense, as the only government that can claim to speak for one of these peoples, the government of Quebec assumes a heightened level of importance. Ensuring that it is afforded this right depends on a continual reinforcement that Quebec represents a French people. On the other hand, the Canadian federation is increasingly seen as partnership among provincial equals. Efforts to introduce levels of asymmetry or to further decentralization must also rest on the extent to which the federal government does an insufficient job of attending to the needs and wishes of Quebecers. This argument can rest on economic terms but also on social value differences between Quebecers and the rest of the country. Particularly when led by PQ administrations, the government of Quebec may further claim that greater devolution of powers rests in the existence of a nation. In both cases, then, context encourages mention of the existence of a nation and the enunciation of its markers in one nation and not in another. Although the recent federal motion recognizing the Quebecois as a nation does not provide constitutional protection and thus fails to link national status and differential treatment for the nation, it does appear to have the capacity to alter the context in which political debate occurs. Internal political debate in Quebec now appears closer to Scotland, where the acknowledgment of national status is not linked to position on the political spectrum, but rather is an entirely predictable element of party manifestos.

A second difference in context may be seen in political events. At times the nation is relevant, and other times it is not. It is worth asking when it might be useful to focus on the nation, to identify its borders and enunciate the pillars of its identity. Election campaigns, certainly, would be times of heightened importance. These provide an opportunity for those with differing visions of the nation to make their appeals to voters. When it is a state election, conducted throughout the UK or Canada, voters in Scotland and Quebec might find the nation a more salient object. Asked to pass judgment on a government, voters in Scotland might base their decision on the treatment the nation enjoys at the hands of the state. Referendum campaigns are also obvious times when the nation becomes more salient, when identifying what a nation is, who it is, and where it is heading is a more explicit issue in the minds of voters.

Identifying these differences in context protects us against making false assumptions given the records at our disposal. If we are examining the views of political parties, for example, the bulk of that material is produced during election and referendum campaigns. We are investigating what a party thinks about the nation and national identity by examining documents written at the height of its salience. Examining these discourses at their most explicit helps us to perform our task, particularly if we believe that this is when concepts such as nation and identity might assume different roles when they become politicized. We should be wary, however, of assuming that national discourse is always this way.

THE POLITICIZATION OF NATIONAL IDENTITY

Political parties make reference to national identity in an effort to draw boundaries around the electorate, to highlight its characteristics, and often to then show how that particular party or this particular side in an argument is the most consistent with popular understandings of national identity. The link between national identity and political culture emerges in the way political actors and organizations speak about the national project. The salience of identity in political debate, the way national identity is linked to the history of the nation, to rights, and to democracy, and the extent to which identity with the nation is seen as compatible with identity to the state all in turn help to identify the *implicit* boundaries of the nation and national identity.

History and Progress

If, as Edward Said claimed, the process of self-definition is exposed in the practice of writing history, the way in which political parties and constitutional documents view the historical development and progress of the nation betrays certain predispositions in their views on identity (Said 1995). In particular, the documents seek to locate the present with respect to the past. In his examination of Scottish history, Smout notes: "National identities are constructed out of references to history, or more exactly, to received popular ideas about history that achieve mythic status" (Smout 1994). Interpretations of history, much as with debates about which party best represents national interests, can degenerate into arguments over who best understands the development of the nation. Charges that other parties cannot understand the nation are linked with charges that neither can they understand its history: "the SNP have misunderstood not only recent Scottish history but also the real global challenges Scotland must meet" (Labour Party 1999). The following section examines the ways in which diverse political agents view similar historical events and the perceived obstacles to national progress. In part this issue speaks to the perceived compatibility of nation and state identities.

Written after a third Conservative victory, the 1988 Scottish *Claim of Right* is forceful in its assessment of the political system. References to "faulty British policy ... [and] fundamental flaws in the British constitutions" mark the opening section. The language employed by the final report of the Scottish Constitutional Convention also heralded the use of a rights-based dialogue that has continued to dominate nationalist debate. *The Claim of Right* includes an analysis of the union that is unambiguous in its verdict. Although claiming that the 1707 treaty ensured the official recognition of Scotland's status as a nation, it argues that the "Union has always been, and remains, a threat to the survival of a distinctive culture in Scotland." Complimentary analyses of the partnership found elsewhere in academic literature are not mentioned. Rather, it argues that if the union had any benefit, it was in the lack of English interference in Scottish political matters, a point later expanded by Paterson (1994a). The report mentions a series of dates, marking increasing power granted to the Scottish Office (1885, 1926, 1939) and the growing centralization of the British state. The picture drawn is one of a forced political union that has stifled Scotland's political development. In making this argument, it echoes academic discourse in Quebec, which argued in the 1950s and 1960s that the Conquest or the Catholic Church, or both, had stunted Quebec's political and economic development.

SNP documents echo this theme. Two years before the 1997 devolution referendum then SNP leader Alex Salmond argued:

> We have not fared well. Whilst, as an ancient European nation in our own right, we have shared the desire for the building of a new community, we have been too often left on the sidelines as the work of construction goes on in sight, but out of hailing distance ... 100 years ago we were amongst the most prosperous nations of the world, a powerhouse of industry, providing manufacturing muscle at the centre of a major empire. Now we often appear to be a social and economic backwater, perched on the fringes of a third rate, badly focused and perpetually wrong footed power. (Salmond 1995b, 1)

Several of the documents refer to the need for Scotland to "become a normal nation, playing a normal part in the world" (SNP Research Department 1995, 6). Scotland deserves better, argues the SNP, and must "put these wasted, futile years behind ... and be a nation again" (SNP 1992, 2).

In their assessments of the union, both Labour and the Conservatives highlight the strong and vibrant partnership that has guaranteed economic success and political voice for an otherwise small nation. The Labour Party, for example, calls for a "vibrant Scotland within a strong Britain working together for a healthy and prosperous Europe where our children can grow up confident and comfortable in their complementary identities: Scottish, British and European" (SLP 1992). A more tempered view of the union appears in Labour's *New Scotland, New Britain* document: Scotland's new Parliament "addresses both the wrongs of the past and the challenges of the future" (Brown and Alexander 1998). It is in its assessment of the historical wrongs endured by Scotland that the Labour document testifies to a particular view of national development. On the whole, the paper treats Conservative administrations and negative aspects of Westminster as interchangeable. Under Labour, Westminster is seen as a beneficent force in British politics, granting democracy to Scotland. The problem, it would appear, is not the British constitutional settlement but rather Mrs Thatcher. This personification of history attempts to direct the critique away from English power within the union towards "the constitutional consequences of Mrs Thatcher ... NO [*sic*] second Mrs Thatcher could ever inflict such damage on Scottish civic life again" (Brown and Alexander 1998). Needless to say, the document shies away from the generic applications of this statement – that no democratically elected and supported English prime minister could ever control Scottish civic institutions again.

Assessments of the desired future development of Scotland differ along party lines. For Labour, success lies in the creation of a multinational country. "Can Britain become, as we would like, the first successful multicultural multiethnic multinational country?" (Brown and Alexander 1998). Despite the obvious problems with such a statement – in particular, the omission of various other countries already possessing charters of rights, multiculturalism policies, and higher proportions of immigrants – the document clearly outlines Labour's preferred future strategy. The answer is a renewed democracy, new legislatures for Scotland and Wales, a freedom of information act, and legislation protecting individual rights all under the rubric of "a modern democracy." Increased fairness – a fair citizenship law, a fair chance – is seen as a definite marker of progress. In its 1992 manifesto the Conservative Party expressed its preference for a different plan: "The Union has evolved since its inception in 1707. We have seen the establishment of the Scottish Office and the creation of the office of Secretary of State for Scotland. Most of Scotland's government is administered by Scots in Scotland ... it is only as a full and equal partner in the Union that Scotland can remain strong" (49, 50). In an effort to undermine the links established by the SNP between self-confidence and independence, the Conservative Party claimed, "As Scots, we are sufficiently self-confident to be able to share our sovereignty within the United Kingdom, within Europe and in the wider world" (SCUA 1992). Since devolution, Labour and Conservative visions of an ideal future appear remarkably similar: "We can build on what we've started, inside the UK, using the powers of devolution to take our country forward or we can rip it all up and start again with the Nationalist's plans for a separate Scottish state and risk all the upheaval and uncertainty that would create at this difficult and challenging time in Scotland and elsewhere" (4). This statement is from the 2003 manifesto of the Labour Party, but it would be at home in any of the Conservative manifestos since 1979.

Within Quebec the emphasis of separatist partisan programs has changed dramatically over the past twenty years. Where once the Parti Québécois attempted to highlight and reinforce the sense of difference dividing francophone Quebecers and other Canadians, party platforms now approach sovereignty and self-determination as a natural, if long overdue, step in the development of any nation. As the party stated in 1994, "Le peuple québécois existe. Le Quebec comme pays est encore à venir" (Parti Québécois 1994a, 1). Or, in an earlier document by the PQ administration:

> For generations and against all odds, we have maintained an identity that sets us apart in North America ... We must believe that we are mature enough, and big enough, and strong enough, to come to terms with our destiny ... [We have accumulated] all the essential experiences ... The Quebec nation is a family that will soon be four hundred years old. Long before reaching that age, in both the Americas, Anglo Saxons, Spaniards and Portuguese gained their sovereignty. History has delayed our emancipation for a long time, but it has not prevented Quebec society from maturing and painfully reaching a level where it could progress and administer and govern itself. We Quebecers are a nation, the most firmly anchored nation on this continent. Over the vast expanses of our land, our deep-rooted memories and our vital presence are constant reminders that the Quebec people is at home here, in this, its ancestral home ... this home [is] completely ours ... delays have taken a heavy toll. We have also been left with a strong inferiority complex, which is the only real reason for our hesitations. We have the chance now to get rid of it once and for all and we have no right to let this chance go by ... We will not hesitate, then, at the great crossroads of the referendum, to choose the only road that can open up the horizon and guarantee us a free, proud and adult national existence, the road that will be opened by us (Gouvernement du Québec 1985).

In documents that consistently employ the future tense, national sovereignty is portrayed as an essential prerequisite of Quebec's social and economic development. Federalism, not in its direct application but as a theory of governance, is portrayed as a barrier to national development. If Quebec were to transcend its present arrangements, the benefits would accrue not only from the security of an internationally recognized collective identification but also through an end to feelings of inadequacy and disempowerment (Bloc Québécois 1998b). If it is to be an adult and legitimate nation, a step for which it is qualified, Quebec requires independence: "the attainment of sovereignty is a normal process, one that has been undertaken by all nations elsewhere in the world ... As Quebecers, we should be masters in our own house, masters of our destiny" (PQ 1994a, 4).

SNP documents also address the issue of rights, but rather than emphasising the absence of democracy within the pre-devolution settlement, they point out that Scots may choose, at any election, to exercise their right to self-determination (SNP 1983; SNP Research Department 1995; Salmond 1996, 1998a).[5] Scots must rise up and "demand what is [their] birth right" (SNP 1987). Self-determination is projected as a normal progression for a people. Since the 1980s the SNP has compared Scotland to other smaller nations both in Europe and further afield, including Norway, Austria, Denmark, the Netherlands, and Ireland. It is compared unfavourably to other, now independent, parts of the British Empire, including Canada, India, and Ghana (Macartney 1997). Its control over its own affairs is compared negatively to Flanders, the Basque region of Spain, and the Isle of Man (Allan 2002). Here the image is of a nation held back by twentieth-century ties to a faded imperial power. Such documents indicate that independence is a normal step for smaller nations and that its automatic consequence is not economic disorder. "Scotland can be a real and independent nation again," notes the 1997 manifesto of the SNP (SNP 199b, 3). The implication, of course, is that without independence, nationhood is in jeopardy: "Normal status in the world is what independence is about. We stand for a modern vision to transform Scotland with 21st century independence" (SNP 2001, 4). The statement presents something of a paradox, as the very notion of a nation-state is a decidedly nineteenth-century preoccupation. The 2001 SNP manifesto clearly conjures that adage of post-Second World War diplomacy: "Every nation has the vocation and right to form a state. Just as mankind is divided into a number of nations, so the world should be divided into the same number of states. Every nation is a state, every state a nation" (Bluntschli 1866, 17).

Those less supportive of sovereignty have attempted to interpret destiny in their own way. The 1980 No pamphlet reminds Quebecers of the strong francophone leaders of their past, men such as LaFontaine, Cartier, Laurier, St Laurent, and Trudeau, to whom, it is obliquely argued, current voters owe their continued Canadian citizenship (Directeur général des élections du Québec 1980a). In contrast, the 1980 Yes pamphlet and the 1985 Quebec government report *Quebec-Canada: A New Deal* chronicle a list of injustices endured by Canada's francophone population. Beginning with the Conquest, such lists pass through the Manitoba Schools Question and Regulation 17 in Ontario. Earlier lists typically end with anglophone objections to Bills 22 and 101, both of which are portrayed as efforts to maintain a fragile francophone identity. Later depictions, most notably the preamble to Bill 1, An Act Respecting the Sovereignty of Quebec, decry the wasted efforts of constitutional negotiations in 1982, 1987, and 1992: "We were hoodwinked in 1982 ... The failure of the Meech Lake Accord in 1990 confirmed a refusal to recognize even our distinct character. And in 1992 the rejection of the Charlottetown Accord by both Canadians and Quebecers confirmed the conclusion that no redress was possible" (Gouvernement du Québec 1995).

If Scottish political documents differ primarily, though not exclusively, in their understandings of the past, political documents in Quebec offer diverse understandings of collective destiny. In part this difference could stem from the stage and focus of each separatist movement. This is not to deny that Scottish documents deal with future political issues or that the Scottish parties hold different preferences for future institutional development. That devolution offered to Scotland a constitutional step which was less radical than that attempted in Quebec could account for the relative degree of consensus in Scotland. The Scottish National Party, standard-bearer for independence, was initially not supportive of devolution, but a considerable portion of civil society backed the project. The Scottish Constitutional Convention outlined the various ways in which devolution could correct the specific injustices of the past. Calls for gender equality, for example, constituted a specific attempt to deal with inequities in the existing system and highlighted the ways in which a changed future could provide for greater political equality. As 1997 approached, even the SNP backed the devolution option advocated by Labour, the Liberal Democrats, and other elements of civil society. Before devolution the difference between Scotland and Quebec stemmed from notions of destiny. Future political change in Scotland was seen as necessary, not because it was owed to Scots, but rather because the present situation had to be changed. Separatists within Quebec have argued, in contrast, for the fulfillment of a natural and evolutionary step in national development, a tactic now adopted by the post-devolution SNP.

Rights and Democracy

Rights and democracy, particularly collective rights and self-determination, provide a second theme within the public documents. An examination of each of these themes highlights the ways in which organized groups have undermined the democracy of the pre-devolution settlement and the current situation in Quebec. In Scotland one of the most effective critiques of the unitary system of government concerned the "absence of democracy" (Brown, McCrone, and Paterson 1998; Kellas 1989). Unionism was seen as anti-democratic because individuals were not receiving the governments for which they voted. If one sees a democratic system as the political rule of the majority over the minority, however, the democratic deficit years of 1979–97 can be understood as unfortunate for Labour voters in Scotland but not necessarily undemocratic. The argument is made possible by the use of Scotland as a meaningful aggregate that deserves its own democratic results. Efforts to link the democratic spirit of Scotland with the anti-democratic political system are on shaky ground for two reasons: one, because it is not clear that the democratic spirit is more vibrant in Scotland than elsewhere in the UK and, two, because the nature of Scottish representation in Westminster remains largely unchanged post-devolution.

According to *New Scotland, New Britain*, "Those of us who had consistently supported Devolution had always believed that the absence of democracy in Scotland diminished Scottish civic life" (Brown and Alexander 1998). The report adds that the Scottish Constitutional Convention attempted to preserve all that was good in Scotland. It "did not seek to destroy what was British that was of benefit to Scotland. It was for Scottish democracy, not against British democracy" (Brown and Alexander 1998). While one could be confused easily by such a statement – what does it mean, for example, to be for Scottish democracy, not against British democracy – a closer reflection reveals an attempt to define Scotland as a collection of constituencies worthy of democracy. It would be a particularly difficult argument to make that the Scots prefer democracy more than their English counterparts, or than their French and German counterparts, for that matter.

If we are assessing democracy in Britain, the test of its success apparently lies in a government elected by a majority within Britain. To say that a settlement is undemocratic because a portion of Britain does not support it ignores the practical functioning of a democracy. In the absence of elections where every single vote falls to the government, there will always be groups that did not support the government. What is interesting here, however, is that those who did not support the government were located in a geographic pocket of Britain, and the particular pocket had national boundaries. Throughout the 1980s the number of constituencies voting for parties other than the Conservatives in Scotland was lower than the number of English constituencies supporting Labour. In 1983, 209 English constituencies voted for parties other than the Conservatives. In that same election 41 Scottish constituencies voted for parties other than the Conservatives. While it is true that in 1997 not a single Scottish constituency elected a Conservative MP, it is not fair to compare elections that produced Conservative governments with those that produced Labour governments. While the Tories were in power, up to 50 Scottish constituencies were voting for parties other than the government. In England as many as 271 constituencies backed parties other than the Tories. In short, both English and Scottish constituencies continued to vote for the Labour Party in the face of Conservative governments. Why, then, is it accurate to claim that 200 constituencies voting Labour is not an affront to democracy, while 40 voting Labour is evidence of a democratic deficit? In part, the answer could lie in the proportion of seats won by parties other than the government. In the United Kingdom as a whole, the percentage of Labour seats between 1979 and 1992 ranged from 23 in 1983 to 42 in 1979 and 1992. In Scotland the percentage of Labour seats ranged from 57 in 1979 to 70 in 1987. More relevant, a national boundary distinguishes one group from the other: Scotland is portrayed as a meaningful aggregate, while the disparate Labour-voting constituencies in England are not. Only then does it become useful to note that those voting Labour represented a greater proportion of the Scottish electorate than they did in England. The Scottish electorate must be seen as a meaningful entity, separate within the UK, for its diverse preferences to be marshalled in nationalist argument. None of this is articulated by political documents in Scotland but, rather, is an assumed premise. The majority preference in Scotland was not the same as the majority preference in Britain. So while nationalism is not necessarily at the heart of devolution, arguments about a democratic deficit rely on the existence of a nation to make their case.

Aligning itself with strong democratic traditions, the Parti Québécois notes that it was the first in North America to elect a leader through universal suffrage (Parti Québécois 1994a). Statements such as this not only reinforce the dedication of the PQ to use existing channels to achieve self-determination but also emphasize the weight of democracy in the national debate. PQ justification for self-determination stems, as stated earlier, from notions of cultural particularity and common destiny. This in itself is not particularly remarkable. The way in which opponents of separatism rebut these claims, however, highlights the relationship between rights and self-determination in Quebec. The anglophone-dominated Equality Party defines itself as a "100 per cent Canadian voice" and encourages voters to move beyond choices offered by the "separatist PQ and the nationalist Liberals" (Equality Party 1994, 3). Promising to reverse "twenty years of provincial economic nationalism which benefits an educated, privileged French-speaking elite," the Equality Party in its policy booklet pledges to reject the special status of Quebec, sign the constitution, and declare the distinct society clause as racist, given its basis in ethnic origin and mother tongue. Several pages later the party, which at its electoral height held four seats in the National Assembly, pledges its support for self-government for Canada's Aboriginal people. The ideological link between self-determination for Quebec and self-government for the First Nations and Inuit peoples is not addressed. In arguing that Quebec separatism is unfounded but that Aboriginal self-government remains a worthy goal, the Equality Party suggests that the rights of one group to self-determination – rights grounded in a distinct culture, language and history – carry more weight than those of another collective. This tension, between self-determination and minority rights, dominates political literature in Quebec.

More recently, nationalist parties in Quebec have adopted the language of a democratic deficit. In its 2004 manifesto the Bloc Québécois suggested that democracy in Quebec was weakened by the federal state; democratically elected members of the National Assembly arrive at decisions within their areas of jurisdiction which are then overruled by the federal government, and when decisions are not overruled, they are so underfunded that MNAS cannot enact policy which reflects a Quebec democratic consensus. Furthermore, representatives in Quebec are denied the opportunity to express the wishes of their constituents in international forums. Together, these three features contribute to what the Bloc Québécois sees as a democratic deficit, driven primarily by a fiscal imbalance that violates the political rights of Quebecers, a feature all the more galling given the apparent emphasis that Quebecers place on democratic values.

The preceding implicit statements about rights and democracy provide us with cues about the inclusive nature of national identity. The rhetoric of the Equality Party, for example, appears to suggest that the fault lines of inclusion are linguistic. Anglophones receptive to the arguments of the Equality Party might believe that the dominant constructions of national membership have no room for them. In Scotland, that the national boundaries are animated around a Labour-voting public could have an impact on the self-ascribed national identity of Tory supporters. Typically, we assume that individuals are drawn to the Conservative Party because of a pre-existing attachment to Britain. If political parties such as the SNP and Labour point to the existence of the nation because of people who support parties other than the Conservatives, this rhetoric might have an impact on the extent to which Tories feel the dominant construction of the nation includes them. In so doing, it might encourage Conservative voters to feel greater attachment to another nation or to describe themselves as British rather than Scottish. In this case, partisan attachment can influence one's sense of inclusion or exclusion from the nation. In Quebec, by contrast, parties such as the BQ and the PQ discuss rights in terms of the federal government's treatment of Quebec. Because the jurisdictional meddling and persistent underfunding is negatively linked to the rights of all Quebecers, not just a particular subset of Quebecers, sovereignist rhetoric about rights and democracy in Quebec is implicitly more inclusive than that in Scotland. If violations of national rights are based on the existence of a Labour-voting public in Scotland and on federal mistreatment of provincial citizens as a whole in Canada, the boundaries are animated by different characteristics. In one case the national pillar is voting preference; in the other it is province of residence.

The Compatibility of National and State Identities

The third implicit treatment of inclusiveness surfaces in debates over the compatibility of dual or multiple national identities for those living in Scotland and Quebec. While the explicit messages of inclusion in political documents of both the SNP and the PQ suggest that holding a sense of national identity to Quebec and Italy or Scotland and Pakistan poses few problems, identification with the larger state provides an entirely different discourse.

Until recently, Scottish historiography highlighted the oppositional nature of nations within Britain. As Smout has noted, Scottish history was often described as a litany of defeats and victories at the hands of the English (Smout 1994). Finlay likewise argued that the nineteenth century produced few Scottish histories of significance, largely because the Scottish identity was seen as secure (Finlay 1994b). Scottish history, together with the trinity of institutions, prevented Scottish identity from aligning itself entirely with the state, but it is also credited with the promotion of a low sense of collective esteem (Beveridge and Turnbull 1989). The presumed static nature of this situation is seen to have negatively affected Scottish historiography. Recent attention to how Scotland has historically asserted its difference seeks to correct this trend (Colley 1994; Devine 2000; Lynch 1992). Within this context, Britishness has been treated as an artificially forged political identity that, when it suited the interests of its constituent members, was only just appealing enough to ensure its continued existence (Colley 1994). The identity amalgam was less linked to values fostered in daily lives and more to the political projects of an imperial state (Brown, McCrone, and Paterson 1998). Thus if Scottish identity could be considered a national identity promoted and sustained by social institutions that were perceived to touch the daily lives of members, British identity was equated with a remote, political state (Cohen 1994). The extent to which one could possess dual national identities to Scotland and Britain is, in this interpretation, context-dependent. At times it is the norm, at others less likely.

Since devolution, the compatibility of British and Scottish identities has drawn much attention as academics, political commentators, and politicians attempt to predict whether institutional boundaries will further weaken a sense of Britishness. For Macmillan, devolution has emphasized national difference to such a degree that it cannot be overpowered by a rebranding of Britishness as "Cool Britannia" (Macmillan 1999). In part, Colley explains, this shift has occurred because devolution alters the reference points for individuals (Colley 1999). The front pages of newspapers report events in the Scottish Parliament, and the additional layer of politicians is physically closer to its electorate. For some, this new-found freedom detracts from the oppressive nature of Britishness, making it easier to hold dual identities, rather than more difficult (A. Wilson 1999). In both analyses devolution is perceived to have strengthened national identity in Scotland.

Within political documents, however, we see little change in the rhetoric of compatible identities. One of the typical tropes of the Scottish National Party is to portray its partisan counterparts as less Scottish than they might be, and thus less adept at protecting the interests of the Scottish electorate, by referring to them as British or London political parties, beholden to the power centres in England. By so doing, the party seeks to align Scottishness with an identity and values that are distinct to the nation and not found beyond its borders. At the same time, though, such claims establish a natural opposition between that which is British and that which is Scottish. "Every other party to a greater or lesser extent still takes its orders from London" (Salmond 1998b, 1). Earlier in 1998 Salmond referred to New Labour as the "Blairite London Expeditionary Force" being sent north on regular occasions to try to "dish the Nats" (Salmond 1998a, 1). Before 1997 it was the Tory party and its secretaries of state for Scotland who earned most of the invective: "The Stone of Destiny and Michael Forsyth wearing a kilt won't soften the blows. The Tories are anti-Scottish" (SNP 1997a). At the 1997 SNP conference, leader Alex Salmond questioned the Scottish credentials of both the Tories and Labour in a speech that marked the end of Tory bashing and the escalation of attacks on New Labour: "It's good that Scotland has learned to laugh at the Tory party and their anti-Scottish scaremongering ... the Tories have rendered themselves irrelevant. But new Labour, London Labour, are also more and more out of touch" (Salmond 1997, 1, 4). In such statements England and Britain are often conflated, reflecting a perceived unity that is often made by those less well informed across the ocean. In this case, however, the perceived unity between England and Britain should be taken as a conscious effort to align the two, rather than a flippant or inaccurate reference. Since the establishment of the Parliament, the Scottish credentials of the coalition Liberal Democrats have also come into question. SNP MSP Margaret Ewing announced to the party conference in 2002, "I have been appalled by the attitude of the LibDems who so regularly claim a radical and Scottish Tradition" (M. Ewing 2002, 3). Such attacks, delivered to the party faithful, are obviously designed to score partisan points, and thus we should be cautious reading between the lines for coded statements about national identity. That opponents are criticized for representing another possible national identity suggests that the compatibility of British and Scottish identities is not a foregone conclusion. The notion that one might feel both Scottish *and* British has been largely absent from SNP documents and speeches, both before and after devolution. On the other side of the partisan divide, the Conservative Party has been equally consistent in its claims that Scottishness and Britishness are not mutually exclusive. "We are Scottish and British – proud to be both and proud of what our partnership has achieved in the past and confident of what it can achieve in the future" (SCUP 2003, 2). Interestingly, for both the SNP and the Conservatives, it seems that holding a sense of national identity to both Scotland and England would be rather difficult. This interpretation suggests that in their discourse the parties can conceive of identities to the constituent nation and to the larger state, but not necessarily to two constituent nations at once. Nowhere do documents on either side of the nationalist or separatist divide speak of the possibilities of being both Scottish and Welsh, for example. This absence suggests that one might hold two identities, Scottish and British, but that both are not necessarily national.

The comparison of nation to state appears frequently in political documents dealing with Quebec. While campaign literature within Quebec has opted to reinforce the distinct characteristics of Quebecers, constitutional documents that the federal government commissioned, supported, or in some cases wrote systematically attempt to reinforce the common bonds between Quebecers and other Canadians. The argument that similarities outnumber whatever differences might exist appears to have been the preferred tactic of federal governments from Trudeau to Martin. In his 1978 pre-referendum document, former prime minister Pierre Trudeau argued that Canadians share a history, a sense of national solidarity, and democratic values. A new constitution, promised Trudeau, would further encourage Canadians to "enjoy full pride and satisfaction in belonging and contributing to this great country" (Trudeau 1978, 26).

The compatibility of Québécois and Canadian identities is complicated by the fact that Canada grew out of the territory currently occupied by Quebec. Quebecers were the first Canadiens, a fact that thus makes any sense of oppositionalism between Quebec and Canada more difficult. In its task force on the anglophone community the PQ addressed this point directly, noting, "To some extent, English-speaking Quebecers have the impression that they must choose between their pride in being Quebecers and their chance to be Canadian" (PQ 1993, 5). Within Quebec the rhetoric of the provincial Liberal Party is far closer to that of the Conservative Party in Scotland: "La plupart des citoyens du Québec se définissent d'abord comme Québécois. Ce sentiment ne nous empêche pas de nous considère aussi comme Canadiens ... Notre apparetenance canadienne nous apparaît comme le complément de notre identité québécoise" (PLQ 1997, 3).

If individuals living in Scotland and Quebec feel that their identity is best described as British or Canadian, then the extent to which they will feel included in the nation depends in part on whether the dominant messages allow for dual identities. If it is suggested that holders of British national identity should consider themselves less Scottish, then there is evidence that Scottish national membership might at the very least be questioned. What is interesting here, of course, is that nationalists in Scotland have been far more likely to argue for single national identities than have nationalists in Quebec. Obviously, we must distinguish between nationalists and non-nationalists, between separatists or those seeking independence, and those happy either with the status quo or with more modest gains in autonomy. Such a distinction shows that nationalists in both Scotland and Quebec point to the existence of dual national identities. The ADQ and the Labour Party, for example, both point to the existence of a Québécois or Scottish nation, but also emphasize shared identities. Even parties less enamoured with the nationalist label, whether the Conservative Party in Scotland, which acknowledges the existence of a nation, and the Liberal Party in Quebec, which acknowledges that Quebec is distinct, advocate shared identities. The case of the Liberal Party is, of course, an interesting one. Because the party tends not to employ the term "nation" but refers to Quebec as a distinct society, it is possible that what it is advocating is shared identities but not necessarily dual *national* identities. If we look at the parties advocating independence, however, the Parti Québécois and the Bloc Québécois have long identified a Canadian identity as the root of a Québécois identity. The SNP, however, has taken great pains to identify British political parties as anti-Scottish. The documents note that the two are incompatible identities for a political party, as the interests of each are in conflict. Such a rhetoric suggests that it is the Scottish separatist party which advocates a more exclusive notion of identity.

If we have evidence that all political parties in both Scotland and Quebec point to similar pillars of identity within their nation, that some employ a language of history and rights to firmly draw boundaries around the national population, and that some parties are better than others at emphasizing the potential for dual national identities, what might we say about the relative levels of inclusiveness in Scotland and Quebec? Part of the answer lies in the debate about civic and ethnic national identity.

Academic literature often portrays Scottish national identity as civic and inclusive, in contrast to Québécois identity (Hobsbawm 1990). But in both nations, markers emphasizing blood and ancestry, what could be considered ethnic markers of identity, are used alongside more "civic" notions of membership. Thus if contemporary identity debates in Scotland ponder the compatibility of multiple national identities – if Scots can also feel British – the multiple identity debate in Quebec wonders whether English Canadians within the provincial boundaries can ever feel Québécois.

Those who would argue that national identity in Quebec is linked to a civic nationalism claim that identity has less to do with pillars of collective association and more to do with a profound sense of distance within the Canadian federation (Imbeau and Laforest 1991/92; Laforest and Gibbins 1998; Nemni 1994). That the population is French and Catholic matters less than the fact that it is not English (Robitaille 1999; Laforest and Gibbins 1998; McRoberts 1988). Charting increased support for sovereignty in the 1970s and 1980s, McRoberts hints that the Québécois identity lies as much in English Canada's – or rather, the federal government's – intransigence as in a self-directed sense of difference (McRoberts 1988). Such a view is supported by quantitative examinations of opinion poll data (Pinard and Hamilton 1986; Coleman 1984; Meadwell 1989; Guntzel 1997). Thus, whether in reaction to federal deadlock or as a play for greater social mobility, national identity remains divorced from the traditional pillars of society. In this sense, the project of national self-determination drives the sense of identity. And yet the correlation between support for an avowedly nationalist-sovereignist party and national identity detracts from the diversity of Quebec identity.

For some, the very phrase "Québécois identity" warrants attention since it denies anglophones and allophones a descriptive label in their own language (Jenson 1995). For others, the seemingly thwarted attempts of individuals other than French, Catholic Quebecers to feel that they belong within society leads to charges of an ethnic national identity (Breton 1988). Academic literature on identity in Quebec, that created both within the nation and outside, has in the past equated Quebecers and francophones. While lamenting the lack of attention to the diversity within Québécois nationalism and national identity, Jean-Louis Roy claims that the underlying common factor among all notions of national identity is, for example, a sense of destiny as francophone (Roy 1987). This tendency to equate Quebecers and francophones prompts Keating to argue that "Quebec nationalism has in any case only partly made the transition from ethnic to civic" (Keating 1995a). While the movement has developed beyond inward-looking protectionism, it remains civic by ideal rather than by membership.

The reason that identity in Quebec has earned itself the ethnic label, while such charges are rarely levelled in Scotland, has much to do with early ethnic analyses of Quebec national identity. For the previously mentioned Abbé Groulx, the nation was a historical community rather than a racially bounded entity. That said, Groulx believed in the superiority of French civilization, although supporters are quick to point out that the anti-Semitism that appears in his work was peripheral to his understanding of the nation (Trépanier in Gougeon 1994). Charting the changing use of history and collective memory, Sarra-Bournet notes that what was once the call of separatists – "Le Québec aux Québécois" – has now become "Le pays pour tous les Québécois" (Sarra-Bournet 1999b). This view of Quebec as a multicultural civic nation has been present in Quebec research and writings both before and after the most recent referendum (Balthazar 1994; G. Bouchard 1999; Laforest 1993, 1995; Seymour 1999a; Venne 2000; Salée 1997; Maclure 2003), but it has not always permeated English Canadian understandings of Quebec nationalism. Partly this absence stems from the role of language as a determinant of Québécois national identity. Seen as something attached to birth and ancestry, language acquires ethnic properties. Seen as something acquired or learned, language can become a civic pillar. The conditions of membership depend on the comprehension of a tool for social communication, nothing more, nothing less. At its more inclusive, national membership is open to residents of Quebec, regardless of their language and dependent only on their willingness to belong.

Clearly, the views of academics do not drive public perception. The distillation of ethnic language being used by individual nationalists and separatists further reinforces the civic character of Québécois national identity. And yet ethnic traces remain. Former Quebec premier Jacques Parizeau did little for his party when he announced on referendum night that the Québécois had been defeated by "l'argent et le vote ethnique" (Parizeau 1995a). Government pamphlets on the history of Quebec entitled *Qui étaient nos ancêtres*? only serve to reinforce the view that identity in Quebec has more in common with the primordial attachments analyzed by Smith, Geertz, and Brass than the modern construct of Gellner and Hobsbawm.

CONCLUSION

The acceptance of Scotland as a nation has meant that calls for greater political control need not focus on the criteria of nationhood and how Scotland fulfills these. Instead, national attention is directed to the democratic deficit. In Quebec, however, the lack of recognition as a nation has forced those who seek greater autonomy to argue, first, that Quebec is a nation and, second, that it deserves greater autonomy as a result. If national identity does not have an explicit role in political debate in Scotland, it certainly does in Quebec. By articulating sovereignty as a goal of a collective group bound by national identity, Quebec separatists have made national identity a central issue in political debate and in so doing have increased its salience in society. This focus, in conjunction with a readily identifiable marker such as language, alters the extent to which Scotland can be seen as similar to Quebec. In Scotland the attainment of devolution has been portrayed and understood as a problem of political inequality among citizens (Brown, McCrone, and Paterson 1998; Mitchell 1996). Constitutional change was necessary because of the democratic deficit. The existence of a nation is implicit in this argument but it is not the central issue, whereas in Quebec change is viewed as necessary *because* of the existence of the nation.

This chapter has provided a comprehensive examination of political literature in Scotland and Quebec, but where does that leave constructions of identity and political culture in both nations? In particular, how might individuals who would consider themselves on the margins of national society, whether because they are new arrivals to the country or because they possess a particular mix of social characteristics, integrate themselves into the nation? The literature in Quebec makes explicit mention of non-Québécois, but the Scottish literature is more circumspect. For Québécois separatists, independence would "clarify the often uncomfortable situation of many new Quebecers who feel a dual allegiance to Quebec and to Canada" (PQ 1994a). Both the SNP and the Parti Québécois have described themselves as tolerant and open, welcoming of immigrants and allophones. The reaction of individuals to such claims forms the focus of chapter 4.

4

Measuring National Identity

How might we measure an individual's identity? We might ask people to talk about their vision of their own identity and who they feel they are. Or we could ask them to fill out surveys and track over time how the different ways that people describe themselves change. The former approach lends itself more to qualitative analysis, while the latter often relies on quantitative measurement. These measurements are gathered for a sample of the population that allows researchers to track identity changes over time. Often criticized as blunt instruments of social investigation, aggregate indicators of identity and the measures used to extract such data provide a picture of changing patterns of attachment and belonging within a population. Quantitative measures not only allow us to track changes in identity within one nation but also enable us to compare identity patterns in one nation and another. What such measures miss, however, is the more personal aspect of identity. Though they provide an incomplete vision of identity for any one individual, in the aggregate these measures prove quite useful.

This chapter examines the contribution of quantitative data to understandings of national identity in Scotland and Quebec. It explores the different approaches to quantitative identity measurement and highlights questions raised by the research. It then turns to the civic-ethnic debate to determine what light quantitative measures shed on identity and the extent to which distinctions between civic and ethnic national identity contribute to a greater understanding of national identity in Scotland and Quebec. Although we might have formed opinions about what we expect to find in the two nations, particularly given the themes of discourse mentioned in chapter 3, this chapter argues that the distinction between civic and ethnic identity is not as clear as we might assume. The key difference between the two cases is not the content of identity – what individuals think it means to be Scottish or Québécois – but the salience of identity in political debate.

Analyses of identity and its measurement allow us to better understand the way that individuals define themselves and the extent to which they feel themselves part of a collective. This perception in itself is of academic interest, but equally important is an assessment of the ways that individuals identify their own political community. We know at present that individuals are participating less in formal avenues of political activity and that they feel disengaged from their fellow citizens and their political system. We know that efficacy, trust, and satisfaction with politics and politicians are low. When asked to explain their identities, individuals very rarely mention their role as citizens. We also know, however, that attachment to sub-state entities remains strong. Individuals identify with their national unit in a way that they do not identify with the state. Understanding why and the extent to which they do so helps political scientists to better comprehend the views of individuals towards the state and their fellow citizens.

IDENTITY MEASUREMENT IN SCOTLAND AND QUEBEC

Part of the problem of measurement stems from the moving "target" of identity. The importance and substance of identity vary both in context and over time. Within the literature, identity has been used as a sense of belonging (Tajfel 1982; Wetherell 1996a), a particular outlook (Erikson 1974), or a self-ascribed label (Hall 1996). Efforts to problematize identity highlight the frustration with existing measurement attempts (Mendelsohn 1999, 2003; McCrone et al. 1998). Criticism addresses issues of definition and measurement, such as the construction of identity scales (Mendelsohn 1999), the operationalization of identity theory (Hall 1996), and the treatment of identity data in the search for meaningful correlations. In particular, researchers point to the low salience of political beliefs and the disputed relationship between attitudes, values, beliefs, and behaviour. Each of these, when compounded by the questionable ability of individuals to explain their own identities, proves a stumbling block for any empiricist attempting to capture the true meaning of national identity.

Aggregate measures of identity in Scotland found little consistency before the introduction of the Moreno question in 1986 (Moreno 1988). Prior to this, votes for the Scottish National Party served as proxies for measures of increasing Scottish identity at the expense of British allegiance. Moreno's scale asks respondents to classify their identity according to the following: Scottish not British, more Scottish than British, equally Scottish and British, more British than Scottish, or British not Scottish. The equivalent poles in the Canadian version usually require respondents to choose between their Canadian and Québécois identities, although questions probing attachment rather than identity have proved most popular.

In Scotland results since the beginning of the decade show a gradual preference for a Scottish identity, allowing for a sense of Britishness at the expense of a uniquely territorial vision of self. In most years, almost 90 per cent of respondents held a sense of Scottish national identity that was at least equal in importance to their sense of Britishness. Around three-quarters either prioritized their Scottish identity or held it exclusively. Complaints that the Moreno question itself encourages a false opposition of Scottishness and Britishness find little support from those who accept that the approach, for all its methodological faults, provides as robust a measure as the public is willing to accept. As McCrone states, people seem to understand what the question is getting at (McCrone 1996). This understanding in itself makes the Moreno scale a more valuable measure than other more complicated tests of allegiance or sense of self.

The Scottish data illustrate the extent to which identity preferences change over time although for the most part the movement occurs within the top three categories (see fig. 4.1). Data from the Moreno scale often come to us from election studies, conducted during British general election campaigns or elections to the Scottish Parliament. The question posed to respondents asks, "Which, if any, of the following best describes yourself?" References to nations and national identity are thus absent from the question in many incarnations, although the wording changes slightly from election study to election study.

In two of the UK election campaigns the proportion of individuals who reported that they felt "more Scottish than British" rose from the pre-election period. At the same time the proportion who felt

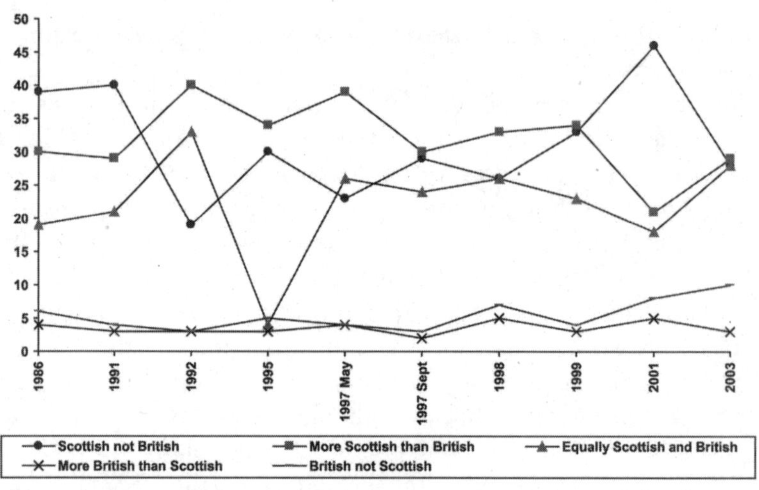

Fig. 4.1 National identity in Scotland, 1986–2003

"Scottish not British" decreased. This apparent paradox could stem from the participation of Scots in a British political rite. Scottish voters might place a greater emphasis on their Scottishness because the election presents an occasion to speak "as a collective" within the political system. For the September 1997 devolution referendum, the proportion of individuals reporting that they felt "more Scottish than British" fell, perhaps because within an electorate composed almost entirely of Scots, the importance of Scottishness is mitigated. In the UK general election immediately following devolution, however, there was a marked increase in the proportion who claimed to be "Scottish not British" and a decrease in the proportion of those who held both Scottish and British identities, regardless of whether both were held equally or Scottishness was prioritized. In other words, before devolution general election campaigns reinforced a sense of shared identity but prioritized Scottishness, while after devolution a single and Scottish national identity has seen the largest increase in its proportion. That the proportion of Scots describing themselves this way fell dramatically for the 2003 elections to the Scottish Parliament reinforces the belief that Scottishness is more important during British election contests than in domestic ones.

In Quebec private polling firms, rather than university-based election study teams, have employed variations of the Moreno

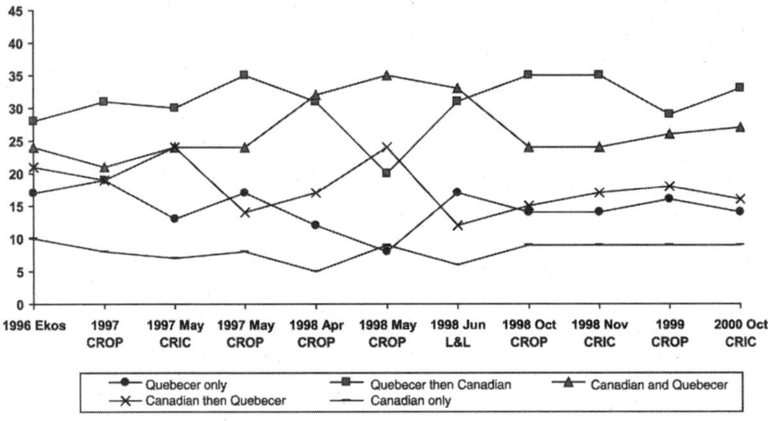

Figure 4.2 National identity in Quebec, 1996–2000

question. The preamble to the question is different from that posed in Scotland, stating, "Different people have different ways of defining themselves. Do you consider yourself ... ?" The options that follow are then similar to those on offer in Scotland, asking individuals to indicate whether they are a Canadian only, Canadian first but also a Quebecer, equally a Canadian and a Quebecer, a Quebecer first but also a Canadian, or a Quebecer only. This question also lacks an explicit reference to national identity. It also begins with the Canadian label, whereas in Scotland the British label appears last.

Although the Quebec data stem from a relatively restricted period of time, several results are worth highlighting (see fig. 4.2). First, unlike in the UK, where data are collected by a relatively stable group of academics and often use the same survey house, the data here are from four different polling houses, each of which seems to produce different trends. In May 1997, for example, both CRIC and CROP were in the field asking the same question. The results for CROP produced higher support for "Quebecer only" or "Quebecer then Canadian" identities than did the CRIC data. More than one year later both firms were again in the field, this time a month apart. Here the results were far more consistent between the two houses. We should proceed with caution in our interpretation of these results.

For the ten data points included here, the identity category "Quebec then Canada" represents the largest proportion of respondents in all but three circumstances. Data collected during federal and provincial elections do not appear to demonstrate significant variations in identity preferences. The data also show consistent identity preferences in Quebec that distinguish it from Scotland. Whereas in Scotland the three largest categories are for those holding a Scottish identity either wholly or in part, in Quebec there is stronger attachment to Canada. While "equally Scottish and British" is typically the middle category preferred by Scots – preferred less than Scottish identities but more than those prioritizing Britishness – dual and equal identities are more popular in Quebec. Though the proportions of respondents in these "equal" identity categories are relatively consistent, the smaller proportion of Quebecers emphasizing their sub-state national identity makes this category appear more important than in Scotland. As in Scotland, an identity solely to the larger state is the least popular category. The numbers themselves are higher than in Scotland, occupying one-tenth of the samples rather than half that number for Scots, but the trend is clear. Unlike in Scotland, those holding an exclusively Quebec identity represent a far smaller proportion of the population. Dual identities, whether equal or nested, are thus more popular in Quebec than they are in Scotland; those holding a Quebec identity, equally or stronger, occupy a majority as in Scotland, but the proportion is much smaller: between 70 and 76 per cent rather than almost 90 per cent in Scotland. Scots appear more likely than Quebecers to prioritize their sub-state identity over their state identity.

These results are clear when averages over time are compared for Scotland and Quebec. Over time Scots have been far less likely to prioritize a British identity. Almost one-quarter of Quebecers, by contrast, usually describe themselves as Canadian first or Canadian only. The results include the average of all survey results since 1997. They also indicate the most recent results for Scotland from the 2001 election study and a 2000 CRIC poll (see table 4.1). The perceived decreased salience of nationalism in Quebec could account for the absence of identity questions on more recent surveys. The results show that in the immediate post-referendum period in Scotland and Quebec results are generally consistent with the more recent trends.

Identity changes in Canada address not only the issue of shared identities but also the changing self-definition from French Canadian to Québécois. Since 1970 the proportion of Quebec residents who describe themselves as Canadian has dropped from 34 to 15 per cent (Mendelsohn 1999). While the proportion describing

Table 4.1
National identity in Scotland and Quebec, average, 2000 and 2001

	Percentage agreeing with each statement			
	Scotland average	*Scotland 2001*	*Quebec average*	*Quebec 2000*
x not British, Canadian	30.8	28	14.4	14
x more than British, Canadian	31.0	29	31.0	35
Equally x and British, Canadian	24.2	28	27.0	24
British, Canadian more than x	3.7	3	17.6	15
British, Canadian not x	6.0	10	7.9	9

SOURCES: CES 2000; BES 2001.
x=Scottish or Québécois.

themselves as French Canadian has remained relatively stable, the greatest change has occurred within the label "Québécois." In 1970, 21 per cent of Quebec residents described themselves as Québécois. By the turn of the century, this figure had more than doubled, to 52 per cent (Mendelsohn 1999). The increase has not been steady but rather has seen two periods of increase, the first in the mid-seventies, during the decade when the sovereignist Parti Québécois was first elected, and the second in the early 1990s, a period that witnessed the failures of both the Meech Lake constitutional agreement and the Charlottetown Accord. The initial transition of the label, from French Canadian to Québécois, occurred in the 1960s, when the provincial government of Quebec took on a stronger role not only with respect to social and economic provisions but also as a guarantor of Québécois culture and identity. As a result, the most dramatic change in identity labels might have occurred before quantitative measurement of identity began. And yet within twenty years, an additional 40 per cent of the Quebec population have described their identity in terms of their province or nation, rather than in terms of the Canadian state.

Within Canada a diverse package of identity questions has sought not only to track identity changes over time but to understand the reasons why identity appears malleable. These measures have not been employed in the Scottish case, and thus a direct comparison between the two remains, for the moment, impossible. An analysis of how these questions relate to one another does raise issues about the accuracy with which social scientists and private polling firms measure identity. In an adaptation of the identity-poles questions offered by Moreno, the polling firm Ekos sought to compare identity trends throughout Canada. The results, published in the English-language daily Montreal *Gazette*, show that there is little to distinguish the provincial allegiances of all Canadians, regardless of place of residence. Quebecers are not more attached to their province than residents of British Columbia or Alberta or New Brunswick. In the 1990s three-quarters of all Canadians, regardless of their province of residence, reported attachment to their sub-state entity. In 1995 this proportion reached a high of 87 per cent for Quebecers and 81 per cent for other Canadians, a predictable result given attention to the referendum of that year. The figure that separates Quebecers from other Canadians is thus not an inordinately high attachment to the province but a below-average attachment to Canada. In the 1990s between 86 and 95 per cent of all Canadians reported an attachment to Canada. Over the same period just over half of Quebecers reported similar levels of attachment (Ekos 1998). Among Quebecers the sense of belonging to Canada is less than that of other Canadians by an average of 35 points. In part, these figures may be tapping different forms of attachment. Whether one sees Canada as a nation or as a state, for example, might account for varying levels of support. For now, though, it appears that support for autonomy in Quebec stems more from a lack of attachment to the federal entity than from a stronger sense of belonging to Quebec.

The distinction between measures of attachment and measures of identity emphasizes different aspects of the identity debate. Moreno-type questions tracking identity labels suggest that a similar proportion in each location feel that they possess sole identities as either Scots or Québécois. In addition, a greater proportion express an attachment that prioritizes their national identity. The results suggest that a sense of identity does not automatically accompany a sense of attachment, but that attachment is more prevalent than identity.

The wealth of Canadian data on issues of attachment and belonging suggest that the long-standing Canadian identity crisis has led to a level of reflection and measurement that attempts to come to grips with some of the more slippery aspects of identity. Within Scotland, a consistent application of the Moreno question has provided a reliable tool for measuring identity over time. And yet even this useful tool cannot clarify the content and salience of identity. Some of these issues are highlighted in the following section.

ISSUES IN IDENTITY MEASUREMENT

As stated earlier, most survey work using national identity as an independent variable exerting influence over partisan preference or voter turnout relies on a variation of Luis Moreno's five-point identity scale (Moreno 1988).[1] Developed while comparing national identity in Scotland and Catalonia, his scale lends itself to straightforward quantification and cross-national comparison. Despite the importance of creating data to test relationships between variables, what Moreno's scale gains in applicability it lacks in description. The scale fails to identify the strength with which national feelings are held, what such self-identification actually means to the individual, or the components of identity itself. What, for instance, are the distinguishing characteristics of the Scottish or Québécois national identity? How is the identity of an individual who self-identifies as solely Scottish different from the identity of an individual whose self-definition allows for a minimal sense of Britishness? Does "national" identity mean the same thing in different contexts? If used in isolation, Moreno's categories, while valuable in their ability to demonstrate the effect of national identity on political behaviour, fail to provide a sense of context to national identity, what it is about national identity that affects subsequent behaviour. Although Canadian newspapers have been quick to commission opinion polls using the Moreno identity scales, the election surveys in Canada rely on a different instrument to measure the varying levels of identity within the country. Asking respondents to indicate their level of attachment to their province and country on two scales of 0 to 100, while avoiding the binary opposition of the British scale, provides little insight into the motivations of belonging.

A second issue concerns the notion of multiple national identities. While Hall has adequately argued that individuals possess multiple social identities (Hall 1992), the proof of multiple *national* identities comes from the measurement side of the debate rather than from theoretical understandings of national identity. The use of scales in which individuals may choose between polarized identity options emphasizes the supposedly multiple nature of identity. Students constructing scales for surveys are warned that a five-point scale in which three of the answers are generally positive and two are negative will skew the results in favour of the positive. If, for example, respondents are asked to score their answers according to

Table 4.2
Statistical measures of identity in Scotland

	Percentage agreeing with the statement "I feel ..."					
	2001			1997		
Moreno 2001	%	*SES 2001*	%	*Moreno 1997*	*SES questions 1997*	%
Scottish not British	27.8	Scottish	74.2	23	Scottish on both	74
More Scottish than British	29.4			38		
Equally Scottish and British	28.3			27	Scottish but not primarily	9
More British than Scottish	3.3	British	18.5	4		
British not Scottish	9.5			4	Not Scottish at all	17

SOURCES: BES 2001 (n=948), BES 1997 (n=882).

a scale that runs from excellent, very good, good, and fine to terrible, the results will be biased. The same can be said of identity scales in which three of the five options refer to a shared identity and the remaining two refer to a sole identity in relation to the "other." A comparison of the Moreno question and three other identity questions found in the 1997 and 2001 Scottish election surveys, collected under the rubric of the British Election Study, proves this point (see table 4.2).

The 2001 data include a forced-choice question on national identity that asked respondents to indicate whether they felt Scottish, British, or European. Almost three-quarters of the sample indicated Scottish, while just under one-fifth said that they felt British. If in the Moreno question only 18 per cent of respondents indicated that they felt more British than Scottish or exclusively British, it is not clear who this 18 per cent includes. It appears the group involves not only those who prioritize a sense of national identity but also those from among the "equally Scottish and British" category who, when forced to choose, opt to describe their identity as British. Different questions probing identity produce different results. An earlier question experiment further proves this point. In the 1997 SES two identity questions ask: do you feel Scottish? what is your primary identity? (See table 4.3.) Those who indicated that they felt Scottish and would consider it their primary identity form 74 per

Table 4.3
Identity-related questions in Scotland

	Number of respondents indicating yes to following questions (%)					
	Scottish not British	*More Scottish than British*	*Equally Scottish and British*	*More British than Scottish*	*British not Scottish*	*Total*
Best identity Scottish	194 (96)	306 (91)	134 (56)	3 (9)	1 (3)	638
Best identity British	7 (4)	28 (9)	85 (36)	27 (77)	22 (63)	169
Total in SES	203	335	238	35	35	

SOURCE: SES 1997 (n=882).

cent of the sample. This proportion compares with 61 per cent of those asked the Moreno question who indicated that they felt primarily Scottish (Scottish not British, more Scottish than British). According to these measures, either Moreno underestimates Scottish identity or the 1997 SES questions overestimate Scottishness. Cross-tabulations for these three questions indicate that the distributions for the Moreno question and the two other questions fail to prove that the two bind together perfectly. For those who indicated that their identity was equally Scottish and British, almost 60 per cent described their "best identity" as Scottish and 40 per cent describe themselves as British. For a measure that seeks to prove that individuals hold both identities in equal regard, the tendency to prioritize a Scottish identity over a British identity should not happen more than 50 per cent of the time. Despite claiming under some circumstances that they feel equally Scottish and British, individuals do not include the British label when it is not presented to them in the question, choosing instead to describe themselves as Scottish.

When not offered the option of combining their British and Scottish identities, fewer Scots suggest they are carriers of dual identities. While the existence of multiple national identities is possible, researchers should be wary that the way in which the questions are asked will influence the results. This is not to say that Moreno is incorrect, but rather than it should not be used as a single proxy question for identity; nor indeed, should any of its possible replacements. Those involved in the Canadian election survey have opted for a different tactic. Perhaps wary of employing questions that combine multiple identity options, the researchers have relied upon

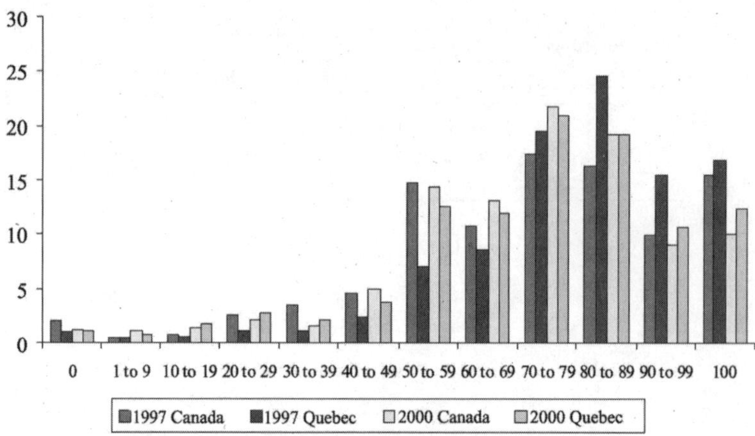

Fig. 4.3 Identity in the Canadian Election Survey, 1997 and 2000: percentage of respondents according to each identity thermometer decile
SOURCES : CES 1997 (n=1034); CES 2000 (n=1251).

two thermometer scales with which to test the identity of Canadians. Respondents are asked to indicate how they feel about Canada and, in a separate question, how they feel about their province on a scale of 0 to 100, where 0 represents minimal attached and 100 maximum attachment. The results for the 1997 and 2000 election studies – the last for which the scale was used – are shown in figure 4.3. The results indicate that over half of Quebecers feel a strong attachment to both Canada and Quebec. Very few indicate minimal attachment to Quebec or Canada. In both 1997 and 2000 less than 10 per cent of the sample indicated a level of attachment that is less than the mid-way point on the thermometer scale.

The thermometers, while useful in analyzing the depth of feeling among respondents, do not allow for a comparison of attachment to Canada and Quebec. Table 4.4 provides such a tool. The results from the Canadian Election Study have been recoded to approximate the results provided by the Moreno question, for despite the previously mentioned limitations of that tool, the accurate reflection of attachment and identity to nation and to state proves an obvious index. For the above data, respondents whose attachment to Canada was greater than that to Quebec were coded as "Canada more than Québec" and vice versa for those whose attachment was greater for Quebec. Those respondents who indicated an equal attachment to both, whether that level was twenty, fifty, or eight,

Table 4.4
Dual attachment in Quebec, 1997 and 2000

	Number in each reconstructed identity group			
	1997		*2000*	
	No.	%	No.	%
Quebec not Canada	14	1.8	9	0.8
Quebec more than Canada	334	42.4	322	32.0
Equally Quebec and Canada	261	33.2	341	33.9
Canada more than Quebec	172	21.9	227	22.5
Canada not Quebec	6	0.8	8	0.8

SOURCES: CES 1997 (n=1034, 247 missing values); CES 2000 (n=1251, 335 missing values).

were coded as "equally to Quebec and to Canada." Last, respondents who listed zero for attachment to either Quebec or to Canada were listed as possessing binary identities, as in the poles of the Moreno question. Table 4.4 summarizes these results.

When compared with data collected by private polling firms, the CES thermometers reveal a higher proportion of residents who indicated that their attachment was to Quebec more than to Canada. In addition, the data show a very small proportion of individuals who proclaimed attachment only to either Canada or Quebec. It should be noted that the question asked by the CES team deals with feelings towards Quebec and Canada – attachment to an entity – rather than self-perception. In each case, a combination of multiple-identity options – or rather, asking about one identity with respect to another – and questions offering only a reflection on national or state identity would provide for a more robust understanding of identity in Scotland and Quebec.

In 2000 the CES team also included a question on identity labels. Asked only of francophone respondents in Quebec, the question allowed individuals to indicate whether they saw themselves as Canadian, Québécois, or French Canadian. The results show that 16.6 per cent of the sample saw themselves as Canadian, 31.4 per cent saw themselves as French Canadian, and the remainder, over 50 per cent of the total sample, preferred the label "Québécois." This outcome confirms what we might expect about identity labels in Quebec. If we examine the mean thermometer scores for each of these identity groups, we find interesting and statistically significant differences among them. The attachment to Canada mean score for those who preferred the label "Canadian" or "French Canadian" was 77.2 and 74.2 respectively. The mean score for the thermometer of Quebec attachment was slightly lower for both groups: 69.2 for Canadians and 67.5 for French Canadians. That these two groups are so similar is a noteworthy finding. Perhaps most important, though, are the results for those who consider themselves Québécois. Here the mean score for attachment to Canada was 61.5, while the mean score attachment to Quebec was 74.0. If we compare Quebecers to other Canadians, we know that they hold their province in similar regard and feel far less attached to Canada as an entity. Within Quebec, however, those who consider themselves Québécois exhibit lower levels of attachment to Canada than do those who consider themselves Canadian or French Canadian. In short, Quebecers are not more attached to their province than are other Canadians, unless they prefer the label "Québéçois." Even those who prefer that label hold levels of attachment to Canada that are far above the mid-point of the scale. These findings are consistent with what we already know of national identity in Scotland and Quebec. They also help us to clarify the extent to which dual national identities are held by residents of Scotland and Quebec.

The questions explored thus far seem to produce different results. Thermometer questions are most likely to indicate levels of attachment to the sub-state nation *and* the larger state, while the options for the Moreno question are least likely to indicate support for the state. Scottish and Québécois results for the Moreno question consistently produce far smaller proportions of those who consider themselves "Canadian first" or "British only" than do forced-choice questions where respondents must choose between the sub-state nation and the state. All three produce different responses, in some cases emphasizing attachment to the state or identification with the nation. What all three also demonstrate is a consistent support for dual identities. It is worth exploring, though, whether these are dual national identities or one identity for a polity and another for a nation.

It is possible that when choosing options emphasizing a shared identity, respondents distinguish between an allegiance to nation (Scotland/Quebec) and an allegiance to the state (Britain/Canada). Respondents in different regions of the country might opt for similar answers (for example, "both Albertan and Canadian"), but in this case Canada might be seen as the nation and Alberta as the political jurisdiction. Someone who describes him or herself as both

Nova Scotian and Canadian might, for example, view Nova Scotia as a nation in possession of a distinct history, language, and culture and Canada as an amalgam state. Just because the same words are used by different respondents should not suggest that the words possess the same meaning. So far, identity measurement has failed to gauge the extent to which the identity selection reflects the existence of a meaningful aggregate or an association with political rights or citizenship. Two individuals within Quebec might each select the option "Quebec first then Canada." For the first individual, Quebec could signify the nation, a meaningful aggregate of shared customs and values, myths and symbols, while Canada refers to the state in which she lives, which provides her a passport and currency and which collects taxes. For the second individual, Quebec could refer to the political jurisdiction in which he lives, works, and votes, while Canada is the meaningful aggregate of shared history. This tension between meaningful aggregate and salient presence lies, in part, in the tension between static label and dynamic process.

Further evidence of this tension may be found in the SES. When asked to describe his identity, only one respondent indicated that he was both Scottish and English. This outcome suggests that it is near anathema to hold simultaneous identities to the constituent nations within the UK and instead lends further credence to the notion that "Scottish" and "English" identities are seen as mutually exclusive ethnic components within Britain. Instead, we are more likely to find a sub-state identity and one to a larger polity, either of which might or might not be seen as a nation.

That multiple identities are possible is without question. It could be argued, however, that they are not the automatic consequence of federal or asymmetrical political systems in which individuals can have dual allegiances: an attachment to two entities, yes; two examples of national identity, not necessarily. As stated earlier, just because the option chosen is understood by some as a nation does not mean that it is seen by the respondent as a nation or chosen as a representation of national identity by all. These differing understandings of identity in Canada and the UK could explain why some individuals believe their respective sub-state units to be, or are capable of being, "multinational."

Identity measurements have failed to capture this notion of a meaningful aggregate and the interactive processes associated with identity. Thus, while the provision of open-ended questions might inhibit quantitative analyses of identity, it might further a greater understanding of widespread changes in identity preferences over time. Identity measurement also contributes to one of the key assumptions of Scotland-Quebec comparisons, namely, that they occupy different sides of the civic and ethnic definitions of nationalism.

CIVIC AND ETHNIC MARKERS OF IDENTITY IN SCOTLAND AND QUEBEC

How might one distinguish between civic and ethnic markers of national identity? Individuals cannot alter ethnic markers. These include where a person was born, his or her race, and her or his ancestry. In an ethnic nation, membership in the desired group is automatic, should one possess the necessary ethnic conditions. The most explicit use of ethnic characteristics in Canada would concern membership in First Nations bands based on Aboriginal ancestry or beneficiary status for land claim settlements. Typically, ethnic markers also include things that can be changed but are associated with a particular ethnic culture, such as religion. Civic national identity, by contrast, relies on mutable characteristics to ensure membership, such as region of residence. Such factors can be changed with relatively little hassle. Civic markers might also include aspects that cannot easily be tested, such as political views. The premise that Scotland and Quebec occupy opposing positions on the civic-ethnic divide rests entirely on two assumptions: first, that Quebec relies on ancestry, language, and religion to determine membership in the nation and that these are ethnic characteristics; and second, that Scotland lacks a reliance on ethnic markers and depends on residency and political support for the existence of a Scottish nation to determine national membership.

We can assume that indications of who is and who is not a member of the nation come from two sources: official pronouncements from arbiters of identity, such as the press or political parties, and the public, who gauge their own and others' membership in the nation. The previous chapter explored the explicit and implicit pronouncements of political actors in order to better understand how individuals might evaluate their own identity. The rest of this chapter explores who is more likely to hold a particular identity and proves that the traditional view of Quebec as home to ethnic nationalism and Scotland as an example of civic nationalism is not only incorrect but not particularly helpful to understandings of how national identity affects political debate. Political parties in Quebec consistently emphasize the civic nature of Quebec national identity, while the general public in Scotland prioritizes ethnic markers over civic markers. The difference between the two is not that one is ethnic and the other is civic, but that the context of political debate makes identity salient in one nation and less so in the other. Furthermore, if the mark of a civic nationalism is whether it is inclusive or not, both Scotland and Quebec can be portrayed as inclusive movements with self-excluding individuals.

DO I BELONG?

Regardless of messages promoted by political parties or the media, individuals are ultimately left with the decision of whether to claim that they belong in the nation or not. We can get a sense of who feel they belong and who exclude themselves if we explore the type of person who applies the label "Scottish" or "Québécois" to characterize themselves. If Scotland is an example of civic nationalism, we might expect that those who see themselves as Scots are not different in terms of ethnicity, religion, or language from those who describe themselves as British. If Quebec possesses an ethnic national identity, we might expect to find indicators of blood or ancestry as predictors of Québécois national identity. The following section uses data from the two most recent comparable election studies in Canada and Britain to explore the self-ascribed identity of Scots and Quebecers. Although more recent data are available – for example, for the 2003 Scottish Parliament election study – it is more useful to compare data collected under similar circumstances. In this case, it involves election campaigns for the Canadian and British Houses of Commons. If we know that in Scotland the political context has an impact on self-ascribed identity, then a context that is as similar as possible across the two cases will help to provide comparable results.

Table 4.5 contains coefficients for OLS regressions. This approach tests the independent impact of certain variables (age, religion, ethnicity) on a dependent variable – in this case, identity. The coefficients describe the expected change in the dependent variable given

Table 4.5
Predictors of Scottish and Québécois identity

	Scotland		*Quebec*	
Female	+	+	+	$+^{***}$
Age	-	+	$-^{***}$	$-^{***}$
Catholic	$+^{***}$	$+^{**}$	+	+
Presbyt/Prot	$+^{***}$	$+^{**}$	-	+
vis. minority	-	-	na	na
Can-born	na	na	$+^{**}$	+
Con feel/Lib feel		$-^{*}$		-
SNP feel/BQ feel		$+^{***}$		+
Indep		+		$+^{***}$
Right-wing		+		-
No assembly		+		na

SOURCES: BES 2001; CES 2000.
NOTE: Results indicate direction of predictors.
$^{*}p < .1$ $^{**}p < .05$ $^{***}p < .01$

a one-unit increase in the independent variable. Using the Quebec data, for example, a one-unit increase in age, which translates here into about a decade, produces a negative change in the dependent variable. Older people are therefore less likely to describe themselves as Québécois. When the independent variable is binary – either male or female, either Catholic or not – the expected change in the dependent variable is for possession of the independent characteristics. In Quebec being Catholic produces a positive change in the dependent variable. Not all coefficients are equally important. Some demonstrate clear effects on the dependent variable, but with others we cannot be certain that the perceived changes are not subject to chance. If we know that there is less than a 10 per cent chance of making a false claim about impact, we say that the result is statistically significant (at the .1 level). If there is only a 1 per cent chance of making a false claim about impact (what we sometimes refer to as a type I error), we say that the result is statistically significant at the .01 level.

The results, which report the signs and levels of statistical significance for logistic regressions, produce three interesting findings. First, religion is a significant predictor of national identity in Scotland. Catholics are more likely to believe that they are Scottish rather than British, than are those describing their religious denomination as Presbyterian or Church of Scotland. In Quebec, where one might expect religion to play a similar role, however, neither Catholicism nor Protestantism plays a significant role. Catholics are not significantly more likely to describe themselves as Québécois; nor are Protestants more likely to hold other identities. Visible-minority status is not a negative predictor of membership, although immigrant status in Quebec clearly matters. Canadian-born respondents are more likely to describe themselves as Québécois than French Canadian or Canadian. Clearly, the variation within the dependent variable might play a role here. Scots and Quebecers were each given three options. Scottish respondents were asked to indicate whether they felt Scottish, British, or European, while Quebecers were allowed to indicate whether they felt Québécois, French Canadian, or Canadian. In both cases respondents could select a label that corresponded to the sub-state nation or to the state. In Scotland, however, the third option was a supra-state entity, whereas in Quebec the third option provided a label that would distinguish Quebecers within Canada. The latter likely explains the negative coefficients for age and Québécois national identity. Older respondents were less likely to describe themselves as Québécois.

In Scotland as in Quebec, the fully specified model, which includes a series of political or civic predictors of national identity, provides statistically significant gains in the total model fit. The adjusted R^2 for the Scottish model increases to .130, while in Quebec it increases to .64. Civic variables are clearly important in both cases. In Scotland, attachment to political parties, measured on a thermometer scale, produces significant results. Conservatives are less likely to describe themselves as Scottish, just as those with greater degrees of attachment to the SNP are more likely to employ that label. This is not a particularly surprising result in itself. We know that Conservative voters are more likely to describe themselves as British, whether equally British and Scottish or more British than Scottish. That this dependent variable provided a forced choice, though, suggests that when we are considering exclusive identities, greater attachment to the Conservatives is a negative predictor of Scottishness.

In Quebec, attachment to political parties, measured by a similar scale, is not a significant predictor of national identity. Although the coefficient signs for attachment to the Liberals or the BQ are in the appropriate direction, in neither case is the coefficient significant. Here support for sovereignty is a greater predictor of a Québécois national identity. Those more supportive of sovereignty are more likely to describe themselves as Québécois. Interestingly, the same is not true in Scotland. Supporters of independence are not more likely to describe themselves as Scottish; nor are those who would prefer a unitary British state less likely to choose Scottishness as their preferred national identity.

The results from table 4.5 demonstrate that a mix of immutable characteristics and political dispositions plays a role in the labels that individuals use to describe themselves. Understanding the labels people assign to themselves is, of course, only one part of the story. Equally important are our perceptions of national boundaries. It is one thing to self-ascribe national identity. It is quite another to hold views on those included or excluded by national boundaries.

References to perceptions of national difference in Scotland suggest that Scottish nationalists, whether supportive of independence or not, believe in the existence of a Scottish people with certain characteristics. Although the size of the Gaelic-speaking population, currently at approximately 2 per cent, inhibits that particular language from occupying a central position as a criterion of membership, the presence of a population that believes the Scots language is relevant suggests that here language itself is seen as relevant. That even the Conservative and Unionist Party articulates a belief in Scottish distinctiveness, "a clear Scottish identity" (SCUA 1997), suggests that no one doubts the existence of the nation or a Scottish people. But does the absence of reference to ancestry or blood or the minimal role of language in official pronouncements on nationalism mean that Scottish national identity eschews ethnic markers of belonging? The following section demonstrates that public opinion prioritizes ethnic markers, even over more inclusive notions of belonging.

Statistical examinations in Scotland and Quebec provide little evidence of a hierarchy of belonging. In part, this outcome has much to do with the methods used to examine identity. In Scotland as in Quebec the available data, by its content and its presentable form, limit examinations. The Scottish Election Study (SES) asked a variety of identity questions during the 1997 general election cam-

Table 4.6
Identity components in Scotland

number agreeing with the following statement "It is ... to be considered Scottish"		
	No.	%
Important to have been born in Scotland	723	82
Important to have Scottish ancestry	643	73
Important to live in Scotland	573	65

SOURCE: SES 1997 (n=882).

paign. Research using these data emphasizes the continued preference for a Scottish identity over a British identity (Brown, McCrone, Paterson, and Surridge 1999). Recent data also allow for an examination of different components of Scottishness. The data in table 4.6 show a subtle ranking in the minds of respondents, with a preference for ethnic rather than civic characteristics. Fewer Scots believe that Scottish residence is more important than Scottish birth.

Despite this view, it is likely that when faced with different combinations of the three previously mentioned components of national membership, alternative hierarchies could form. An individual who lives in Scotland and was born there, for example, might be seen to have a greater claim to Scottish identity than an individual with Scottish ancestry, despite the weight assigned to ancestry over residence in the previous table.

Table 4.7 tracks whether these categories vary according to self-assigned identity label. The table shows that those who consider themselves primarily Scottish place less stock in place of residence as a determinant of identity and more emphasis on birth. At the same time, place of residence as a determinant of identity is even less important for those individuals who are living in Scotland but do not consider themselves Scots. Such data make sense on an intuitive level: those who live in Scotland but do not consider themselves members of the Scottish nation indicate that residence does not correlate with Scottish identity. Perhaps this group is more aware of the ephemeral "other" characteristics that are necessary to acquire a sense of belonging in Scotland.

Seeking to tease out the relationship among blood, place of birth, and residence, David McCrone points to three definitions of Scottishness. The first, based on blood, appears to have been less popular in the twentieth century, largely because of the negative

Table 4.7
Moreno hierarchies of identity in Scotland

Percentage of those within identity group claiming characteristics are "important"			
	Born	*Ancestry*	*Living*
Scottish not British	88	76	72
More Scottish than British	90	81	72
Equally Scottish and British	78	75	66
More British than Scottish	80	74	60
British not Scottish	57	54	37
All	82	73	65

SOURCE: SES 1997 (n=882).

connotations of "ethnic" national identity. A second definition grounds Scottishness in place of birth, which he sees as an attempt to "short-circuit the lineage issues" (McCrone 1994a). The third and final definition is based on territory, a seemingly inclusive definition in which Scottishness is available to all within its borders. McCrone notes the pattern of Scots to domesticate potential aggressors and invading forces (McCrone 1994a). The view sits well with Malcolm Dickson's analysis of the political values of English-born Scottish residents, who show very little deviation from their Scottish counterparts (Dickson 1994). Recent attempts to measure public perceptions of citizenship regulations devote still further attention to this trio of characteristics. In its survey of Scots, polling company ICM and the 1999 Scottish Parliamentary Elections Survey created a hierarchy of characteristics that would determine an individual's right to a Scottish passport. In broad terms, support decreases when one moves away from place of birth towards more civic markers.

Between the two studies there are very few differences (see table 4.8). There is overwhelming support to extend Scottish citizenship to those born and living in Scotland, and to those born there but living in other parts of the UK or further afield. Residency itself is seen as a sufficient criterion for over half of those in the samples. When one explores issues of ancestry, support for extending citizenship decreases. In 1998 only half of Scottish residents supported the provision of a Scottish passport to those who were not born there. The proportion that supported the same provision in 1999 fell by fifteen points. Together these findings must appear a stumbling block to those who claim that Scottish nationalism is resolutely civic and

Table 4.8
Scottish citizenship and identity

Which of the following types of people should be entitled to a Scottish passport? (percentages)		
	1998	*1999*
Born and live in Scotland	94	98.4
Born in Scotland but live elsewhere	81	81.7
Not born in Scotland, live in Scotland	55	56.1
Neither born nor live in Scotland but one Scottish parent	50	35.8
Neither born nor live in Scotland but one Scottish grandparent	26	16.3
All within the UK	31	na

SOURCES: ICM November 1998 (n=1010); SSA 1999 (n=1482).

inclusive. Civic it may be, but not necessarily inclusive. Although it would be accurate to note that the projected provision of Scottish citizenship on the basis of parentage is more liberal than in any other state in Europe, the conditions under which passports would be delivered sufficiently alters the context of these claims. Conditions prompting the very existence of Scottish citizenship would follow a departure from the United Kingdom, where at present all Scots hold citizenship. Thus moving from a situation where all share citizenship to one with divided citizenship would perhaps encourage a more liberal policy than under "normal" circumstances. In short, residency itself, a marker of inclusiveness that is not dependent on ethnic characteristics such as birth or ancestry, is seen by over half of the two samples as sufficient grounds for citizenship. Ancestry alone is seen as a weaker justification for Scottish citizenship. Documents from political parties have already shown a distinction between membership in the state, as offered by citizenship, membership in a Québécois or Scottish society, and membership in the nation. Citizenship was treated with the most inclusive language, and arguments from both the SNP and the PQ emphasized that citizenship would be extended to all residents of Quebec or Scotland, regardless of ethnicity, should the nation achieve independence. In this context the Scottish electorate appears to hold more restrictive definitions of citizenship. Two questions are worth considering. First, are such views distributed equally among Scots, and second, to what extent can we see similar results in Quebec?

When determining if all Scots share similar views of citizenship, a first approach could divide respondents according to their place of birth. One perspective would suggest that those who were born in Scotland would be more ambivalent to extending citizenship rights to others, knowing that they would be included in any definition of citizenship, while those born outside Scotland might be more likely to pursue an inclusive notion of membership. Simple cross-tabulations for place of birth and extending passports to those living but not born in Scotland note that there are statistically significant differences among the groups. While over three-quarters of those born outside Scotland, whether in England and Wales (75 per cent) or outside the UK (77 per cent), support extending citizenship to resident Scots, just over half, or 53 per cent, of Scots-born respondents feel the same way. This finding suggests that respondents tend to hold views that would include themselves, but are more hesitant to extend membership in the state to others.

A second approach focuses less on where individuals were born and more on their own conception of identity. If we compare respondent answers to the Moreno identity question with support for citizenship to those who were not born but now live in Scotland, we can see that those who identify themselves as British are more likely to have an inclusive definition of citizenship. Among those who prioritize their Scottishness, 51 per cent believe that passports should be extended to those living but not born in Scotland. For those who see themselves as equally Scottish and British, 64 per cent feel the same way, as do a slightly higher proportion of those who describe their identity as primarily or exclusively British. This finding shows that support for inclusive membership increases as one encounters those likely to benefit from them, but that such conceptions are also attached to self-ascribed identity. In other words, Scots-born respondents may be less likely to extend citizenship to others, but within this group those who consider their primary identity to be British hold the most inclusive conceptions of membership. A more systematic explanation summarizes the impact of several predictors of support for citizenship.

The regression results in table 4.9 test two models. The first examines whether religious variables, place of birth, and ethnicity have an impact on inclusive definitions of citizenship, in addition to standard control variables such as age, gender, and university education. The second, fully specified model explores whether a range of political or identity variables affects support for the dependent variable. The results in table 4.9 show that demographic character-

Table 4.9
Extending citizenship to those living in but not born in Scotland

	Scotland	
Female	+	–
Age	+*	+*
Catholic	+	+*
CofScotland	–	–
Vis. minority	+	+*
UK-born	+***	+***
Non-UK-born	+**	+**
University degree	+***	+***
British identity		+
Scottish identity		+
Voted Yes		+
Attachment to Conservatives		+
Attachment to SNP		–
Support for independence		+

SOURCE: SPES 1999 (n=1491).
NOTE: Results indicate direction of predictors.
*$p < .1$ **$p < .05$ ***$p < .01$

istics, including place of birth, ethnicity, and religion, have an impact on perceptions of citizenship. Those born in the UK but outside Scotland, those born outside the UK, Catholics, and visible-minority respondents were all more likely to hold an inclusive view of citizenship, supporting the extension of passports to those living in but not born in Scotland. Given the pillars of national identity in Scotland, these groups could be considered at the margins of a more ethnic definition of national membership. It is perhaps not surprising to find that members of such groups advocate an inclusive definition of citizenship.

Equally worth noting, political attitudes and behaviours, such as support for independence, voting Yes in the referendum, or viewing the Conservatives or the SNP positively, have a minimal impact on perceptions of citizenship. The coefficients for all but support for the SNP are positive but non-significant. Last, it is worth noting that the results do not include any statistically significant negative coefficients. Although those supportive of the SNP and members of the Church of Scotland are less likely to extend citizenship to those living but not born in Scotland, the results are not significantly different from answers provided by other groups.

Surveys used for the Canadian Election Study do not include questions similar to those used in Scotland. Post-referendum surveys con-

Table 4.10
Identifying "peoples" in Canada (percentages)

	All	*French*	*English*
Canadians form a people	86.2	88.1	82.9
Quebecers form a people	65.3	70.4	56.4
Cree/Inuit are peoples	78.4	71.4	90.3
Anglophone minority are part of Quebec people	72.0	69.3	76.8
Cree/Inuit are part of Quebec people	62.5	59.4	68.0
Respondent is part of Quebec people	72.5	76.5	65.5

SOURCE: CROP 1998 (n=1000).

ducted by CROP, however, address the issue of national membership. Whereas the Scottish survey questions concern themselves with citizenship, the surveys in Quebec explore the existence of peoples: a Canadian people, a Québécois people, whether the Cree and Inuit are peoples, and who belongs to each of these groups. A number of results are worth noting. First, as the results in table 4.10 demonstrate, respondents indicated overwhelmingly that Canadians form a people. In comparison, a smaller majority said that Quebecers form a people. Asked to evaluate their own membership in the Québécois people, almost three-quarters of respondents believed that they belonged. These results are not, however, distributed equally among the population. Anglophones are less likely to believe that they are part of the Quebec people than are francophone respondents.

The survey also asks whether anglophones and the Cree and Inuit are part of the Québécois people. A higher proportion of respondents (72 per cent) indicated that anglophones in Quebec belonged to the Quebec people than believed that the Cree and Inuit belong (62.5 per cent). An examination of these results within the population shows that francophones are less likely to support a definition of "Québécois people" that includes anglophones. Sixty-nine per cent of francophones believe anglophones belong. Among anglophones the results are quite interesting. First, three-quarters of anglophones believe that as a group they belong to the Québécois people. When asked whether they themselves belong to that people, however, only 65.5 per cent said yes. In other words, anglophones appear to believe that their *group* as a whole belongs to any construction of the Quebecois people, but *individually* respondents are not convinced of their own membership. The results in table 4.11 show that anglophones have a more inclusive definition of the Que-

Table 4.11
The anglophone minority is part of the Quebec people

	Model 1	*Model 2*
Female	+	–
Age	+	+
University	+***	+
English mother tongue	+*	+
Independence		–
PLQ vote		–
Q anglos more Q than English		
Have dual identities		

SOURCE: CROP 1998 (n=1000).
NOTE: Results indicate direction of predictors.
*$p < .1$ **$p < .05$ ***$p < .01$

bec people than do francophones, preferring in higher numbers that anglophones, Cree, and Inuit may be included. Chi square results for each of these questions – whether anglophones belong and whether respondents are part of the Quebec people – show statistically significant differences between linguistic groups.

Regression results test the impact of various predictors of support for the membership of anglophones in a Québécois people. The results in table 4.11 confirm what was suggested earlier: anglophones are significantly more likely to believe that the anglophone minority is part of the Quebec people, as are those with university degrees. Consulting the political variables, however, we note that support for independence and intentions to vote for the PQ are negatively associated with an inclusive membership. Taken together what do these results mean?

We should be cautious comparing results gathered in Scotland and Quebec. It is one thing to compare data collected under the rubric of election results in different years and by different teams, even when the individual questions asked retain the same wording across samples. Data discussed in this section, however, draw on surveys administered in different contexts, using different questions, and at times testing different concepts. The Scottish results were collected during the first election campaign for the Scottish Parliament. Data collected by CROP were gathered in 1998, the same year as a provincial election but outside the campaign period. The concepts measured in each case are also different. Scottish questions probed the conditions under which respondents would extend the right of citizenship to various groups, while the Quebec surveys probed the existence of and membership in various peoples. If we keep these limitations of our comparison in mind, however, we can draw several salient points from the available data.

First, there is clear majority support for the existence of a Quebecois people, a Canadian people, and Aboriginal peoples. In addition, there is a clear consensus that anglophones, Cree, and Inuit are members of the Québécois people. Less clear, however, is whether individuals within these groups would consider themselves part of this people. Second, as with the Scottish results, we can detect a difference in the rhetoric projected by separatist or nationalist political parties and the beliefs of voters. The resolutely inclusive messages promoted by the PQ, ADQ, and PLQ all speak to the membership of individuals, regardless of ethnic origin, language, or religion, in Quebec, although whether that entity refers to a future independent state, a society, or the nation depends on the particular party involved. Individuals, regardless of their mother tongue, appear to support this construction: a majority in all cases included anglophones, Cree, and Inuit in the Québécois people. The last step, however, that anglophones would then feel that they belong, is less clear.

Taken together, these results suggest that the rhetoric of the nationalist or sovereignist movement is not exclusive, that individuals do not perceive it to be so, and that the public at large maintains an open and tolerant vision of national membership. Individuals who might feel themselves at the boundaries of national identity, possessing some but not all of the relevant markers, however, continue to exclude themselves, regardless of the messages from political parties and their own assessments of general inclusiveness; individuals continue to exclude themselves from membership in the nation, even in the face of generally inclusiveness messages.

5

National Political Cultures

If we are hoping to examine the impact of national identity on political culture in Scotland and Quebec, it is important not only to identify the broad themes within the political cultures in Scotland and Quebec but also to articulate clearly what we mean by political culture. The definition provided in the introduction includes subjective orientations and the objective relationship between individuals and the state. It also includes views of fellow citizens. These factors mandate us to explore the dominant values, attitudes, and behaviours within the polities, as described by existing research and available data. They also require us to explore what political parties and voters have to say about the political cultures in which they live.

Political culture is a valuable tool for analyzing polities. It allows us to understand the dominant beliefs and behaviours within a political system, and it enables researchers to comprehend the link between institutions and individuals. Political institutions are the product of the political culture, created by individuals who have visions of the way the political world should operate. At the same time, they continue to exert an influence over the attitudes and behaviours of future generations. When we examine political culture, we look at the institutions of a political system and the dominant beliefs, attitudes, and values within that system.

Often political-culture research focuses on the relationship between citizens and the state. In so doing, it examines how the state treats citizens and how citizens feel about that treatment. It is worth noting that political culture is grounded, on the one hand, on the way things really are – the way the state actually treats its citizens – and public perception. Citizen reactions to government or political parties are grounded in personal beliefs, which may or may not be informed by fact (Jowell and Topf 1988). Perhaps the first thing to note about political culture is that it is grounded both in the actual relationship between citizens and the state and in the perceived relationship between citizens and the state. This distinction is a useful one, for as we have already seen, political pronouncements about national membership are not necessarily matched by public perceptions.

Another useful way to examine political culture is to focus on the relationship among citizens. Political culture often examines the types of policies that are popular in one country but not in another (Lipset 1990). Variations in support for the death penalty or free trade or subsidized health care are often explained by differences in political culture. While we could classify these topics according to perceptions of the role of the state, in that those supportive of subsidized health care would likely welcome state involvement more than those supporting privatized medicine, policy support also addresses views of fellow citizens. How we feel about our fellow citizens – the rights we think they should access or whom we include as fellow citizens – can also be seen as an integral part of political culture. For this reason, this book relies on the following definition of political culture: the relationship, both perceived and actual, between citizens and the state and the relationship, both perceived and actual, among citizens.

One of the criticisms in this study is that political culture has long ignored the influence of national identity. This is not the only concern that one might have. Political culture has been criticized for being too positivist (Pateman 1989), for ignoring economic factors (Jackman and Miller 1996a, 1996b) or behavioural factors (Reisinger 1995), and for being methodologically slippery (Whitefield and Evans 1999), in addition to the usual charges that it has been applied incorrectly (Inglehart 1988). And yet its appeal is understandable for it seeks to explain the dominant values in a polity. It explores how individuals think of themselves, their fellow citizens and the state, and it incorporates in this view the institutions that structure our political life. Efforts to understand why people in one country approach politics in one way and those in another hold different views has led to a resurgence of political-culture analyses even in the face of economic or rational-choice efforts to show that individuals consistently behave in a way that maximizes benefit and minimizes cost. Political-culture researchers would argue that while this criticism might be true, the way that individuals identify costs and benefits is culturally defined. Rational decisions can thus occur within a political culture. Concepts such as social capital, which attempts to link the aggregate level of citizen interaction with the stability of society or democracy, still rely on examinations of political culture to provide a sense of context to the work (Colemen 1988; Putnam, Leonardi, and Nanetti 1993; Bennett 1998; Boix and Posner 1995; Johnston and Jowell 1999; Portes 1998). For these researchers, the methodological issues involved are outweighed by the benefits of a cultural approach.

Early studies in political culture focused on impressions of a culture. De Tocqueville , in his examination of American political culture, sought to describe and account for the patterns of political interaction and leadership in the United States. Since the mid-1950s, however, political-culture studies have often relied heavily on comparative survey data to provide a summary of attitudes and behaviours. Often such studies focus on attitudes such as trust, deference, efficacy, confidence, and satisfaction. The subjective orientations of individuals can be directed at the state – its structures, policy outputs, and symbols – or at fellow citizens.

Do Scotland and Quebec possess national political cultures? Both nations exist within larger democracies, each of which has its own institutions that structure political debate and in turn influence the dominant political attitudes and behaviours of its citizens. The development of a Western and liberal political culture thus provides the context for the Scottish and Quebec debates. Canada and the United Kingdom, and within them Quebec and Scotland, are liberal democracies, with elected lower houses of Parliament and unelected or absent upper houses. Both are examples of parliamentary democracies in which the head of government is the leader of the largest political party in the lower house. They possess similar democratic structures, elect governments on the backs of similar turnout levels, and view politicians, judges, journalists, teachers, and other authorities with similar levels of trust and cynicism (Gwyn 1995). When Russell argues that the basic values of popular sovereignty, political equality, majority rule, and protection of individual rights can be found in convention and constitution in Canada (Russell 1993), he could as well be speaking of the United Kingdom. According to these criteria, the only difference for the UK would be a greater belief in parliamentary sovereignty and the absence of a written constitution. Indeed, such similarities extend beyond Canada and the UK and include most Westminster polities and, with minimal adaptation, many other Western ones. Given these broad institutional similarities, two things stand out.

First, within Westminster polities there is a considerable range in policy provision in terms of health care, education, and social services. Liberal democratic welfare states provide differing policy options and solutions for the approval of the electorate than do Nordic or continental welfare regimes. Institutional similarity does not guarantee a similarity of policy preferences. At the same time, we know that there are broadly similar attitudes towards the state, in terms of efficacy, deference, satisfaction, and confidence. Cross-national studies performed by academics in a variety of locations produce surprisingly similar results (Inglehart 1977, 1990; Nevitte 1996; Halman and Nevitte 1996; Nevitte and Gibbins 1990). Whatever gap existed among first-world Western nations when Almond and Verba began the fieldwork for *The Civic Culture* has been closed by years of unprecedented economic and political security, an increasingly powerful global communications network, international trade, and political alliances. Within advanced industrial countries we are dealing with decreasing variations in attitudes, something that makes diagnosing differences in the political cultures of Scotland and the UK, Quebec and Canada, more difficult than it might have been at the start of the twentieth century.

CITIZENS AND THE STATE

The first thing to note about political culture in our two cases is that by traditional measures, there are interesting differences. The results in table 5.1 show that a higher proportion of Canadians than Britons are likely to believe that MPs lose touch. We can consider such questions measures of external efficacy or a sense that the system is responsive to influence or change. In this case it appears that on one indicator, levels of external efficacy are lower in Canada than they are in the UK. Other measures listed in table 5.1, such as whether politics is difficult to understand or too complicated or whether "people like me have no say," could be considered indicators of internal efficacy or a sense that individuals can effect change. The results in table 5.1 show that levels of internal

Table 5.1
Attitudes to the political system in Canada and the UK (percentages)

	Canada	*Quebec*	*UK*	*Scotland*
MPs lose touch	78.4	76.3	65.4	70.9
Parties/gov't don't care what I think	26.4	37.5	50.6	55.6
Politics complicated	50.2	56.9	56.4	61.4
People like me have no say	45.2	16.3	56.1	60.1

SOURCES: BES 2001; CES 2000.
NOTE: Canadian responses do not include Quebec; UK responses do not include Scotland. In the second question the wording was slightly different in Canada: UK asked, "Government doesn't care what people think," whereas Canadian survey asked, "Parties don't care what people think."

efficacy are lower in the United Kingdom. UK residents are more likely to believe that politics is difficult to understand and more likely to feel that they have no say. These results show that there is not a sense of low efficacy in one country and evidence of high efficacy in another. Instead, they show generally low levels of efficacy, with results lowest in the UK on three of the four measures.

If we compare results in Quebec to those in Canada and results in Scotland to those in the UK, we find that there are remarkable differences. First, residents in Quebec and Scotland are more likely to believe that parties or government are inattentive. One of the indicators of poor internal efficacy is also higher in Scotland and Quebec. Over half of Quebecers and Scots believe that politics is difficult to understand. When we turn to the last indicator, whether people have a say in politics, we find that Quebecers demonstrate a higher level of internal efficacy than do other Canadians, a pattern not matched in Scotland, where 60 per cent of respondents feel they have no say.

The differences are interesting, but are they significant? The Canadian results show that there are statistically significant differences between the responses of Quebecers and those of other Canadians for each of the indicators listed in table 5.1. When we turn to the Scottish results, there are only significant differences between Scots and other Britons for the indicators that tap internal efficacy. On measures of external efficacy, however, the results are not significantly different. In short, Quebecers exhibit consistently different attitudes from other Canadians on all measures of efficacy, while in Scotland voters differ primarily in terms of internal efficacy.

From this brief table we are able to point to interesting differences between the constituent nations and their larger states. These measures are, of course, among the more traditional indicators of political culture. If we employ these as a starting point, it is useful to determine how they feed into debates about attitudinal and behavioural differences between the nation and the larger state. Political actors, academics, and voters each have their own estimations of whether political culture within the nation is distinct within the state. An investigation of each of these three sources shows that there is a consistent perception that the nation holds a different political culture, but also that it is different in consistent and meaningful ways.

PARTISAN PERSPECTIVES ON NATIONAL POLITICAL CULTURES

Political actors have at times occupied themselves with the relationship between national values and the political culture of the larger state. As with the discourse surrounding national recognition, perspectives on nationalism (rather than constitutional change) appear to dictate perceptions of national political cultures. Nationalist parties point to the existence of Scottish or Québécois values. In the tenth Donaldson lecture, given in 1995, former SNP MP and current MSP George Reid claimed that identity "implies a return to separate, national roots" (Reid 1995). Other SNP documents further elaborate on this theme. The 1999 party manifesto declared that "traditionally, Scots have believed in values of compassion, community and the common weel [*sic*]" (SNP 1999). In 2002 then SNP leader John Swinney argued, "My job is to restore Scotland's values to Scotland's Government. Those Scottish values are deep-seated and cherished. They are values of fairness, honesty and equal opportunity" (Swinney 2002, 3). Swinney then added, "This party has those traditional Scottish values running through its very core" (4). Clearly, the SNP possesses a belief that Scottish values are distinct from the values prioritized elsewhere in the UK. In addition, in an effort to curry favour with voters, the party has attempted to align itself with those values. Other parties perform a similar task.

The Conservative Party outlines "Scottish" values that are consistent with those raised by the SNP. The 1999 Conservative manifesto confirms that "a sense of community is deeply ingrained in the

Scottish psyche" (SCUP 1999, 32). The Labour Party raises similar themes. Former Labour leader Donald Dewar argued, "For me, what makes our country special is not just the beauty of our land but the strength of our values. It is a country where equality of opportunity and social justice are central to our sense of self." He adds, "These traditional Scottish values are also the values of Scottish New Labour" (SLP 1998). This quotation shows not only that parties of diverse political views share a vision of Scotland's key institutions, shared values, and distinctiveness, but also that they try to align the views of their party with the historically justified views of Scots. In 1988 Margaret Thatcher declared, "Tory values are in tune with everything that is finest in the Scottish character, and with the proudest moments in Scottish history ... Scottish values are Tory values – and vice versa" (*Scotsman*, 14 May 1988).

Political debate has also involved efforts of parties to paint their opponents as out of tune with traditional Scottish values. The SNP, in particular, has often adopted this approach, criticizing Thatcherite values as "anti-Scottish", contemporary Conservative policies as "anti-Scottish elitist dogma," and Blairite policies as evidence of a "contempt for traditional values and lack of respect for the "common weel" [*sic*]" (Salmond 1996, 3). In a speech two years later Salmond repeated the attack on new Labour values as anathema to Scottish "culture and identity" (Salmond 1998a) and stated derisively, "The current social orthodoxies of Blairism – the orthodoxies of Thatcherism with a grinning face – are being challenged in Scotland not just because they do not reflect Scottish values, but because they are inherently wrong in the Scottish situation" (Salmond 1998a, 5). More recently Swinney promised to "replace the warped values of New Labour with the decent values of the decent people of Scotland" (Swinney 2002).

Within Quebec, references to common values surface far more frequently in the discourse of federalist parties and organizations than they do in the documents and speeches of Quebec nationalists. In its 1991 final report, the Citizens' Forum on Canada's Future returned to the Trudeauist vision of the Canadian federation, maintaining that "Canadian citizenship is an emotional tie, a sense of shared values and commitments to our country ... [a] focus for unity" (Citizens' Forum on Canada's Future 1991, 1). The report seems to mark a halfway point between the views advanced by Trudeau and Mulroney by adding that "being Canadian does not require that we all be alike. Around a core set of values, Canadian citizenship accommodates a respect for diversity that enriches us all" (1). The common bonds are characterized by a belief in freedom, dignity, respect, equality, fair treatment, and opportunity to participate. The extent to which these values distinguish Canadians from, for example, Americans or Britons, Germans or Norwegians, remains open to debate.

Within Quebec, however, there is far less attention to the existence of Québécois values. Documents and speeches for the Bloc Québécois place far greater emphasis on "la défense des intérêts de l'ensemble des Québécois" than on its values, although there are isolated examples of the latter. In 1998 the party argued that "Quebecers [have] never lost sight of the values they had always cherished: respect for others, tolerance and solidarity" (BQ 1998b, 7). Later the same document notes that Quebecers are "tolerant, peace-loving and concerned for the well-being of their fellow man." As is typical of documents in Quebec, the BQ argues that Quebecers and other Canadians have different policy preferences, something that is certainly linked to distinct values in the Scottish documents: "les choix des Québécois sur les plans socials, économiques et politiques sont incompatibles avec ceux des Canadiens" (BQ 1999, 7). Such differences are frequently referred to as the Quebec consensus or the Quebec model: "un modèle original de concertation et d'action de gouvernement, combinant le progrès social à la res- ponsabilité budgétaire" (PQ 1999, 6). When the Quebec Liberal Party suggested that the Quebec model be revisited, PQ leader Lucien Bouchard clearly linked the model to distinctiveness: "En s'attaquant à ce qui nous distingue, en posant la prémisse que ce qui est différent est mauvais nécessairement, il prépare le terrain du grand moule de l'uniformité canadienne ... Il fait le travail des tenants de l'union sociale et du rouleau compresseur canadien" (Bouchard 1999a, 2). In response, the Quebec Liberal Party later acknowledged, "Unfortunately, some people want to associate every attempt to reflect on the "Quebec model" with an attack on Quebec's identity" (PLQ 2001, 30).

As in Scotland, political parties attempt to align themselves as well as possible with what are perceived to be the dominant national values. "Le Parti libéral du Québec est l'héritier d'une longue tradition politique fondée sur la défense des droits et libertés, voué au progrès économique, social, culturel et politique du Québec. Ces valeurs ont contribué à former la société québécoise" (PLQ 1997). Of course, the most explicit example of this tactic may be found in "Liberal Values and the Modern-Day Quebec," in which the party demonstrates how the values of the Quebec Liberal Party have had an enduring influence on public life in Quebec. At the same time, the Liberal Party in Quebec has taken pains to emphasize that the values common to Quebecers are values shared by other Canadians. These include a belief in the importance of individual liberties, diversity, social programs, and solidarity (PLQ 1998c).

The more limited presence of explicit references to values in the Quebec documents could have something to do with the fact that the provincial government provides a venue where policy may be affected by the particular attitudes and values of Quebecers. Much of the dialogue about value difference in Scotland stems from the pre-devolution period and was used as evidence that a Scottish parliament was necessary. It is likely that the centrality of values to political discourse in Scotland derives from the context of political debate, rather than from a greater belief that the nation is distinct. It is also worth noting, however, that since 1999 rhetoric in both Scotland and Quebec has paid more attention to values, not less. Here, though, values have been linked less to policy and portrayed instead as the civic glue that binds national members together.

SCOTLAND AND QUEBEC: RESEARCH ON NATIONAL POLITICAL CULTURES

If political actors have a specific interest in claiming that "national" values exist, academic research should provide dispassionate proof whether these claims are true. Such research focuses on two questions: first, to what extent is the political culture of the nation distinct from the larger political culture of the state? and second, to what might we attribute any differences should they exist? In Scotland research tends to emphasize the causes of difference, while in Canada far greater attention to a possible "Quebec political culture" focused in the 1960s on the impact of a cultural fragment from New France and since the 1970s on interprovincial differences in attitudes. The following section addresses the two questions raised by academic research: do national political cultures exist, and if so, why?

Within Canada, research on a distinct political culture in Quebec surfaces in two literatures. The first addresses whether the cultural fragment of New France had a long-lasting effect on Canadian political institutions and approaches to political life, tempering the liberalism that one sees in the United States and providing in Canada a Tory-touched view of politics (Hartz 1964; Horowitz 1966, 1977, 1985; Christian 1978; McRae 1978, 1964). This literature sits with others arguing that it was the United Empire Loyalists (Bell 1970; Bell, and Tepperman 1979) or the decision not to rebel against the British (Lipset 1968) that served to distinguish Canadian political culture within the continent. This literature on fragments was joined by later research seeking to identify empirically the boundaries of political cultures within Canada. J. Wilson (1974) and Simeon and Elkins (1974, 1980) pointed to the role that federalism has played in the development of distinct political cultures within Canada. Here it was not that Quebec was distinct from the rest of Canada but that the existence of provinces and their legislatures, bureaucracies, and sociological boundaries served to create interprovincial differences within regions. Simeon and Elkins noted, of course, that provinces tended to cluster regionally, so that the Atlantic provinces tended to exhibit more deference and less trust than other provinces. Gidengil likewise noted that provincial political cultures were motivated by centre-periphery relations both within and across provincial boundaries (Gidengil 1990). Henderson confirms the existence of regional rather than provincial political cultures in Canada (Henderson 2004).

If evidence of distinct political attitudes in Quebec is rather thin on the ground, explanations for its existence are not. Quebec political culture is portrayed as an illiberal culture where democracy was slow to develop thanks to an underdeveloped rural economy and a powerful Catholic Church (Trudeau 1958). The retarded-development thesis, which argues that Quebecers are much more collectivist than other Canadians, runs as follows: in the post-Conquest period a dominated population lost its natural elites (Brunet 1962, 1964; Frégault 1956; Iguarta 1974; Séguin 1970) and vigilantly protected its language and culture by prioritizing the values of *survivance* (Cook 1989), simultaneously developing a suspicion of the (British) state (Bernard 1977). This view has been supported by francophone and anglophone academics. More recently, however, research tends to argue that the original analysis overestimated the influence of the church, if not in the everyday lives of individuals, then certainly in the formation of their overtly political attitudes (Létourneaou 1997; McRoberts 1997; G. Pelletier 1988). The extent to which the Quiet Revolution is seen as a dramatic break with the past or an adaptation to previous practice depends on the initial perception of Quebec's development. Those arguing for the dominant role of the church tend to stress the caesura between *la grande noirceur* of the immediate postwar period and the big-government days of the 1960s. More recent efforts to describe political culture in Quebec emphasize modernity rather than traditionalism. A greater spirit of continentalism (Lachapelle 1999) and post-material values (Pelletier and Guérin 1996; R. Pelletier 1997) suggests that Quebecers distinguish themselves from other Canadians by their attention to continental pragmatism and quality of life.

A final cluster of research explores political behaviour. The fact that a significant proportion of the population votes for a nationalist political party and public support for independence are seen not as generators of a distinct political culture but as proof of its existence. Efforts to identify predictors of support for self-determination (Blais, Martin, and Nadeau 1995; Drouilly 1994, 1997a, 1997b; Guérin and Nadeau 1998; P. Martin 1994, 1998) point to the importance of subjective boundaries around a cultural group, a theme that surfaces in the research on political culture in Scotland.

Works addressing Scottish political culture have, in the main, emphasized the similarities in political attitudes across the UK and have argued that if any difference exists, it is small. Data from the British Social Attitudes Survey, which began in 1983, emphasize that differences are typically small. Relying on British Rights Survey data, Dickson also notes that "the degree of similarity outweighs any small empirical difference" between the views of Scots and other Britons (Dickson 1996). Even so, he identified greater Scottish support for reducing unemployment, providing help for the disabled, protecting ethnic minorities, strengthening law and order, taking care of the needy and less support for self-reliance. Most measures seem to indicate a greater willingness among Scottish residents for a proactive and implicated state.

Data on political behaviour, however, provide better evidence of a distinct political culture. For Curtice, the uneven distribution of partisan support within the UK provides indirect evidence of different attitudes towards policy (Curtice 1988), although he cautions that variations in partisan support could also be attributed to neighbourhood effects (Books and Prysby 1991). Indeed, for him, there is evidence of attitudinal variation between the south and north of mainland Britain but not of a distinctly Scottish political culture (Curtice 1992). The research teams exploring data from the Scottish Election Study have also pointed to greater support for social-democratic parties as proof of a distinct national political culture (Brown, McCrone, Paterson, and Surridge 1999)

Within Scotland, a heightened belief in governmental responsibility could be linked to a greater sense of cohesion fostered by a strong civil society. The greater willingness to accept state activity does seem to provide proof that Prime Minister Thatcher's program of limited government was anathema to Scottish political culture. This attitude would certainly explain greater support for social-democratic parties, something identified as a key pillar of national political cultures. Both Dickson and Curtice suggest that socio-economic particularities of the region, rather than identity, account for variations in attitudes and partisan support. Scots are not inherently more socialist but, rather, vote according to their needs. The structure of society, with its higher dependence on public-sector employment, council housing, and heavy industry, creates needs that were traditionally met by the (old) Labour Party (Dickson 1994, 1996; Curtice 1988, 1992, 1996). A sense of separateness does not appear to be the motor for distinctly national values. When seeking to explain support for devolution, Brown and colleagues have argued that voters were motivated by welfare rationality – by the potential benefits to society as a whole (Brown, McCrone, Paterson, and Surridge 1999). Just as national identity provided a poor predictor of support for devolution, so too does it fail to account for variations in attitudes within the UK.

For other researchers, it is the absence of key characteristics that accounts for variations in attitudes. According to Pye and Verba, the way in which history infuses a people with a sense of common experience and of self can have an impact on contemporary political culture (Pye and Verba 1965). For Eatwell, diverse references to King Arthur and Boadicea, Robin Hood and the Dunkirk spirit, have coloured British political culture. The absence of such references in Scotland, in addition to the symbolic difference of national flags, patron saints, bank notes, sports teams, churches, and governmental institutions, reinforces a view of separateness in Scotland that filters through to political culture (Eatwell 1997). This sense of separateness presents one of the interesting conundrums of political culture in Scotland. Even though little evidence of a distinctly national culture exists, explanations abound for *why* it might exist, and political parties – even parties opposed to constitutional change – emphasize its existence. The psychological borders erected before devolution have ensured that much of the population sees itself in possession of a distinct political culture, even if the attitudes and behaviours they exhibit are almost indistinct within the United Kingdom. How and why this perception occurs forms the focus of the next section and the following chapter.

NATIONAL POLITICAL CULTURES AT THE TURN OF THE CENTURY

If we want to test for the existence of national political cultures in Scotland and Quebec, we have sufficient data at our disposal. Each of the election studies in Canada and the UK contains a series of questions that provide insight into political attitudes and behaviours. This section identifies key value sets for each location and focuses primarily on two areas: first, attitudes towards the state and, second, attitudes towards fellow citizens. This approach deliberately excludes attitudes towards the election itself, the perceived issues of importance in each election, attitudes towards party leaders, and methods of accessing electoral information. The desire here is less to identify different positions of each nation within a context of electoral competition than to probe the existence of national political cultures, cultures which may survive more short-term factors such as election issues.

The 2000 Canadian Election Study contains a number of questions probing different aspects of political culture. These include perceptions of the state, civic roles, and attitudes towards fellow citizens. Table 5.2 summarizes the attitudinal differences between Quebecers and other Canadians. It includes average scores for six additive indices. The possible answers for each index range from 0 to 1, and each index was created by summing the results for the constituent indicators and locating an average score. Full descriptions of the constituent indicators, including alpha scores, are given in the notes.

The results demonstrate two key findings. First, Quebecers display significantly different attitudes on five of the six measures examined.

Table 5.2
Variations in attitudes in Canada and Quebec

	Canada	*Quebec*
Cynicism	.60	.67***
Voting	.75	.73*
Traditional values	.59	.24***
Anti-discrimination	.61	.69***
Anti-immigration	.54	.53
Free trade	.57	.64***

SOURCE: CES 2000.
NOTE: Results are predictors for OLS regressions.
*$p < .1$ **$p < .05$ ***$p < .01$

Cynicism index: Alpha Canada .460, Quebec .350
Those elected to Parliament soon lose touch with the people.
I don't think the government cares much what people like me think.
Voting index: Alpha Canada .676, Quebec .632
People who don't vote have no right to criticize the government.
It is the duty of every citizen to vote.
It is important to vote, even if my party or candidate has no chance of winning.
If I did not vote, I would feel guilty.
Free-trade index: Alpha Canada .553, Quebec .473
Overall, free trade with the US has been good for the Canadian economy.
International trade creates more jobs in Canada than it destroys.
Anti-discrimination index: Alpha Canada .818, Quebec .629
Discrimination makes it extremely difficult for women to get jobs equal to their abilities.
How much do you think should be done for women?
How much do you think should be done for racial minorities?
How much should be done to reduce the gap between the rich and the poor in Canada?
Are you very sympathetic towards feminism: quite sympathetic, not very sympathetic, not at all sympathetic?
We have gone too far in pushing equal rights in this country (change direction).
It is more difficult for non-whites to be successful in Canadian society than it is for whites.
The best way to protect women's interests is to have more women in Parliament.
Anti immigration index: Alpha Canada .775, Quebec .786
Too many recent immigrants just don't want to fit into Canadian society.
Immigrants make an important contribution to this country (change direction).
We should look after Canadians born in this country first and others second.
Political parties spend too much time catering to minorities.
Traditional values index: Alpha Canada .756, Quebec .633
Only married couples should children.
Gays and lesbians should be allowed to get married (change direction).
The Bible is the literal word of God and is to be taken literally word for word.
The world is always changing, and we should adapt our view of moral behaviour to these changes (change direction).
Do you think it should be very easy for women to get an abortion (change direction)?

These include both attitudes towards the state and attitudes towards fellow citizens. Second, the direction of differences are not what we might expect. Quebecers are more likely to express cynical values towards the political process and more likely to feel that MPs lose touch and that the government doesn't care, but are less likely to believe that voting is important and that it is a civic duty.

In terms of attitudes towards other citizens, Quebecers possess less traditional values than other Canadians. This area presents the largest gap between the two solitudes and confirms what we might expect, given higher than average rates of common-law marriages and children born out of wedlock in Quebec. The indicators included in the traditional values index, however, span more than visions of marriage and focus also on support for gay marriage, the adaptation of moral views, the ease with which women should be able to procure an abortion, and interpretations of the Bible. Lower scores on this index thus suggest that Canada outside Quebec is far more traditional in its approach to religion, marriage, and morality than are Quebecers. In terms of anti-discrimination, Quebecers are more supportive than those beyond their borders. Items included in this index tap into support for feminism and whether more should be done for women and racial minorities, in addition to perceptions of the role that discrimination plays in the lives of women and visible minorities. Last in this section, the index on anti-immigration includes indicators that tap the perceived role of immigrants within society. These include whether immigrants attempt to fit in, whether Canadian unity is affected by ethnic diversity, and whether Canadian-born citizens should be "looked after" before immigrants. The results show surprisingly high scores for both Quebecers and other Canadians, with both groups scoring over the midpoint on the index. There are, however, no differences between Quebecers and other Canadians. Quebecers do not harbour anti-immigrant sentiments at a rate that is different from other Canadians.

A final index dealt with the role of trade. Support for free trade speaks, on the one hand, to general economic optimism but also to openness towards other markets and societies. A lack of support for free trade could be indicative of general isolationism and the perceived impermeability of boundaries. Here we find that Quebecers are far more supportive of free trade, believing that it provides jobs and has brought general benefit to Canada. Taken together, the results for the six variables show that Quebecers possess consis-

Table 5.3
Variations in attitudes in the UK and Scotland

	UK	Scotland
Cynicism	.63	.66**
Voting	.65	.66
Traditional values	.59	.56***
Anti-discrimination	.63	.64
Anti-immigration	.53	.48***
Pro-EU	.46	.48**

SOURCE: BES 2001.

NOTES: $^{*}p < .1$ $^{**}p < .05$ $^{***}p < .01$

Cynicism index: Alpha England/Wales .688, Scotland .699
MPs lose touch with people.
I don't think the government cares much what people like me think.
Voting index: Alpha England/Wales .737, Scotland .747
Voting can change Britain.
I would feel very guilty if I did not vote.
Democracy only works if you vote.
Seriously neglect duty if did not vote.
Pro-EU index: Alpha England/Wales .765, Scotland .712
Supportive of joining Euro currency.
Supportive towards British membership in the EU.
Anti-discrimination index: Alpha England/Wales .590, Scotland .602
Men are better suited for politics (change direction).
Husband earns money, woman stays home (change direction).
Anti-immigration index: Alpha England/Wales .832, Scotland .811
Immigrants increase crime rates.
Immigrants are good for the economy (change direction).
Immigrants take jobs from natives.
Immigrations make Britain open to cultures (change direction).
We should send asylum-seekers home immediately.
Traditional values index: Alpha England/Wales .504, Scotland .404
We should tolerate unconventional lifestyles (change direction).
Youth don't respect traditional values.
Censorship is necessary to maintain moral standards.

tently different attitudes towards the state and their fellow citizens than do other Canadians.

The British Election Study contains a similar blend of questions about political culture, although a far greater proportion of the survey deals with attitudes towards parties, party leaders, and facets of the electoral process. It is possible, though, to replicate the indices found in the Canadian Election Study and to create an index to free trade by exploring attitudes towards the European Union. The results show that on some measures Scots and other Britons possess clear value differences; on four of the six indices listed in table 5.3, the differences are statistically significant.

Scots display a greater cynicism towards the political process and are less supportive of traditional values, trends common in Canada, although the gap is clearly not the same as the one distinguishing Quebecers from other Canadians. The cynicism index used for these data contains identical measures to the one used for the Canadian data. The traditional values index taps familiar measures and probes support for censorship, the perception that youth do not respect traditional values, and the belief that unconventional lifestyles should not be tolerated. Unlike in Canada, where there are not statistically significant differences in terms of support for immigration, Scots are less prone to display anti-immigration sentiments. The anti-immigration index contains items tapping the role that immigrants play in society and in the economy. Scots do not show statistically significant variations in opinion with respect to voting or anti-discrimination. This outcome is noteworthy for two reasons. First, such differences do exist in Quebec. Second, if we distinguish between state-directed political culture issues and attitudes towards fellow citizens, there are inconsistent results. Scots may feel differently from other Britons about the state, but they do not hold different attitudes in terms of civic duty. Scots may hold less traditional values and may exhibit less opposition to immigration, but the differences are smaller than those found in Quebec, and insignificant if we examine attitudes towards gender equality or anti-discrimination.

Scots appear significantly more supportive of continued UK participation in the EU and the single currency. This outcome confirms the rhetoric employed by the SNP, Labour, and Liberal Democrat parties. There can be no argument that the Scots are more parochial than their English and Welsh counterparts, if the only test of parochialism is continued support for EU integration.

These differences are what we might expect, particularly given results for Quebec. Both nations appear to exhibit less support for traditional values, greater cynicism with the political process, and greater openness to international integration. We should be cautious, however, of assuming that nation or national identity plays a pre-eminent role here. Dividing respondents by region suggests, certainly, that value differences may be rooted in location, but as the academic literature indicates, they could just as easily be grounded

Table 5.4
Salience of nationhood in political culture, Quebec and Scotland

	Trad. val.	*Anti-imm.*	*Anti-discrim.*	*Vote*	*Pro-trade, EU*	*Cynicism*
Quebec	.051	–.042	.166	**–.055***	**.118****	.019
Age	.007*	.001*	–.001	.002***	.000	.001
Gender	.039	–.031	–.035	–.001	–.092**	–.070**
University	–.190	–.052**	.096	–.014	.139***	–.089**
Income	–.037	.005	–.005	.000	–.001	.000
Union	–.035	.036	–.067	.039	–.059	.001
Vis. minority	.008	–.078	.150	–.139**	–.048	.013
Married	.020	–.013	–.196***	.013	.025	.028
R^2	.36	.08	.38	.08	.14	.05
Scotland	–.019	**–.043*****	.008	**.036*****	.013	.024
Age	.191***	–.056	–.305***	.301***	–.093***	.049
Gender	.008	–.040***	.058***	.033***	–.012	–.009
University	–.066***	–.137***	.048***	.052***	.103***	–.061***
Income	–.029	–.052*	.105***	.082***	.127***	–.064**
Union	–.006	–.015	.033**	.033***	.031**	–.039***
Vis. minority	.050*	–.118***	.004	.062**	.080**	.015
Married	.025*	.042***	–.039***	–.005	–.029*	.004
R^2	.10	.16	.17	.13	.08	.05

SOURCES: CES 2000; BES 2001.
NOTE: Results are unstandardized OLS coefficients.
$^*p < .1$ $^{**}p < .05$ $^{***}p < .01$

in the social and economic variations within the state as in any national political culture. In short, such measures lack controls for other important factors such as religion, economic station, education, and ethnicity. A second step in determining whether national political cultures exist warrants a more restrictive test of national influence. The tables discussed below summarize the impact of national residence on value dispositions, while controlling for typical socio-demographic factors. If national residence remains a significant predictor, then we can say that there is something to the claim of national political cultures in Scotland and Quebec.

Table 5.4 contains results for the six indices created earlier. Residence in the nation – in Scotland or Quebec – is included as one possible predictor of value dispositions, along with other typical control variables. Age, gender, whether the respondent holds a university degree, union membership, income, visible-minority status, and marital status surface repeatedly as significant indicators of civic behaviour and political attitudes. It seems fruitful then to pit them again the nation. The results show that for both Scotland and Quebec, residence in the nation is a significant predictor of attitudes for two of the six possible indices. In Canada, residence in the nation is a significant predictor of support for free trade and a negative predictor of voting as a civic duty. On all other measures, other socio-demographic variables were more successful in their predictive capacity. Overall, nation fared worse that university education and age as consistent predictors of attitudes, each of which was a significant predictor for three of the items. In Britain, living in Scotland is a significant predictor for the voting variable, as in Quebec, and for anti-immigrant sentiment. In other words, Scots are significantly less likely to express anti-immigrant sentiments than are other Britons. When compared to the various controls, nation performed least well. Each of the control variables proved a more significant predictor of attitudes than did residence in Scotland.

This model has two weaknesses, one of which will be addressed here. First, it does not include other regional or national variables. In other words, national political cultures may exist in the United Kingdom, but they may be manifest in England and Wales rather than in Scotland. Excluding those two variables allows us to pronounce on the importance of "Scottish political culture" but not national political cultures writ large. The same is true in Canada, as the model excludes the importance of living in Ontario or Alberta, factors we might expect to have an impact on support for traditional values, for example.

The second weakness deals with the importance of socio-demographic variables in the nation. The model excludes religion. In part, this was done because of the variations in religious denomination across the UK. It is also fruitful, as in Canada we have come to expect that Catholicism may be a predictor of support for traditional values outside Quebec but a predictor of support for social libertarianism within the nation. It is appropriate to test the importance of nationhood in basic indicators of political culture by pitting nation against a range of typical socio-demographic factors. One way in which national boundaries may be relevant, however, is the way in which different socio-demographic variables exert influence. If union membership is a significant predictor of behaviour in Scotland but not elsewhere in the UK, or if visible-minority status is not important within Quebec but salient outside its borders, then these too may point to the existence of national political cultures.

Table 5.5
Significant predictors of value dispositions, Scotland and Quebec

	Trad. val		*Anti-imm.*		*Anti-discrim.*		*Vote*		*Pro-trade, EU*		*Cynicism*	
	Q	C	*Q*	C	*Q*	C	*Q*	C	*Q*	C	*Q*	C
Catholic								+			+	
Age		+						+				
Gender				–					–			–
University										+		–
Income										+		
Union										+		
Vis. minority				–				–				
Married						–						
	Sc	UK	Sc	UK	Sc	UK	Sc	UK	Sc	UK	Sc	UK
Catholic												
Age	+	+			–	–		+		+		
Gender				–	+	+	+	+				
University		–	–	–				+		+		–
Income						+				+		–
Union						+		+			–	–
Vis. minority				–		+			+	+		
Married			–								+	

SOURCES: CES 2000; BES 2001.
NOTE: Results indicate direction of significant coefficients.

This conclusion suggests that national political cultures may exist, first, in the distinct value dispositions that individuals may hold. Quebecers may support one policy, while other Canadians back another. National political cultures might also exist, however, in the links between socio-demographic predictors and values: gender might be relevant to attitudes within Quebec but not elsewhere. The last step in determining the boundaries of national political cultures is to examine the impact of a range of predictors on support for the six indices, both inside the nation and outside its borders.

The results in table 5.5 indicate the signs for statistically significant predictors at the .1, .05, or .01 level. For example, age is a statistically significant and positive predictor of traditional values outside Quebec, but within Quebec it is not. Within Quebec, gender is a significant and negative predictor of pro-free-trade attitudes, but it is largely irrelevant elsewhere in Canada, where holding a university degree, having a higher income, or belonging to a union are significant, positive predictors. The results also highlight cases where variables display similar influence within and outside the nation. As we might expect from the Canadian results, age is a significant predictor of traditional values in the UK and is also a significant and positive predictor of support in Scotland.

The results show that in the United Kingdom socio-demographic factors work in similar directions some of the time. In no case did a significant predictor change direction within or outside the nation. What we did not find, for example, was that age served as a significant positive predictor of pro-EU attitudes in the UK and a significant negative predictor of attitudes in Scotland. The overwhelming trend, though, is for an indicator such as age or gender or income to serve as a significant predictor either outside national boundaries or within the nation, but not both. A similar trend is evident in Canada, where significant predictors of behaviour for Canadians do not appear to be driving attitudes within the province of Quebec. These results appear to confirm what we might expect: that national boundaries are significant not only because they structure general preferences but also because the links among preferences, and the factors dictating them, vary within the state. To understand value differences within the *nation*, however, warrants an additional degree of attention, something that forms the focus of the final chapter.

6

National Identity and Political Culture

Do nations have centres and peripheries? The previous chapters show that nations can be distinct within a larger state and that claims to this effect can be used by political parties and other actors to reinforce the boundaries of the nation. In addition, we have evidence at our disposal that significant proportions of residents within Scotland and Quebec feel that they hold a national identity, as well as dispositions that are different from those living beyond their borders. Thus far we have robust evidence of national difference within the state. If we are exploring the impact of national identity on political culture, one obvious first step is to determine whether people feel differently about their own identities and whether they hold ideas and values that set them apart. Evidence to this effect suggests that national identity has an impact on political culture in Scotland and Quebec. National identity can also affect political attitudes *within* the nation.

If we are hoping to evaluate the impact of national identity on political culture within the nation, we must return to the salient features of identity discussed at the beginning of this book. First, we must distinguish between the identity label that people use to describe themselves and the process of identifying with the nation. Second, we must recognize that identities are not zero-sum. They can be prioritized over others, or they can be subordinate. They can be shared equally with other identities. These characteristics hold not just for other national or state identities but for other groups to which individuals feel they belong, whether those groups are structured by gender, race, religion, or class. In addition, we must recognize that national identities can be more or less salient depending on context.

Certainly, we have evidence that recognition of the nation in Scotland and a lack of explicit recognition in Quebec has affected public debate on national identity. The same is also true of individuals. At times, national identity can be salient, at other times less so. At times it might be shared; at other times it might be held exclusively. Although we are able to divide individuals into national groups and measure their attitudes and beliefs, doing so tells us less about identity than it might. Understanding the impact of national identity on political culture must acknowledge that national identity is more than just a zero-sum label.

If this is the case, how might we go about capturing the nuances of national identity and their various political impacts? The most obvious first step it is to examine value differences among the different identity groups in Scotland and Quebec. This process allows us to answer three questions:

1 Are those who consider themselves "Scottish only" or "Québécois only" different from others who consider themselves "British only" or "Canadian only"?
2 Are those who prioritize their Scottish or Québécois identity different from those who prioritize other state or national identities?
3 Are those who hold exclusive identities different from those who hold shared identities?

Together, these three questions allow us to speak to the hierarchies of belonging that may exist within a nation. They will help us to determine, for example, whether the particular identity label plays a significant role in attitudinal variations, or whether labels are less relevant than whether they are exclusive or shared, and if shared, whether they are shared equally or prioritized.

The Canadian Election Study contains one question on identity delivered only to those completing the survey in French in Quebec and a number of questions on attachment. The identity question asks individuals, "Vous considérez-vous comme canadien(ne), canadien(ne) français(e), ou québécois(e)?" We can analyze the relationship between identity and value indices by conducting ANOVA tests.

One-way analysis of variance, or ANOVA, reveals F test figures that allow us to determine whether there is meaningful variation among groups on a single interval-level measure. Although comparisons between two groups may be analyzed by using a T test, comparisons between more than two groups rely on a test with fewer restrictions. The F test allows us to test the null hypothesis: that the factors do not contain items which produce varying results among the different identity groups. These F tests do not, however, indicate where this difference lies. In order to determine which identity groups differ, a further post-hoc or a posteriori test is required. For this purpose, a Scheffé test is used. This test is useful for comparisons of groups with uneven numbers. Because the identity groups created by the identity questions range in size considerably, a Scheffé test is appropriate. Most important, the test provides a conservative estimate of significance, thus reducing the likelihood of incorrectly crediting identity with influence. This test, a conservative estimate of variance, compares the scores of each combination of identity groups for each factor. In so doing, it is able to determine which group accounts for the variance recorded in the F test.

If we explore the attitudes of individuals within each of the identity categories Canadian, French Canadian, and Québécois, we can see clear differences among the identity groups on three of the six indices. ANOVA results show that for attitudes towards immigration, trade, and public cynicism, the three identity groups possess statistically significant differences. Post-hoc Scheffé tests reveal that those francophone Quebecers describing themselves as "canadien français" are significantly more likely to have negative attitudes towards immigration than those describing themselves as Québécois. Those describing themselves as "canadien" are more likely to be sympathetic to free trade than those describing themselves as Québécois. This outcome addresses an earlier point. We know that Quebecers as a group are more supportive of free trade, and we know that nationalist political parties have argued in favour of free trade. Putting these two facts together, we might assume that a strong sense of Québécois national identity would serve as a predictor of pro-trade attitudes. It is not, however, individuals who describe themselves as Québécois who are most supportive of free trade but, rather, Quebecers who use alternative national identity labels.

It is cynicism, however, that produces the clearest divisions among identity groups. The cynicism index is also the measure of political culture that best conforms to its original formulation by Almond and Verba, as it evaluates attitudes towards the operation of the state as a political system, rather than tapping attitudes towards fellow citizens. Francophone Quebecers who describe themselves as "canadien" are less cynical about politics than those describing themselves as "canadien français" or "Québécois." The most cynical group are Canadiens français. The differences among these groups are significant, but they should not suggest that these groups represent wildly different evaluations of political life. The average cynicism score for Canadiens is .608, while for Canadiens français it is .680.

We know from data discussed earlier that there are demographic variables distinguishing these groups, and such data can help to examine why, for example, self-described French Canadians might feel more cynical about politics than do francophones who describe themselves as Canadian. If we know that the French Canadian label was popular in the 1950s and 1960s and has generally been supplanted by the label "Québécois" since the Quiet Revolution, then we can hypothesize that this older identity group is expressing a level of cynicism common to its age cohort. A more political examination, however, might suggest that those who align themselves with a label describing a political state might feel a greater sense of proximity to the state itself and therefore might evaluate its operation in more positive terms than those who eschew state-inspired labels for their identity. Quebec, while clearly a nation by criterion-based and sociological definitions, is also a polity. This factor raises two key caveats to this investigation.

First, these identity questions were asked only of francophone Quebecers and thus excluded those who might typically find themselves the subject of debate about national belonging. This omission warrants a repeated examination using questions directed to the entire sample on attachment to Canada and to the province. Second, these results cannot yet confirm for us whether identity plays a more significant role than, for example, age, ethnicity, language, or religion.

The Canadian Election Study contains a number of questions on attachment, two of which are relevant to us here. First, participants are asked to assess their level of attachment to Canada and, second, to assess their level of attachment to their province. These thermometer scales allow us to compare not only whether individuals feel attachment to one entity over another but also how much that entity is preferred over another, something that the standard Moreno question in Scotland does not allow. If we rely on both of these questions, we can subtract attachment to Quebec from attachment to Canada and create a unified scale of attachment where positive numbers indicate greater attachment to Canada, negative numbers indicate greater attachment to Quebec, and 0 represents equal attachment to both. What such a unified scale lacks is the original metric. An individual with a score of −10 might have assessed her original attachment to Canada as 70 and attachment to Quebec as 80 or might have selected numbers such as 20 and 30. The reconstituted scale thus tells us only about relative attachment, rather than absolute intensity of attachment. Using such a scale, though, we may assess what impact attachment has on political values.

We can examine correlations between attachment scales and index scores to see whether, as attachment to Canada increases, so too does support for free trade or immigration. The results show that for three of the indicators, there are significant correlations between attachment to a particular entity and our indicators of political culture. First, with regard to civic duty, greater attachment to Canada at the expense of attachment to Quebec produces greater levels of support for the act of voting. This outcome confirms what we discovered earlier when comparing Quebec to the rest of Canada. The same can be said for traditional values and attitudes towards trade. If we are examining positions on an attachment pole, with near-exclusive attachment to Canada at one end, shared attachments in the middle, and near-exclusive attachment to Quebec at the other end, that same spectrum fits across our indicators for traditional values and trade. Those at the Quebec end are significantly less likely to exhibit traditional values and less likely to support free trade. As with voting, the results for traditional values confirm what we knew before: that Quebecers as a whole are less traditional in their morality than are other Canadians. Within Quebec those who feel a greater attachment to the nation are also less traditional than their provincial counterparts who identify more closely with the Canadian state. The trade results show, however, that although Quebecers as a group are more supportive of trade, within the province attachment to Quebec is negatively correlated with support for free trade.

Having expanded the sample to include both anglophones and francophones, we can now turn to results for demographic groups. It is one thing for us to claim that identity is relevant to political attitudes. It is another to show that it remains relevant when we control for other demographic factors such as age or gender. Relying on our six variables as dependent variables, we can test the ability of our attachment scale to predict values in light of six control variables. These are age, gender, university attainment, income, union membership, and marital status. If we run OLS regressions for each of the six variables, we find that attachment is a significant predictor in only one circumstance: for anti-immigration sentiment. Here attachment to Quebec is a significant and negative predictor of hostility to immigrants.

Two things are relevant here. If we see views towards immigrants in the general sense of views towards fellow citizens, then this is clearly a relevant issue for political culture. Second, if we view perceptions of immigrants as a corollary to views towards outgroups within the nation, then it also speaks to inclusion and exclusion within the nation. These findings certainly question claims that nationalists hold exclusive visions of their own nation and are unwilling to admit members who cannot rely on traditional ethnic markers of belonging. Although the individual questions within the "anti-immigration" indicator do not tap membership in the nation explicitly, they speak implicitly to fair treatment and general inclusion within society, themes raised in nationalist and separatist discourse.

The spectrum of attachment that we have been using allows us to address only general preferences. We can examine differences between those who express a strong attachment for one of two entities: Quebec or Canada. We are comparing people at one pole to people at the other pole. What such a formulation does not allow us to do, however, is examine whether the people in the middle – those with equal attachment to both Canada and Quebec or those who prefer one identity over the other only slightly – are different from those with more exclusive attachments. We can reconstitute the attachment scale so that it provides a better conceptual comparison to the Moreno scale. Those from –100 to –21 are coded as being most attached to Quebec; those from –20 to –1 are attached to Quebec more than Canada; those scoring 0 on the combined attachment scale are coded as having equal attachment to Quebec and Canada. The positive side of the scale mirrors the negative side. The results show statistically significant differences among the reconstituted Moreno groups for traditional values and for cynicism (see table 6.1).

Table 6.1
Value differences among identity groups in Quebec

	Traditional values	*Cynicism*
Most attached to Quebec	.34	.71
Quebec more than Canada	.39	.68
Quebec and Canada equally	.55	.60
Canada more than Quebec	.52	.58
Most attached to Canada	.47	.64

SOURCE: CES 2000.
NOTE: Results are mean scores on 0 to 1 scale.

The results not only show that those with greater attachment to Quebec hold fewer traditional views, but they also demonstrate for us that the difference is between those who prioritize their attachment to Quebec and those who are equally attached to Canada and Quebec. Prioritizing attachment to Quebec is significantly aligned with less traditional values. Quebecers as a whole are less traditional, those who are more attached to Quebec than to Canada are less traditional, and those who prioritize their shared Quebec identity, rather than hold dual identities equally, are also less traditional. This is an interesting finding, for it suggests that it is not a sense of exclusive Canadian identity that is correlated with conservatism, but that even when one holds both identities equally, there is a significant increase in support for traditional values.

Turning to the results for cynicism, we see a steady decrease in cynicism as we move towards a prioritized Canadian identity. Those most attached to Quebec are far more likely to exhibit cynical attitudes towards the state than are those prioritizing their attachment in Canada. If we perform a separate analysis distinguishing between only those who hold shared and exclusive attachments or between shared and equal, on the one hand, and prioritized, on the other, there are not significant differences among them. This result may in part be due to the small numbers of individuals involved. Using a reconstituted scale is less useful than using one that builds into its architecture a comparison of identities.

The 2001 British Election Study asked a wider range of questions about identity, determining whether respondents felt Scottish or not, whether they felt Scottish, British, or European, and, with the Moreno question, whether they felt Scottish not British, more Scottish than British, and so on. If we focus first on whether respondents felt Scottish, British, or European, we can see that there are statistically significant variations among the identity groups on two of our six indicators. Those attitude clusters most likely to produce variations among the groups concern anti-discrimination, or equality among genders and ethnicities, and attitudes towards the EU. On approaches to political life, whether cynicism or voting, the identity groups do not appear to differ significantly.

Post-hoc Scheffé tests reveal that those who describe their identity as either Scottish or European are more likely to record anti-discrimination feelings than are those who record their identity as British. The average score for the British identity group on the anti- discrimination indicator was .575, while for Scots and Europeans it was .648 and .786 respectively. In the face of concerns about the inclusiveness of Scots, those who prioritize their sense of Scottishness are more vociferous in their condemnation of unfairness than are those describing their identity as British. Perhaps not surprisingly, those who describe their identity as European are significantly more supportive of the EU than those who describe themselves either as Scottish or as British. Here self-described Scots are slightly more supportive than those who hold a British identity, but the difference is not significant.

If we turn to the typical Moreno identity question, we find different results. If we ignore the importance of Europe to the identity of individuals and focus primarily on the relationship between Scottish and British identities, we find results more interesting from a traditional political-culture perspective. Again, on two of the six indicators, the identity groups hold significantly different results. Here, though, the attitude clusters deal with anti-immigration and cynicism. If we explore attitudes towards cynicism, that factor which we might consider in the mainstream of most political-culture definitions, we find that the significant difference is between those who hold a Scottish identity exclusively and those whose identity is both shared and equal. Those who hold an exclusive identity are more likely to be cynical of the state than are those who hold both identities equally. With respect to attitudes towards the state, a sense of Scottishness is positively correlated with cynicism, but only if that identity is held exclusively.

In terms of support for immigration, we find that those who prioritize their sense of Scottishness are less likely to hold anti-immigrant views than are those whose identity is exclusively Scottish or exclusively British. The issue, then, is not with Scottishness. Holding a Scottish identity is not a source of or aligned with prejudice. What we find, however, is that holding only one identity, whether that identity is Scottish or British, is more closely aligned with anti-immigrant sentiment. This link applies not just to those who hold an exclusive Scottish identity but also to those who hold an exclusively British identity. It appears that dual identities, whether equal or uneven, are positively associated with supportive attitudes towards immigrants. If we hold to the notion that political culture refers not just to the state but also to how one feels about fellow citizens within the state, national identity in Scotland has an important impact in two ways. One, among residents of Scotland, those who prioritize their sense of Scottishness are more cynical about the state, and second, those who hold dual identities are more welcoming to those who might be considered "outsiders" in the nation. These results mirror almost perfectly the findings for Quebec.

We know, however, that the same criticism of the tests used for Quebec may be levelled here. Identity may be a salient feature in determining attitudes, but this link could also stem from the demographic variations of each of these identity groups. Those who describe themselves as European might be younger, while those who describe themselves as British not Scottish might be older. In order to understand whether identity remains significantly aligned with each of these attitudinal clusters, we must evaluate its impact when controlling for other factors, such as age, union membership, university attainment, gender, and income. If we run regressions in which each of the indices serves as a dependent variable and the independent variables include identity and a number of demographic controls, what can we say about the relationship between national identity and political culture?

The regression results indicate that only for cynicism does national identity matter, when we control for other demographic variables (see table 6.2). When we say that national identity matters, though, it is not that a sense of Scottishness makes one more or less likely to feel cynical towards the state, but whether one holds a shared identity or an exclusive identity. In other words, when we control for other factors, individuals who feel both Scottish and British, regardless of whether they hold both identities equally or prioritize one over the other, feel less cynical than do those who

Table 6.2
Predictors of cynicism in Scotland

Age	.595 (.106)
Female	.005 (.041)
University	.091 (.057)
Income	–.272***(.099)
Union	.043 (.045)
Married	.172*** (.048)
Catholic	.026 (.055)
Dual identity	–.133*** (.049)
Constant	(.595)***.076)
R^2	.251

SOURCE: BES 2001.
NOTES: Results are un-standardized OLS correlation coefficients with standard errors in parentheses.
$^{*}p < .1$ $^{**}p < .05$ $^{***}p < .01$

hold one identity only. Here people who describe themselves as Scottish not British behave exactly as do those who describe themselves as British not Scottish, when we control for other factors. This notion of control is an important one. If we look purely at identity groups, those who consider themselves Scottish appear more cynical than those who consider themselves primarily British. If we control for demographic variables, variables that we know from earlier factors are likely to distinguish those who define themselves as Scottish and those who define themselves as British, then the impact of national identity changes. No longer is it a case of self-defined Scots appearing more cynical than self-defined Brits, but rather that we can distinguish between those who hold one identity and those who hold two. Income is also a significant predictor for cynicism. Here those with higher incomes are less likely to be cynical about the state, while married persons are more likely to be cynical. One possible explanation for these results has to do with the nature of dual identities.

If we argue that holding dual identities implies attachment to the nation and to the state, regardless of which entity is deemed the nation and which is seen as the state, then we might expect that someone employing an identity based on the borders of the larger polity might feel more positively towards the polity than someone who refers only to the nation. The answers to these questions were provided during a British election. Indicating a sense of identity that is both Scottish and British during a British election in itself likely implies a greater comfort with the state. Such an explanation is, however, merely hypothesis and not possible to test, given our current data. It suggests, though, that the context of the surveys is likely salient to our findings.

The initial six variables included here were chosen because they appeared salient when examined through factor analysis. The additive indices were designed to tap attitudes general to political culture that were less subject to short-term variations in policy preferences or electoral context. The analysis ignored variables related to election campaigns, such as partisan support, perceptions of debate winners, or salient electoral issues. They also excluded assessments of confidence with particular institutions, because such attitudes could themselves be the focus of partisan electoral campaigns. It is an uncommon election in the UK, for example, when the Conservative Party does not make reference to confidence or satisfaction with the police, whether in a positive or in a negative sense. Such a decision excludes from our analysis variables that may not be considered part of the bedrock of political culture but might be politically relevant. These include self-placement on the left-right spectrum, measures of post-materialism, and satisfaction with the civil service or with particular parties, in addition to evaluations of parties, their leaders, or constitutional options. These factors are more attitudinal, more short-term, less built into our evaluations of the state and citizens, and more aligned with particular policy preferences on any given day. It is useful to determine, though, for which indicators there are significant variations among national identity groups.

The data identify two key findings (see table 6.3). First, those at one end of the identity spectrum are different from those at the other. For example, we see that while most Scots prefer to read the *Record*, among those who describe themselves as British not Scottish, most read a regional or local paper. If we look at party support, which takes the modal answer among a number of party-identification questions, those who describe themselves as Scottish not British are more likely to back the SNP, those who describe themselves as primarily British are more likely to back the Conservatives, and everyone else is more likely to feel more closely aligned to the Labour Party. It is worth noting that those who describe themselves as British not Scottish are more apt to prefer the Labour Party unless we ask which party they are leaning towards, in which

Table 6.3
Attitudinal variables among identity groups in Scotland

	Sc x B	*Sc > B*	*Sc=B*	*B>Sc*	*BxS*
Left-wing	.45	.42	.43	.38	.41
Most important issue	NHS	NHS	NHS	NHS	NHS
Paper read*	*Record*	*Record*	*Record*	*Record*	regional or local paper
Party support***	SNP	Labour	Labour	Conservative	Labour
Attention to politics*	4.62	5.46	5.35	6.19	6.33
Respect for:					
Parliament***	4.39	5.5	5.58	6.63	6.45
Civil service	4.8	4.81	4.86	6.60	5.81
Police	6.7	6.69	6.90	7.56	7.27
EU	3.81	3.94	4.39	4.93	4.63
Politicians ***	3.6	3.94	4.39	4.93	4.63
Active in voluntary ass'n***	3.55	4.64	4.95	4.88	4.0
Participate in demo*	1.98	2.51	3.0	1.69	2.45
Work with group to solve problem	2.73	3.36	4.08	4.44	3.39

SOURCE: BES 2001.
NOTE: Results are mean scores on indicators, or modal entries were relevant.
$^{*}p < .1$ $^{**}p < .05$ $^{***}p < .01$

case the modal response is Conservative. We can see, then, that there are differences among the identity groups, primarily between those who are Scottish identifiers and those who are British identifiers. Attention to politics also functions in this way. Those who consider themselves British not Scottish are far more attentive to politics than are those who consider themselves Scottish not British. Attention to politics increases steadily as one moves through the Moreno categories. We find a slight trend with left-right spectrum, where those who prioritize their Scottishness are more likely to place themselves on the left of the spectrum, but the differences among groups are not particularly large.

If we examine levels of respect for different political or civic institutions, we find that support increases steadily as we move through the Moreno categories, from those who prioritize Scottishness to those who prioritize their sense of British identity. Two factors could be at work here. First, we know that those who prioritize their sense of Britishness are Conservative supporters and that respect for institutions is a particularly Conservative trait. The other interpretation, however, is that a greater respect for British institutions could be feeding a sense of British identity. While we cannot confirm the direction of the causal arrow, regressions with each of the respect variables as dependent variables and identity and Tory support as independent variables show that both remain significant predictors of respect. That British identifiers also tend to identify with the Conservative Party cannot alone explain higher levels of respect for political and civic institutions.

The second finding shows that individuals at the respective ends of the identity spectrum behave in a relatively similar manner, but they are distinct from those with shared identities. This holds particularly for what we might consider measures of social capital. If we probe involvement with community groups, participation in voluntary associations, or even activity levels in demonstrations, we find that those with shared identities are more active than those with exclusive identities. This result could explain some of the findings raised earlier; namely, that identity labels appear to inform views of the state, while shared versus exclusive identities appear to influence how one views fellow citizens.

The results for Quebec in table 6.4 provide a useful comparison to those from Scotland. The table reports mean results on a number of indicators of reconstituted identity groups. Although a strict reformation of the attachment scale into reconstituted Moreno categories may be conceptually appealing, it creates an imbalance of group size. The groups used here represent ranges on the attachment scale. Within Quebec there are significant differences among the identity groups on many of the indicators listed here. Many of these are subject to change more readily than the more enduring elements of political culture, and many will vary from election to election. With that caveat in mind, though, we can identity indicators on which there are clear differences between those who prioritize a Québécois identity and those who prefer a Canadian identity and between those with exclusive identities and those with shared identities. If we are looking for indicators that distinguish people more attached to Quebec from those more attached to Canada, the party supported is an obvious example. Those exhibiting greater attachment to Quebec are significantly more likely to back the Bloc Québécois in federal elections and to vote for the Parti Québécois in provincial contests. This correlation in itself is not particularly surprising. What is noteworthy, though, is that those holding equal attachment to both entities appear to have more in common with

Table 6.4
Attitudinal variables among identity groups in Quebec

	Most attached to Quebec	Q>C	Q=C	C>Q	*Most attached to Canada*
Support for sovereignty***	.78	.60	.29	.15	.09
Left wing	.40	.25	.26	.25	.27
Most important issue	health care	health care	health care	health care	health care
Federal party supported***	BQ	BQ	Lib	Lib	Lib
Provincial party supported***	PQ	PQ	QLP	QLP	QLP
Protects interests?***	Quebec	Quebec	Quebec	Quebec	Canada
Boycott	.33	.28	.25	.24	.24
Demo	.26	.23	.19	.25	.26
Occupy***	.08	.03	.01	.01	.03
Confidence in:					
Organized religion	.47	.50	.49	.47	.46
Armed forces***	.49	.52	.59	.55	.59
Public schools*	.65	.61	.60	.60	.58
Supreme Court***	.54	.57	.62	.64	.58
Civil service**	.46	.44	.50	.48	.46
Unions	.48	.39	.40	.37	.36
Police***	.60	.60	.68	.67	.65
Federal government***	.27	.39	.49	.50	.51
Provincial government***	.52	.49	.49	.45	.33
Big business*	.38	.43	.43	.41	.38
Media *	.44	.47	.44	.41	.37

SOURCE: CES 2000.
NOTE: Results are mean scores on indicators or modal entries where relevant.
$^{*}p < .1$ $^{**}p < .05$ $^{***}p < .01$

those who prioritize their Canadian attachment than they do with those who prioritize their Québécois attachment.

On other measures there is clear evidence of difference between the two ends of the scale. Those most attached to Quebec are, predictably, more likely to support sovereignty, but they are also more likely to participate in the occupation of a building as a form of protest, more supportive of public schools, more likely to have confidence in the provincial government, and more likely to have confidence in the media. At the same time, they are least likely to have confidence in the armed forces and in the federal government. This view of the federal government is reinforced when we examine perceptions of who best protects interests. Only those most attached to Canada believe that it is the federal government that best protects their interests. All others believe that it is the provincial government. Here the difference is not between those who prioritize a sense of Quebec attachment and those who are equally attached, but between those most attached to Canada and everyone else. As in Scotland, there are also cases where those at the poles of attachment appear remarkably similar and distinguish themselves from those with shared or equal attachments. In this case, those with equal attachment are more likely to support the Supreme Court, the civil service, and big business. Those most attached to Quebec or Canada are significantly less supportive.

What then can be said of the quantitative data on national identity and political culture? First, we should be cautious in our comparisons of Scottish and Québécois data. The presence of two thermometer scales in the Canadian Election Study inhibits a full comparison with Scottish data. In an effort to make the two data sets more comparable, the amended attachment variable seeks to retain the conceptual distinctions within the Moreno question. And yet the new Quebec scale cannot be assumed to function as well as the Moreno categories. Individuals classified as having greater or lesser attachment to Canada and Quebec may have answered differently if they were responding to a question that demanded an explicit comparison of identities, as does Moreno. Survey data analyzed in chapter 3 suggests that the amended scale underestimates the proportion of individuals who profess an attachment to Quebec not Canada (CROP 1998). This limitation coexists with the use of different question items probing political attitudes in the Canadian and Scottish surveys. Any comparison must take care to compare the interaction of items within each data set, rather than the two sets of results directly. With this consideration in mind, it is possible to explore the relationship between national identity and political culture in each nation.

The data for Scotland and Quebec reveal that in each case, identity groups react differently to some of the items listed above and that the differences at times are statistically significant. Overwhelmingly, however, the evidence suggests that whatever differences do exist are subtle rather than profound. In the majority of cases the statistical analysis presented here confirms evidence provided by earlier studies of identity (Brown 1979; Pammett and Whittington 1976;

Westle 1993): that identity groups possess dissimilar views on identity issues such as sovereignty and that they may possess different views of the state, but that when we control for other factors, differences disappear. Those who prioritize their identity with Scotland or their attachment to Quebec are more cynical towards the state than are those who prioritize British or Canadian identities.

If we do not explore identity as a dichotomous variable but choose instead to consider the operation of shared identities, we find that those who hold dual identities tend to be less cynical and in Scotland they are also less hostile to immigration. In Quebec those who hold equal attachments are also more supportive of traditional values. This finding raises two key conclusions. First, we must expand our definition of political culture to include not just views of the state but also views of fellow citizens. The boundaries of the nation and the treatment of citizens within those boundaries are a logical feature of political culture. The results in Scotland and Quebec show that there are significant differences among the identity groups on attitudes towards fellow citizens. In each case, support for national identity is correlated positively with more welcoming, less hostile attitudes towards immigrants and is more opposed to discrimination. Second, we must treat identity as more than an either-or category and recognize that differences emerge not just between people who consider themselves Scottish or Canadian or Québécois but between those who hold one identity exclusively and those who claim two identities at the same time. Those with shared identities hold different views not only towards the state but also towards fellow citizens. Even when we control for other factors, dual-identity respondents are less cynical towards politics than are other respondents.

7

Cultural Boundaries and National Inclusion

In its investigation of the relationship between national identity and political culture, this work has explored the promotion of identity markers, the identity process, and the interaction of identity and political attitudes. In part, the study was motivated by the under-explored relationship between national identity and political culture. Recent increased attention to political-culture studies and the growth in social-capital research suggest that cultural analyses of the polity have much to offer political science. At the same time, such analyses have often avoided references to national identity. As a result, these two literatures have only rarely crossed paths. In its analysis of the way that national identity functions, how political actors promote markers of identity, and the way that individuals articulate their own sense of belonging, this work has brought these two research traditions together. Throughout, a wide definition of political culture has been used, one that includes the relationship, both perceived and actual, between individuals and the state and the relationship, both perceived and actual, between individuals and their fellow citizens.

Comparisons between Scotland and Quebec are useful because of their similarities. Upon integration into a larger polity, both received protection for institutions of public life that later became pillars of national identity. Both contain peaceful and democratic nationalist movements that claim to be examples of civic nationalism and seek to use the political process to gain greater autonomy. Both contain autonomist political parties that gained parliamentary seats in the 1960s and currently espouse left-of-centre or social- democratic values. The path to self-determination has offered referendums to electorates in each polity. Scotland and Quebec occupy similar economic roles within the larger state and have at times articulated political preferences at odds with that state. And yet the components of national and political life in each case are sufficiently different that the comparison is not a needless repetition of similar material. The absence of a Scottish parliament before 1999 and the role of language within Quebec, for example, serve to distinguish the two nations. More salient, the comparative homogeneity of the population in Scotland and the absence of national recognition for Quebec have structured the context in which debates about national identity and national destiny take place. By employing two case studies that possess comparable parliamentary designs and particular national characteristics, the comparison provides for more general conclusions about the impact of national identity on political culture. The arguments in this book make two contributions to our understanding of identity and politics, the first about boundaries and the second about inclusion.

The first recurrent theme in the book deals with the operation of objective and subjective boundaries. Research on both national identity and political culture provides several examples of the often inconsistent relationship between objective or empirical conditions and subjective perception. Sometimes the two work in tandem; at others they are at odds. The very definition of a nation has both objective and subjective elements: a nation exists if it fulfills a list of objective criteria (common history, common territory, common language, common culture) or if its population wills it into existence, even in the absence of objective markers. By both objective and subjective definitions, Scotland and Quebec can be considered nations. Not only is the demographic profile of each case distinct, but a significant proportion of their residents hold identities that declare their allegiance and attachment to the nation. The pillars of national identity can also be objective and subjective. The perception that institutions – the education system, church, or legal system – make a nation distinct is often linked to the values that such institutions are supposed to inculcate in national members. Whether such institutions actually produce distinct attitudes and orientations is less relevant than the national myth that this relationship exists. Political culture itself includes objective features such as the institutions that govern political life and subjective orientations towards the state. This theme of objective and subjective difference relates to boundaries in two ways. First, it determines how individuals navigate the borders of the nation, and second, it helps us to understand whether national political cultures exist.

Nations can have both physical and sociological borders. Previously independent nations, for example, have historical borders that provide a physical boundary for the nation. Membership in this type of nation is akin to citizenship in a state. Nations without physical borders, such as those composed of diasporic communities, rely on the sociological boundaries around a people. Marked by language, culture, or shared attachment, such stateless nations have borders more open to dispute. Quebec and Scotland possess recognized borders. It is their sociological borders that are subject to dispute. Because sociological boundaries are rarely drawn explicitly, an ill-defined consensus emerges about membership in the nation. Those who are assumed to speak for the nation, because they are in positions of authority or advocate independence for the nation, provide cues about the markers of belonging in the nation. And yet the list of organizations making pronouncements about national membership extends beyond the government and separatist political parties. The public space in which a dialogue about national identity takes place is a crowded one. This diversity of voices can create confusion about national membership. The more heterogeneous the population within the physical borders of the nation, the more contested are its sociological boundaries.

Whether one feels a sense of belonging to the nation is a function of both personal belief and the expected reception of claims of membership. This negotiation of identity takes place in the muddied field between objective evidence and subjective claims. Individuals might ask themselves whether they possess markers of national membership touted by political elites, and whether claims to belonging might be taken seriously by others should they be made. This point is clearest when exploring the data on national identity. Anglophones in Quebec may believe that the anglophone community is part of the nation of Quebec, but when asked if they as individuals feel part of the nation, a smaller proportion claim to belong. In so doing, they are making a clear distinction between the objective right to belong and a subjective sense of belonging.

The relationship between objective and subjective difference surfaces also in discussions of national political cultures. Whether national identity has an impact on political culture depends on whether we focus on the objective or subjective elements of each. Political culture can be distinct if the institutions governing political life are different from those in neighbouring polities or if the values or behaviours of the electorate appear unique. It is worth asking, though, whether the perception that a political culture is distinct is sufficient proof of its separate existence. If its electorate believes that Scotland has a distinct political culture, does that make it distinct? In this regard, the debate about national political cultures mirrors those about the objective and subjective criteria for nations; Renan's daily plebiscite (1882) can create a political community just as it does a national one.

Certain criteria allow us to determine that national political cultures exist. Some of these criteria are objective; others are subjective. We can argue that a national political culture exists if there is objective evidence that it is distinct. This might include evidence of distinct institutions or evidence of distinct subjective orientations. Second, a national political culture can exist if its members believe it to exist. Third, we can assume that a national political culture exists if the factors affecting attitudes function differently in other cultures. If gender affects attitudes in one culture but not in a neighbouring polity, we might have evidence of national political cultures. By two of these measures we have evidence of national political cultures in Scotland and Quebec. First, there is obvious evidence that individuals in both nations believe in the existence of a distinct national political culture. References to "national" values are common in both cases. Second, if we expand measures of political culture to include more than just deference and efficacy, we have evidence of consistent variations in attitudes between residents of the nation and the larger state. Quebecers and Scots are both more cynical about politics and less traditional in their social values than other Canadians and Britons. Even when we control for other predictors of attitudes, residence in the nation explains political views. In terms of demographic predictors, there are not significantly different patterns of influence on either side of the national boundary.

Discussions of boundaries and borders point to the similarities between Scotland and Quebec. The identity process of individuals, for example, is similar in both cases, and tests for national political cultures provide both objective and subjective evidence of their existence. When we explore perceptions of inclusion and the impact of identity on political culture, however, we see clear differences between Scotland and Quebec.

Previous attention to the civic-ethnic divide in nationalism and in particular the claims that Scotland and Quebec lie at opposite ends of that spectrum provide insufficient attention to the way that national identity is articulated and understood. Neither nation serves as an ideal type. Indeed, the comparison suggests that what distinguishes these two cases is the degree to which the nation and national identity are perceived as inclusive or not. Inclusion, in turn, depends on how political actors articulate a sense of national identity and how individuals use cues about belonging to understand their own position within the nation. Both the selection of national identity markers and the way they are promoted affect whether the nation is seen as a bounded entity in which only a few may claim membership or a relatively porous collective. Each of these claims warrants greater attention.

Neither Scotland nor Quebec represents a pure example of civic or ethnic nationalism. In a civic nation, individual membership in the nation cannot be conditional on the possession of immutable characteristics. Instead, exposure to public institutions or the presence of shared values dominates civic political rhetoric. We have considerable evidence that in both Scotland and Quebec political actors prioritize civic markers of belonging over ethnic markers such as ancestry, race, or religion. Regardless of whether they believe Quebec is a nation or not, political parties within Quebec point to the institutions that distinguish political life in Quebec from other provinces. In Scotland the four main political parties all emphasize the importance of the distinct education and legal systems. In their discussions of national distinctiveness, political actors establish a link between these institutions and political values that provide an additional boundary around the national populations. The rhetoric in each case is explicitly inclusive. Since the 1980s the Parti Québécois has emphasized the role of anglophones within the Quebec nation, and the ADQ claims that all residents of the province are Québécois. For its part, the Parti Libérale du Québec notes that everyone is welcome in the party. Before devolution, Labour, the Liberal Democrats, and the SNP each noted that the Scottish nation included all within its borders, although after devolution only the SNP has addressed the topic, regularly holding up the "mongrel nation of Scotland" as the ideal. The rhetoric of these political actors is both explicitly civic and inclusive. And yet we know that language is an important pillar of identity in Quebec, that religion was the prime motor for the federal system that currently operates in Canada, and that the Presbyterian Church of Scotland was one of the key institutions afforded protection in the Treaty of Union. Whether one assumes that these features invalidate claims that each is a civic nation depends on the importance one places on religion and whether one assumes language is an ethnic marker. Seen as something acquired – albeit slowly – upon arrival, language can be considered as civic a characteristic as residency. Seen as something imparted from birth or as an unchangeable mother tongue, language holds more ethnic connotations.

The waters are muddied further when we look at how individuals understand their own identity. In a civic nation ethnic characteristics such as place of birth, race, and the questionably ethnic trait of language should not predict political attitudes about the future of the nation; if sovereignty is the political project for an inclusive nation, it should appeal to more than members who possess ethnic markers. If only those born in Scotland support Scottish independence, or if only French-speakers support the Parti Québécois, then we might have reason to doubt whether either can claim to be an example of civic nationalism. When we explore the characteristics that serve as predictors of support for sovereignty or sovereignist parties, we find that in Quebec language, religion, and place of birth each serve as statistically significant predictors of support for independence, the PQ, or the BQ. In Scotland, however, the same types of demographic markers do not drive support for independence or the SNP. In short, ethnic markers predict support for sovereignist parties and sovereignty in Quebec, but not in Scotland.

Ethnic markers surface again when we ask individuals to discuss membership in the nation. When asked who should have access to citizenship in an independent Scotland, the largest proportion of survey respondents supported citizenship for those born in the nation, followed by those with Scottish ancestry. The smallest proportion would extend citizenship to those whose claim to belonging is based solely on residency. In Quebec a larger proportion of Quebecers believe that francophones are members of the Québécois nation than believe Aboriginal peoples or anglophones resident in the province belong to the nation. These data do not provide definitive proof that Scotland and Quebec are ethnic nations. Instead, they demonstrate that we have evidence of civic and ethnic markers in operation in both cases and that they function in similar ways. At the macro-level, political rhetoric within the nation is resolutely civic, notwithstanding exceptions present in both cases. At the micro-level, individuals employ ethnic markers to understand national membership, and such markers are clearly predictors of support for the sovereignist movement. Nationalism in Scotland and Quebec is both civic and ethnic.

Part of the appeal of the civic-ethnic dichotomy was that it offered an explanation for why perceptions of exclusion appeared far more prevalent in Quebec than in Scotland. That nationalism in Quebec hinged on ethnic markers appeared to justify greater perceptions of exclusion. Since the political rhetoric in the two places is similarly civic, alternative explanations are required. More helpful is the acknowledgment that the salience of national identity is far more important than whether it is civic or ethnic. Whether national identity is salient or not depends on audience and context. Messages about the nation – whether it exists, the markers upon which it is based, whom it excludes, where its future lies – are delivered to those within the physical boundaries of the nation and those outside its borders. The demographic diversity within the nation, the absence of a sub-state legislature in Scotland, and the absence of national recognition for Quebec all have affected the content of nationalist messages and the extent to which it is a salient feature of political discourse.

Research on sub-state nationalism often treats the nation as a relatively homogeneous entity, distinct within a larger heterogeneous state: Quebec is the French province within an overwhelmingly English Canada. Such research often ignores the fact that nations house within them considerable diversity in terms of language, religion, ethnicity, economic wealth, and political preference. In a homogeneous nation, markers of national membership are relatively undisputed within the borders of the nation. In a heterogeneous nation, however, markers of membership or even the very existence of the nation can be contested. Scotland and Quebec differ in the extent to which they can be considered heterogeneous entities.

Institutions of national distinctiveness received protection in Scotland in the Treaty of Union (1707). The Quebec Act (1774) served the same purpose more than a decade after the conquest of

New France. At the time of this institutional protection Scotland was by far the more heterogeneous nation, housing Protestant and Catholic populations, Gaelic, Scots, and English speakers, Highlanders and Lowlanders. The result was a series of overlapping publics with different attitudes to the monarchy and to the union. In Quebec, however, the population was a more homogeneous French and Catholic one and more united in its views of the Conquest.[1] The result of a process of negotiation, the union would have had both supporters and detractors. Residents in New France, by contrast, were not agents in their own changed destiny.

If we examine the two nations in their contemporary contexts, however, Quebec houses far greater diversity within its population than does Scotland. Aboriginal peoples (now part of the political community), anglophones, allophones, immigrants, and visible minorities stretch the definition of national membership beyond those in the *ancien régime*. Almost one-fifth of Quebecers have a language other than French as their mother tongue. Scotland, by comparison, is a more homogeneous nation, its demographic diversity limited to visible minorities representing 2 per cent of the population and English residents. For the most part, heterogeneity beyond a Presbyterian English-speaking Scots population stems from groups present at the time of the union.

Diversity within the state is relevant because it affects the perceived salience of national membership. It is not necessary to proclaim that a nation is inclusive if all within it would be considered national members by even the most limited definitions of belonging. In a heterogeneous nation, though, political actors seeking the integration of newer arrivals have two tasks before them. Assuming that their vision of the nation is an inclusive one, they must make such newer arrivals feel welcome in the nation. Such a task requires public pronouncements about the extent to which the nation includes those beyond its ancestral members. In addition, political actors adopt a socializing role, educating newcomers about the dominant features of the nation, its history, its markers of identity, the dominant values and behaviours that animate its public life. The absence of a significant outgroup in Scotland has made continued statements about the inclusive nature of Scottish national identity an unnecessary component of political debate. In Quebec, however, the existence of anglophone, allophone, Aboriginal, and visible-minority residents has prompted greater examination of the construction of national identity and in so doing has heightened its place in political debate. Heterogeneity in Quebec feeds a debate about national membership that does not demand the same degree of attention in Scotland.

The key point here is not just that Scotland is distinct within the UK or that Quebec is distinct within Canada – which is the usual way of looking at things – but that each nation houses internal dynamics that affect the context in which discussions of national identity, national history, and national destiny take place. It is less relevant that Canada houses more than one nation or that the UK does than that within each sub-state nation there are important variations in the degrees of demographic, political, and economic diversity and that these variations help to structure political debate about the nation. If the audience is important, so too are the structural factors of political life. Chief among these are the absence of a legislature in Scotland between 1707 and 1999 and the absence of national recognition for Quebec.

While the original impetus for federalism may have been the distinct nature of the predominantly Catholic population in Quebec, the political aspirations of that distinct population were effectively removed from the Canadian political stage by the presence of a separate arena in which to debate and discuss national progress. This is not to say that Quebec's distinctiveness and its role in Canada were never discussed in Ottawa, but that the presence of a separate legislature provided a natural arena for discussions about national policy and national destiny. Key here is not the relative absence of separatist voices in Ottawa, though this was certainly a feature of political debate until the 1990s, but the greater attention to the political wishes of a nation within the boundaries of the nation. In the UK, by contrast, the need to bend policy to the particularities of life in Scotland ensured an almost continuous adaptation of the Westminster legislative process. In the absence of a separate arena in which to debate the benefits of nationalism, independence, or distinct policy preferences, such views were aired in the parliament of a unitary state outside the borders of the nation. Matters of consequence to Scotland were thus debated in London. This disconnect had two effects. First, political debate in London witnessed far greater attention to internal Scottish matters than did political debate in Ottawa. Second, the sheer amount of political debate about the nation, its members, its goals, and its future was far higher in Quebec than in Scotland. With internal political campaigns in Quebec, political parties could debate national membership, policy, and destiny. In the unitary UK, by contrast, the campaign manifestos of Scottish political parties offered near carbon copies of the pledges made by English parties. Obviously, the campaign for independence in Quebec forced politicians in Ottawa to discuss the role of the province within Canada, and the campaign for devolution provided sufficient material for a domestic Scottish media. The absence of a Scottish legislature, however, made debates about the nation itself physically more remote and a less salient feature of political life.

Equally relevant is the absence of national recognition for Quebec. The Treaty of Union recognized Scotland as a nation. The Quebec Act, while providing similar institutional protection to the church and the legal system, fell short of national recognition. Confederation similarly avoided conferring national status on what became the province of Quebec. Given a system of governance that took into account Quebec's distinctiveness, further national recognition was likely seen as unnecessary overkill. Since then it has been portrayed as anathema to the existence of symmetrical federalism in Canada. The refusal on the part of federalist parties and political actors to confer upon Quebec the status of nation has had a clear impact on the way that national identity is discussed and promoted. Constitutional bids for change in Scotland are framed within the context of improved democracy and the principle of subsidiarity. National distinctiveness is mentioned, but it is rarely a significant pillar of separatist argument, in large part because it is an acknowledged fact. In Quebec, however, the bid for constitutional change often begins by establishing the grounds for such a claim, grounds that rely predominantly on the existence of a distinct nation within Canada. By denying that a nation exists, federalist political actors in Canada have ensured that those seeking constitutional change must continually assert the existence of a nation before they advocate political change. Such continual reassertion of the existence of the nation, its boundaries, and its characteristics makes nationhood and national identity a more present feature of political debate in Canada than it is in Britain.

While it is too early to determine whether the federal motion recognizing the Québécois as a nation will have an impact on the constitutional future of the province, it does appear to have had an impact on the rhetoric employed by political actors. If political debate in Scotland has distinguished itself from that in Quebec both in the degree to which political actors of different partisan stripes agreed on national status and in the decreased salience of national markers, national recognition for Quebecois appears to have had one clear effect. There is now greater agreement among political actors in Quebec that a nation exists. Previously, actors of different partisan stripes contested national status, each arguing that the province was distinct but employing different language to make this point. There is now a greater uniformity of rhetoric. Whether this will bring about a decreased salience within political debate, however, remains to be seen.

The presence of a legislature and the absence of national recognition have made the nation and national identity far more salient in Quebec than in Scotland. That the population in Quebec is more heterogeneous has sparked a separate debate about inclusion that also heightens the salience of national identity. Quebec is thus not an example of ethnic nationalism to Scotland's civic comparator but a case where national identity and belonging have been more important features of political debate. Whether the nation is seen as inclusive or not depends in part on its salience. Exclusive constructions of national membership in which national identity is of little consequence to political debate will not produce the same perceptions of exclusion found in polities where national identity and national destiny are more pressing political concerns.

The political use of nationalism and national identity provides the final opportunity to examine inclusion in Scotland and Quebec. Political elites can make individuals feel they belong by deliberately referring to their inclusive nation, one that welcomes outsiders, where members share values rather than blood ties. In so doing, the rhetoric is explicit about the extent to which the nation is inclusive. When references to the nation are pressed into service as justifications for or against greater self-determination, we find more implicit statements about inclusion. And when political parties suggest that self-determination is the fulfillment of national destiny, it is worth determining who they believe is thwarting that destiny. Here we find Scottish political dialogue more exclusive than that occurring in Quebec.

In pre-devolution Scotland, Labour, the Liberal Democrats, and the SNP laid the blame for national problems clearly at the feet of

Conservative governments. For much of the 1980s Margaret Thatcher herself bore the brunt of considerable criticism. England as a whole was not seen as the transgressor, though the union, portrayed as a good idea for eighteenth-century Scotland, was recast by most advocates of reform as an obstacle to truly reflective social policy and national economic growth. The political rhetoric blamed both an institutional settlement and a political party. In Quebec, sovereignist rhetoric blames federalism as a system of governance, rather than federalists, for stymying the democratic wishes of Quebecers. Where pre-devolution rhetoric in Scotland referred to a democratic deficit, in Quebec the deficit is seen in instrumental terms as a financial one: the province is underfunded by federal administrations that off-load policy commitments without sharing the considerable budget surplus. Clearly, pro-change arguments in each case express frustration with the government in the larger state. The distinction is between blame for Conservative administrations and blame for federal administrations of any stripe. We should be cautious with this distinction. Conservatives may have borne the brunt of pro-devolution frustration in part because they were the only anti-devolution party on the political scene. In Canada every federal administration is hostile to sovereignty, regardless of its position on the political spectrum. That said, if in their rhetoric political actors can make certain groups feel alienated from the nation, we have here a construction of the nation that goes out of its way to place Conservative partisanship outside dominant national preferences. This perception includes more than Conservative views of devolution; Conservative values themselves are portrayed as anathema to Scottish values. The rhetoric in Quebec, by contrast, is resolutely inclusive; all Quebecers, regardless of their views of sovereignty, are worse off as a result of the particular implementation of federalism.

That one political party might be portrayed by its rivals as out of step with the wishes of the nation as a whole is not uncommon. In electoral contests all political parties attempt to demonstrate that they and they alone are able to understand the wishes of the electorate. In both Scotland and Quebec political parties have attempted to align themselves with national values and, at the same time, to demonstrate that some of their partisan rivals clearly misunderstand the destiny of the nation and the wishes of its members. This rhetoric is most explicit in SNP documents that portray first the

Conservatives and more recently Labour as not only out of step with Scottish values but anti-Scottish. Even the Liberal Democrats are seen as betrayers of their supposedly Scottish roots. Within Quebec political parties align themselves with national values, but far greater attention is devoted to the schism between the preferences of Quebecers and those of other Canadians. Claims that other parties either misunderstand or misrepresent national values are all but absent. In Scotland portraying political parties as alienated from the nation raises questions about the inclusiveness of national membership. Values typically occupy the terrain of civic nationalism. Political dialogue in Scotland and to a lesser extent in Quebec suggests that constructions of the nation can be both civic and exclusive.

The extent to which the nation is portrayed as an inclusive entity depends, last, on the perceived compatibility of Scottish or Québécois identity with other possible identities. Even with the restricted notion of dual identities, there are several possible incarnations. One can be both Scottish and Pakistani, or Québécois and Italian. Here the second identity is to a nation outside the borders of the state. Second, one can feel a dual identity to both the sub- state nation and the larger state. Here one can feel both Scottish and British, or Québécois and Canadian. Finally, one can feel a sense of national identity to two sub-state entities within the larger state. Thus one can feel both English and Scottish, or Québécois and Albertan. In Scotland and Quebec we find differing efforts to portray these formulations as naturally incompatible and different identity preferences within the nation.

In both Scotland and Quebec there is far less reticence about the existence of dual identities between the nation and an extraterritorial entity. Both PQ and SNP political documents demonstrate a deliberate courting of individuals who feel themselves, for example, Greco-Québécois or Scots Italian. The third formulation of dual identities – that between two sub-state entities – receives limited attention in both cases. When present, it is overwhelmingly ethnic in its formulation. Individuals proclaiming themselves both Scottish and English often juxtapose their current nation of residence and where they were born or where their parents were born. Much of the discussion of multiple identities focuses on dual identities, in particular on whether one belongs to the nation or to the larger state in which the nation resides. Here we find remarkable consistency between political rhetoric and the views of individuals. Sovereignist parties and those supporting independence align themselves with single national identities, while nationalist parties that support the institutional status quo advocate dual national identities. In Scotland the latter included the Conservatives both before and after 1997, and since devolution they also include Scottish Labour and the Liberal Democrats. In Scotland there is greater support for identities that emphasize Scottishness over Britishness. More than 60 per cent of survey respondents describe their identity as Scottish not British, more Scottish than British, or equally Scottish and British. In Quebec there is far greater support for shared identities. Three-quarters of Quebecers indicate a sense of belonging to both Quebec and Canada. Whereas almost one-third of Scots describe themselves as "Scottish" exclusively, half that number hold a similar exclusive identity in Quebec.

We should be cautious with the measures used to explore support for dual identities. The standard Moreno measure is often interpreted as proof of dual national identities. The assumption is that when someone describes her or himself as Scottish or Canadian, she or he is referring to a nation. We have no way of knowing, though, whether that attachment is to a nation or to a bounded polity and no way to determine whether the sense of belonging is to a meaningful national aggregate of shared values or to the provider of goods and services.

If we can identify the ways in which Scotland and Quebec offer varying degrees of inclusiveness, what impact does this understanding have on political culture? When we explore the attitudes of individuals, those who feel themselves excluded from the nation possess different views of the state and different views of citizens from those with an automatic assumption of national membership. Equally important, individuals who hold single identities, regardless of whether it is to Quebec or Canada, Scotland or Britain, hold different views of the state from individuals who possess dual identities. Attachment to multiple groups improves efficacy and makes individuals more supportive of their fellow citizens. Where previous research has sought to determine whether Scots hold different views from those resident in England, an approach that acknowledges the operation of the identity process provides us with compelling evidence of how and why national identity affects political culture.

Notes

INTRODUCTION

1 PhD dissertations on the topic have a longer history. See, for example, Newman 1989; Teghtsoonian 1988.
2 On whether nations are ancient or primordial, see Barth 1969; Brass 1991; Smith 1971, 1981, 1986, 1988, 1992b. For views that they are modern and constructed, see Deutsch 1966; Gellner 1964, 1983; Gellner and Smith 1996; Kedourie 1994; Nairn 1977.
3 The Canadian contribution to political-culture research raises the possibility of rival notions of national identity. According to Pammett and Whittington, the focal point of loyalty, whether city, province, region, or country, will be determined by the way key agents of socialization seek to transmit a sense of history (Pammett and Whittington 1976).

CHAPTER ONE

1 For information on Scottish elites, see M. Lynch 1992; Paterson 1994a; Kellas 1989. For information on Quebec elites, see Brunet 1962, 1964; Frégault 1956; Iguarta 1974; Séguin 1970. Ouellet claims the decapitation thesis overemphasizes whatever influence the economic elite had in pre-Conquest Quebec (Ouellet 1966).
2 See, inter alia, Bouchard 1990, 1993, 1996, 1998, 1999a, 1999b, 1999c; Chrétien 1997; DeVilliers 1997; S. Dion 1998a, 1998b; Johnson 1996, 1997; Parizeau 1995a. The subsequent modification of this compact theory includes Aboriginal peoples, who were not taken into account in 1867.

3 Among the MPs in the current cabinet, four, or 16 per cent, represent ridings in Quebec.
4 The 1871 census shows 1,191,516 residents in Quebec and 3,689,257 in Canada as a whole.
5 Although the prime minister was educated in Edinburgh and although he is known to emphasize that his grannie was from Govan, he is not considered a Scot by either his English constituents or voters in Scotland.
6 The exceptions to this pattern are the 1976–79 Labour cabinet of James Callaghan and the first Thatcher cabinet, which each included three Scots.
7 Although technically these members do not serve as representatives of the church while members of the upper house.
8 The proportion of residents indicating they held "no religion" grew by 50 per cent between 1991 and 2001 in Quebec, while in Canada it increased by 30 per cent.
9 In addition to military campaigns within its borders in 1715 and 1745 and the subsequent proscription of markers of Highland life between 1746 and 1752, the persistent Anglicization of Scotland can be directly attributable to the union (M. Lynch 1992).
10 McCrone subjects Hechter's analysis to careful scrutiny in *Understanding Scotland*, arguing that by splitting Britain between Highland and Lowland areas, Hechter treated Scotland as a Highland region in its entirely, ignoring the diversity within the Scottish economy (Hechter 1975; McCrone 1992). According to McCrone, Hechter's decision to adapt his analysis (Hechter 1982) by arguing that Scotland represented an overdeveloped, rather than underdeveloped, region further limits the degree to which his analysis can be considered useful (McCrone 1992).
11 The Barnett formula calculates the block grant given by Westminster to Scotland. The formula functions on a purely proportional scale, but a falling population in Scotland has meant that it traditionally receives more than its strictly proportional share. The SNP argues that because Scotland's oil revenues are transferred directly to London, it receives a smaller share that it is due, given the contribution of North Sea oil to the British economy.
12 During the 1999 election campaign the Scottish National Party promised to release two manifestos, the first with costings for a devolved Scotland and the second with projected costings for an independent Scotland. In the end, only the one full manifesto was published (SNP 1999), although press releases later in the campaign covered further economic details.

13 Above-average growth in the province of Newfoundland since 1998, in particular, could be credited with such results. Current ratings from Dominion Bond Rating Services indicate that the province has recently upgraded to an A (high) rating, an improvement on the A rating it received in 2000 after four years at the A(low) rating.

14 Partisan choices available to voters in Northern Ireland have consistently deviated from options available to voters in the rest of the UK.

CHAPTER TWO

1 Statcan labour-force characteristics, population 15 years and older, by census metropolitan area 2003.

2 The five constituencies are Abitibi, Charlevoix, Jonquière, Manicougan, and Roberval.

CHAPTER THREE

1 For information on banal nationalism and the role of the heritage industry, see McCrone, Morris, and Kiely 1995; Billig 1995b; Harvie 1981; Smout 1986.

2 Until the 1997 Canadian federal election, political parties rarely provided manifesto booklets containing a full list of policies. Instead, they released policies to the press throughout the campaign in an effort to capture the electorate's interest. The Quebec parties have, since the 1994 provincial election, provided full manifestos detailing their campaign promises. These works, and other constitutional documents from the parties, are considered in tandem with government documents and commission reports.

3 See, for example, Assemblée des évêques du Québec 1973, 1977, 1981, 1995; Assemblée des évêques du Québec, Comité des affaires sociales 1976; Assemblée des évêques du Québec, Comité de théologie 1994.

4 The relative attentiveness to history within Quebec historiography is discussed by Jocelyn Maclure (Maclure 2003).

5 Exceptions include the 1997 party manifesto, which stated that Scotland "is denied its democratic right to self-government" (SNP 1997b).

CHAPTER FOUR

1 For a description of the development of the scale, see Moreno 2006.

CHAPTER SEVEN

1 The territory that became Quebec obviously housed, at the time of the Conquest and the Quebec Act, Aboriginal populations. Unlike in Scotland, these individuals would not have been considered part of the political community but more like extraterritorial allies.

Bibliography

Abercrombie, Nicholas. 1990. "Popular Culture and Ideological Effects." In Nicholas Abercrombie, Stephen Hill, and Bryan Turner, eds., *Dominant Ideologies*. London: Unwin Hyman.

Action démocratique du Québec (ADQ). 1998a. *L'ADQ et le Québec du prochain millénaire.*

– 1998b. *La formation universitaire, priorité à l'emploi.*

– 1998c. *Un Québec 100% branché.*

– 1998d. *Un vent de changement: Programme de l'Action démocratique du Québec.*

– 1998e. *Une vision pour le Québec du prochain millénaire.*

– 2004. *La voie autonomiste.*

Adams, Michael. 1998. *Sex in the Snow: Canadian Social Values at the End of the Millennium*. Toronto: Penguin.

– 2003. *Fire and Ice: The U.S., Canada, and the Myth of Converging Values*. Toronto: Environics Research Group.

Adsett, Margaret, and Michael Willmott. 1999. "Support for the Quebec Independence Movement in Canada: Identity and Affective vs. Rational and Economic Actor Frames." Unpublished paper presented at the Conference on Nationalism, Identity and Minority Rights, Bristol.

Ajzenstat, Janet, and Peter J. Smith. 1998. "The 'Tory Touch' Thesis: Bad History, Poor Political Science." In Mark Charlton and Paul Barker, eds., *Crosscurrents: Contemporary Political Issues*. Toronto: ITP Nelson.

Alford, Robert R. 1967. "Class Voting in the Anglo-American Political Systems." In Seymour Lipset and Stein Rokkan, eds., *Party Systems and Voter Alignments: Cross-National Perspectives*. London: Collier-Macmillan.

Allan, Alasdair. 2002. *Talking Independence*. Edinburgh: SNP.

Allardt, Erik. 1997. "Political Sociology and Comparative Politics." In Hans Daalder, ed., *Comparative European Politics: The Story of a Profession*. London: Pinter.

Alliance Quebec. n.d.a. *Alliance Quebec*. Montreal.

– n.d.b. *Alliance Quebec Achievements*. Montreal.

– n.d.c. *Alliance Quebec and the Electoral Fraud Case: The Basis for Support*. Montreal.

– n.d.d. *Alliance Quebec: What Have We Done for You ... Lately?* Montreal.

– n.d.e. *Because You Care about the Future of Your Country and Your Community*. Montreal.

Almond, Gabriel. 1989. "The Intellectual History of the Civic Culture Concept." In Gabriel Almond and Sidney Verba, eds., *The Civic Culture Revisited*. London: Sage.

– 1992. "The Political Culture of Foreign Area Research: Methodological Reflections." In Richard J. Samuels and Myron Weber, eds., *The Political Culture of Foreign Area and International Studies*. New York: Brassey's.

– 1993. "The Study of Political Culture." In Dirk Berg Scholosser and Ralf Rythlewski, eds., *Political Culture in Germany*. London: Macmillan.

Almond, Gabriel, G. Bingham Powell Jr, and Robert J. Mundt. 1993. *Comparative Politics: A Theoretical Framework*. New York: Harper Collins.

Almond, Gabriel, and Sydney Verba. 1963. *The Civic Culture*. Princeton: Princeton University Press.

– eds. 1989. *The Civic Culture Revisited*. London: Sage.

Alter, Peter. 1989. *Nationalism*. 2nd ed. London: Edward Arnold.

Anderson, Benedict. 1991. *Imagined Communities: Reflections on the Origins and Spread of Nationalism*. 2nd ed. London: Verso.

Angus Reid Group Inc. 1998. *Canadians and the Senate*. 11 May. Ottawa: Angus Reid.

– 2000. *17 Country Poll on Taxes, Spending and Priorities*. March. Ottawa: Angus Reid.

Archand, David. 1995. "Myths, Lies and Historical Truth: A Defence of Nationalism." *Political Studies* 43: 472–81.

Archives Nationales du Québec. 1994. *Qui étaient nos ancêtres? Comment vivaient-ils?* Québec: MinistPre de la Culture et des Communications.

Assemblée des évêques du Québec. 1979. *The People of Quebec and Its Political Future.*
– 1973. *Élections du 29 octobre 1973: Identification de quelques problèmes majeurs au Quebec.*
– 1977. *La Charte de la langue française au Québec.*
– 1981. *Observations des évêques du Québec sur la question constitutionnelle.* Québec.
– 1982. *Éducation religieuse.*
– 1984. *L'enseignement religieux catholique: Orientations pastorales.*
– 1993. *L'Église du Quebec 1988–1993 à l'occasion de la visite ad limina 1993.* Montréal: Éditions Fides.
– 1995. *Le référendum sur l'avenir du Québec.*
– Comité des affaires sociales. 1976. *Élections du 15 novembre 1976: Identification de quelques problèmes majeurs au Québec, qui appellent des décisions politiques urgentes.*
– Comité de théologie. 1994. *L'engagement des communautés chrétiennes dans la société.*
Assemblée nationale du Québec. 1992a. *Journal des débats: Commission d'étude des questions afferentes à l'accession du Quebec à la souveraineté.* Québec.
– 1992b. *Journal des débats: Commission d'étude sur toute offre d'un nouveau partenariat de nature constitutionelle.* Québec.
Assemblee plénière de la conférence des évêques catholiques du Canada. 1972. *Les évêques canadiens et la vie politique au Québec.*
Axworthy, Thomas S., and Pierre Elliott Trudeau, eds. 1990. *Towards a Just Society.* Markham. Viking.
Badie, Bertrand, and Pierre Birnbaum. 1994. "Sociology of the State Revisited." *International Social Science Journal* 140: 153–68.
Balthazar, Louis. 1987. "Québec Nationalism: After Twenty-five Years." *Québec Studies* 5: 29–38.
– 1993. "Faces of Quebec Nationalism." In Alain-G. Gagnon, ed., *Quebec: State and Society.* Scarborough: Nelson.
– 1994. "Reconnaissance et identité dans le contexte canadien." *International Journal of Canadian Studies* 10: 139–43.
– 1996. "Identity and Nationalism Quebec." In James Littleton, ed., *Clash of Identities: Media, Manipulation, and Politics of the Self.* Scarborough, Ont.: Prentice-Hall Canada.
Barry, Brian. 1970. *Sociologists, Economists and Democracy.* Chicago: University of Chicago Press.

Barth, Fredrik. 1969. *Ethnic Groups and Boundaries*. Boston: Little Brown.

Bateman, Derek. 1996. "Quebec: The Second Referendum." *Scottish Affairs* 14: 1–7.

Bauer, Julien. 1991. "Les minorités en France, au Canada et au Québec: Minoritaires ou mineures." *Revue québécois de science politique* 20: 5–34.

Baum, Gregory. 1999. "Nationalisme et mouvement sociaux contre l'hegemonie du marché." *Le Devoir*, 17 July.

Bauman, Z. 1996. "From Pilgrim to Tourist: – or A Short History of Identity." In Stuart Hall and P. DuGay, eds., *Questions of Cultural Identity*. London: Sage.

Beals, Ralph C. 1977. "The Rise and Decline of National Identity." *Canadian Review of Studies Nationalism* 4: 147–66.

Béchard, Fabien. 1998. *Le discours libéral sonne aussie faux au printemps 1999 qu'B l'élection de novembre 1998.*

– 1999a. *Notes pour un discours au Conseil national du Parti Québécois, January.*

– 1999b. *Notes pour un discours au Conseil national du Parti Québécois, April.*

Beer, Samuel. 1982. *Britain against Itself: Political Contradictions of Collectivism*. London: Faber and Faber.

Bell, David, and Lorne Tepperman. 1979. *The Roots of Disunity: A Look at Canadian Political Culture*. Toronto: McClelland and Stewart.

Bell, David V.J. 1970. "The Loyalist Tradition Canada." *Journal of Canadian Studies* 5: 22–33.

Bennett, Lance. 1998. "The UnCivic Culture: Communication, Identity, and the Rise of Lifestyle Politics." *Political Science and Politics* 31: 741–61.

Bennie, Lynn, Jack Brand, and James Mitchell. 1997. *How Scotland Votes*. Manchester: Manchester University Press.

Berelson, B., P Lazarsfeld, and W. McPhee. 1954. *Voting*. Chicago: University of Chicago Press.

Bergeron, Gérard. 1979. "Plus de souveraineté que d'association ou l'inverse." In Panayotis Soldatos, ed., *Nationalisme et intégration dans le contexte canadien*. Montréal: Université de Montréal.

Bergeron, Viateur. 1995. *Sur l'opportunité de realiser la souveraineté: je dis non* . Hull: V. Bergeron.

Bernard, André. 1977. *La politique au Canada et au Québec*. Québec: Presses de l'université du Québec.

Bernard, Claude. 1983. "The Quebec of Tomorrow." Unpublished paper presented at the University of Portland, 23 March.

Berry, Reginald, and James Acheson, eds. 1985. *Regionalism and National Identity*. Christchurch: University of Christchurch.

Beveridge, Craig, and Ronald Turnbull. 1989. *The Eclipse of Scottish Culture*. Edinburgh: Polygon.

Bhabha, Homi K. 1990a. "DissemiNation: Time, Narrative, and the Margins of the Modern Nation." In Homi Bhabha, ed., *Nation and Narration*. New York: Routledge.

–1990b. "Narrating the Nation." In Homi Bhabha, ed., *Nation and Narration*. New York: Routledge.

Billig, Michael. 1995a. *Banal Nationalism*. London: Sage.

– 1995b. "Rhetorical Psychology, Ideological Thinking and Imagining Nationhood." In Hank Johnson and Bert Klandermans, eds., *Social Movements and Culture*. London: University College London Press.

Blair, Rt Hon. Tony. 1999. Speech delivered to the Scottish Labour Party Conference.

Blais, André, Pierre Martin, and Richard Nadeau. 1995. "Attentes économiques et linguistiques et appui à la souveraineté du Québec: Une analyse prospective et comparative." *Canadian Journal of Political Science* 29: 635–57.

Bloc Québécois (BQ). 1998a. *Le Bloc Québécois: un parti souverainiste dans l'arPne fédérale canadienne*. Québec.

– 1998b. *Quebec ... on the Road to Nationhood*. Québec.

– 1999. *Au coeur de la réflexion souverainiste*. Québec.

Bluhm, William. 1974. *Ideologies and Attitudes: Modern Political Culture*. Englewood Cliffs: Prentice Hall.

Bluntschli, J.K. 1866. *Alllgemeine Staatslehre*. 6th ed. Cited in Michael Hughes, *Nationalism and Society: Germany 1800–1945*. London: Edward Arnold, 1988.

Bochel, John, and David Denver. 1993a. "The 1992 General Election Scotland" *Scottish Affairs* 1: 14–26.

– 1993b. "Trends in District Election." *Scottish Affairs* 2: 106–19.

Boix, Charles, and Daniel N. Posner. 1995. "Social Capital: Explaining Its Origins and Effects on Government Performance." *British Journal of Political Science*: 686–93.

Bonenfant, Jean Charles. 1967. *The French Canadians and the Birth of Confederation*. Ottawa: Centennial Commission.

Bonin, Daniel, ed. 1992. *Towards Reconciliation? The Language Issue in Canada in the 1990s*. Kingston: Institute of Intergovernmental Relations.

Bonnett, Alastair. 2000. *White Identities*. London: Prentice Hall.

Books, John W., and Charles L. Prysby. 1991. *Political Behaviour and the Local Context*. London: Praeger.

Bouchard, Gérard. 1999. *La nation québécoise au future et au passé*. Montréal: VLB Éditeur.

Bouchard, Lucien. 1990. "Sovereignty Must Complete Quebec's Quiet Revolution." Speech delivered to the Université du Québec à Hull.

– 1993. "The Bloc's Case for Quebec Sovereignty." Speech delivered to the Canadian Club of Toronto and the Empire Club of Canada.

– 1996. "Living Together before, during and after the Referendum." Notes for a speech to the anglophone community of Quebec.

– 1998. Notes pour un discours au Conseil national du Parti Québécois.

– 1999a. Notes pour une allocution à la journée de reflexion et d'actions stratégique sur la souveraineté du Québec. Saint-Hyacinthe, 5 June.

– 1999b. Notes pour une allocution au Conseil national du Parti Québécois, January.

– 1999c. Notes pour une allocution au Conseil national du Parti Québécois, April.

Boucher, Christian. 2004. "Canada-US Values: Distinct, Inevitably Carbon Copy, or Narcissism of Small Differences?" *Policy Research Initiative Horizons* 7.

Bourdieu, Pierre. 1985. "The Social Space and the Genesis of Groups." *Theory and Society* 7: 723–44.

Bourque, Gilles. 1984. "Class, Nation, and the Parti Québécois." In Alain G. Gagnon, ed., *Quebec: State and Society*. Toronto: Methuen.

– 1999. "Pour un nationalisme ouvert à la citoyenneté pluraliste" *Le Devoir*, 3 July.

Bouthillier, Guy. 1979. "Le Nationalisme Québécois." In Panayotis Soldatos, ed., *Nationalisme et intégration dans le contexte canadien*. Montréal: Université de Montréal.

Brady, Henry E., Sidney Verba, and Kay Lehman Schlozman. 1995. "Beyond SES: A Resource Model for Political Particpation." *American Political Science Review* 89: 271–94.

Brand, J., J. Mitchell, and P. Surridge. 1994. "Will Scotland Come to the Aid of the Party?" A. Heath, R. Jowell, and J. Curtice, eds., *Labour's Last Chance? The 1992 General Election and Beyond*. Aldershot: Dartmouth.

Brand, Jack. 1978. *The National Movement in Scotland*. London: Routledge.

– 1987. "National Consciousness and Voting in Scotland." *Ethnic and Racial Studies* 10: 334–48.
– 1993. "Scotland and the Politics of Devolution: A Patchy Past, a Hazy Future." *Parliamentary Affairs* 46: 38–48.
Brass, Paul. 1991. *Ethnicity and Nationalism*. London: Sage.
Breitenbach, Esther. 1993. "Out of Sight, Out of Mind? The History of Women Scottish Politics." *Scottish Affairs* 2: 58–70.
Breton, Raymond. 1964. "Institutional Completeness of Ethnic Communities and the Personal Relations of immigrants." *American Journal of Sociology* 70: 193–205.
– 1988. "From Ethnic to Civic Nationalism: English Canada and Quebec." *Ethnic and Racial Studies* 11: 85–102.
Breuilly, John. *Nationalism and the State*. Manchester: Manchester University Press, 1993.
Brooks, John W., and Charles L. Prysby. 1991. *Political Behaviour and the Local Context*. London: Praeger.
Broun, Dauvit, R.J. Finlay, and Michael Lynch. 1998. *Image and Identity: The Making and Re-making of Scotland through the Ages*. Edinburgh: John Donald.
Brown, Alice, David McCrone, and Lindsay Paterson. 1998. *Politics and Society Scotland*. 2nd ed. Basingstoke: Macmillan.
Brown, Alice, David McCrone, Lindsay Paterson, and Paula Surridge. 1999. *The Scottish Electorate: The 1997 General Election and Beyond*. Basingstoke: Macmillan.
Brown, Archie. 1979. "Introduction." In Archie Brown and Jack Gray, eds., *Political Culture in Communist States*. 2nd ed. London: Macmillan.
Brown, Archie, and Jack Gray, eds. 1979. *Political Culture in Communist States*. 2nd ed. London: Macmillan.
Brown, Callum G. 1996. "Popular Culture and the Continuing Struggle for Rational Recreation." In T.M. Devine and R.J. Finlay, eds., *Scotland in the 20th Century*. Edinburgh: Edinburgh University Press.
Brown, Rt Hon. Gordon. 1999. Speech delivered at the Edinburgh City Chambers.
Brown, Gordon, and Douglas Alexander.1998. *New Scotland, New Britain*. London: Smith Institute.
Brubaker, R. 1996. *Nationalism Reframed: Nationhood and the National Question in the New Europe*. Cambridge: Cambridge University Press.
Brunet, Michel. 1962. *French Canada in the Early Decades of British Rule*. Ottawa: Canadian Historical Association.

– 1964. *La présence anglaise et les Canadiens: Études sur l'histoire et la pensée des deux Canadas*. Montréal: Beauchemin.

Bryan, Gordon. 1984. *Scottish Nationalism and Cultural Identity in theTwentieth Century: An Annotated Bibliography of Secondary Sources*. Westport, Conn.: Greenwood Press.

Buchanan, Allen. 1996. "Secession and Nationalism." In Robert E. Goodin and Philip Pettit, eds., *A Companion to Contemporary Political Philosophy*. Oxford: Blackwell.

Bulmer, Simon, Stephen George, and Andrew Scott, eds. 1992. *The United Kingdom and EC Membership Evaluated*. London: Pinter.

Burchill, Richard. 1998. "Hiding behind Hadrian's Wall: How the 'Self' of Scotland Is Determined." Unpublished paper presented at the Boundaries of Identities Conference, Abertay-Dundee.

Butler, D.E., and D. Stokes. 1974. *Political Change Britain*. 2nd ed. London: Macmillan.

Cairns, Alan C. 1977. "The Governments and Societies of Canadian Federalism." *Canadian Journal of Political Science* 10: 695–725.

– 1991. "Quebec and Canadian Federalism." Canada House Lecture Series 49. London: Canadian High Commission.

Calder, Angus. 1994. *Revolving Culture: Notes from the Scottish Republic*. London: I.B. Tauris.

Caldwell, Gary. 1998. "The Decay of Civil Society Contemporary Quebec." *Inroads* 7: 176–84.

Caldwell, Gary, and Éric Waddell. 1982. *The English of Quebec from Majority to Minority Status*. Québec: Institut québécois de recherche sur la culture.

Cameron, Ewen A.. 1998. "Embracing the Past: The Highlands in Nineteenth Century Scotland." In Dauvit Broun, R.J. Finlay, and Michael Lynch, eds., *Image and Identity: The Making and Re-making of Scotland through the Ages*. Edinburgh: John Donald.

Campaign for a Scottish Assembly. Constitutional Steering Group. 1988. *A Claim of Right for Scotland*. Edinburgh.

Careless, J.M.S. 1969. "'Limited Identities' in Canada." *Canadian Historical Review* 50: 1–10.

Carr, Edward Hallet. 1965. *Nationalism and After*. London: Macmillan.

Cavanagh, Michael, Neil McGarvey, and Mark Shephard. 2000. "New Scottish Parliament, New Scottish Parliamentarians?" Unpublished paper presented at the Political Studies Association Annual Conference.

Chartrand, Luc. 1997. "Québec 1930–1945: Le mythe du Québec fasciste." *L'actualité*, 1 March, 19–30.

Chevrier, Marc. 1999. "Notre republique en Amérique." *Le Devoir*, 10 July.

Chrétien, Jean. 1997. "Step-by-Step Changes to Strengthen Unity." Speech delivered to the Canadian Club of Toronto.

Christian, William. 1978. "A Note on Rod Preece and Red Tories." *Canadian Journal of Political and Social Theory* 2: 128–33.

Citizens' Forum on Cannada's Future. 1991. *Shaping Canada's Future Together: Report to the People and Government of Canada*. Ottawa: Ministry of Supply and Services.

Clarke, Harold, Jane Jenson, Lawrence Leduc, and Jon Pammett. 1996. *Absent Mandate: Canadian Electoral Politics in an Era of Restructuring*. Toronto: Gage.

Clarke, Harold D., Lawrence LeDuc, Jane Jenson, and Jon H. Pammett. 1979. *Political Choice in Canada*. Toronto: McGraw-Hill Ryerson.

Clift, Dominique. 1981. *Le déclin du nationalisme au Québec*. Montréal: Libre Expression.

Cloutier, Édouard, Jean H. Guay, and Daniel Latouche. 1992. *Le virage: L'évolution de l'opinion publique au Québec depuis 1960*. Montréal: Québec/Amérique.

Coates, Colin, and Ailsa Henderson. 2006. "Scotland-Quebec: An Evolving Comparison." Special issue of the *British Journal of Canadian Studies* 19, no. 1.

Cohen, Anthony. 1996a. "Owning the Nation, and the Personal Nature of Nationalism: Locality and the Rhetoric of Nationhood Scotland." In V. Amit-Talai and C. Knowles, eds., *Resituating Identities: The Politics of Race, Culture and Ethnicity*. Peterborough: Broadview Press.

– 1996b. "Personal Nationalism: A Scottish View of Some Rites, Rights and Wrongs." *American Ethnologist* 23: 802–15.

Cohen, Robin. 1994. *Frontiers of Identity: The British and the Others*. London: Longman.

Coleman, J. 1988. "Social Capital the Creation of Human Capital." *American Journal of Sociology* 94: 95–120.

– 1990. *Foundations of Social Theory*. Cambridge: Belknap.

Coleman, William. 1984. *The Independence Movement in Quebec, 1945–1980*. Toronto: University of Toronto Press.

Colley, Linda. 1994. *Britons: Forging the Nation, 1707–1837*. London: Pimlico.

– 1999. *Millennium Lecture: Britishness in the 21st Century*

Collier, Jane F., Bill Maurer, and Liliana Suarez-Navez. 1997. "Sanctioned Identities: Legal Constructions of Modern Personhood." *Identities* 2: 1–27.

Commission sur l'avenir politique et constitutionnel du Quebec. 1991a. *Minutes and Proceedings of Evidence*. Québec.

– 1991b. *Petit résumé de la Commission Bélanger-Campeau: Audiences tenues entre le 6 novembre 1990 et le 23 janvier 1991*. Imprimerie d'Arthabaska.

Connor, Walker. 1972. "Nation-building or Nation-destroying?" *World Politics* 24: 319–55.

– 1978. "A Nation Is a Nation, Is a State, Is an Ethnic Group, Is a ..." *Ethnic and Racial Studies* 1: 378–400.

– 1990. "When Is a Nation?" *Ethnic and Racial Studies* 13: 92–103.

Conservative Party. 1979. *The Conservative Manifesto*. London.

– 1992. *The Best Future for Britain*. London.

Consultative Steering Group. 1998. *Shaping Scotland's Parliament*. Edinburgh: Scottish Office.

Contogeorgis, Georges. 1998. "L'offre identitaire des médias." *Revue internationale de politique comparée* 5: 53–7.

Cook, Ramsay. 1989. "The Evolution of Nationalism in Quebec." *British Journal of Canadian Studies* 4: 306–17.

– 1996. "Challenges to Canadian Federalism the 1990s." In James Littleton, ed., *Clash of Identities: Media, Manipulation, and Politics of the Self*. Scarborough, Ont.: Prentice-Hall Canada.

Cornell, Stephen. 1996. "The Variable Ties That Bind: Content and Circumstance in Ethnic Processes." *Ethnic and Racial Studies* 19: 265–89.

Cox, Kevin R., and David R. Reynolds, eds. 1974. *Locational Approaches to Power and Conflict*. New York: Halsted Press.

Crabb, Peter. 1985. "Regionalism and National Identity: Canada and Australia." In Reginald Berry and James Acheson, eds., *Regionalism and National Identity*. Christchurch: University of Christchurch.

Craib, Ian. 1998. *Experiencing Identity*. London: Sage.

Créatec. 1996a. *Rapport final sur l'environnement post référendaire*. Présenté au Conseil Privé, March.

– 1996b. *Rapport final sur les rPgles de sécession/renouvellement du féderalisme*. Présenté au Conseil Privé, October.

Creighton, Donald. 1956. *The Empire of the St. Lawrence*. Toronto: Macmillan.

Crewe, I., B. Sarlvik, and J. Alt. 1977. "Partisan Dealignment Britain 1964–1974." *British Journal of Political Science* 7: 129–90.

Crick, Bernard. 1993. "Essays on Britishness." *Scottish Affairs* 2:71–83.

CROP. 1998. *Sondage d'opinion auprPs des québécois*. Montréal. May.

Curtice, John. 1988. "One Nation?" In R. Jowell, S. Witherspoon, and L. Brook, eds., *British Social Attitudes: The Fifth Report*. Aldershot: Gower.

– 1992. "The North-South Divide." In R. Jowell et al., eds., *British Social Attitudes Survey: The 9th Report*. Aldershot: Gower.

– 1993. "Popular Support for Electoral Reform: The Lessons of the 1992 Election." *Scottish Affairs* 4: 23–32.

– 1996. "One Nation Again?" In *British Social Attitudes*, 13: 1–18. Aldershot: Dartmouth.

– 1998. "Reinventing the Yo-Yo? A Comment on the Electoral Provisions of the Scotland Bill." *Scottish Affairs* 23: 41–53.

Curtice, John, and Jowell, Roger. 1995. "The Sceptical Electorate." In R. Jowell et al., eds., *British Social Attitudes Survey: The 12th Report 1995/96*. Aldershot: Dartmouth.

– 1997. "Trust the Political System." In *British Social Attitudes Survey*, 14: 89–109.

Daiches, David, Peter Jones, and Jean Jones, eds. 1986. *A Hotbed of Genius: The Scottish Enlightenment 1730–1790*. Edinburgh: Edinburgh University Press.

Dalton, Russell J. 1996. *Citizen Politics: Public Opinion and Political Parties in Advanced Western Democracies*. 2nd ed. Chatham: Chatham House Publishers.

DeFleur, M.L., and F.R. Westie. 1958. "Verbal Attitudes and Overt Acts: An Experiment on the Salience of Attitudes." *American Sociological Review* 23: 667–73.

Delage, Denys. 1999. "Les trois peuples fondateurs du Québec." *Le Devoir*, 24 July.

Denholm, Andrew. 1996. "SNP's New Scots Attack Anti-English Claims." *Scotsman*, 18 October.

Denver, David. 1994. *Elections and Voting Behaviour in Britain*. 2nd ed. London: Harvester Wheatsheaf.

Deutsch, Karl W. 1966. *Nationalism and Social Communication: An Inquiry into the Foundations of Nationalism*. 2nd ed. New York: MIT Press.

DeVilliers, Paul. 1997. "Why We Must Entrench Quebec's Francophone Heritage." Speech delivered at Lindsay, Ontario.

Devine, T.M . 1988. "Introduction." In T.M. Devine and Rosalind Mitchison, eds., *People and Society in Scotland*, vol. 1, *1760–1830*. Edinburgh: John Donald.

Devine, T.M., and R. Mitchison, eds., 1988. *People and Society in Scotland*. Vol. 1, *1760–1830*. Edinburgh: John Donald.

Devine, Tom. 1998. "Unless Irish Immigration Was Curbed, a Racial and Religious War Was Feared." *Herald*, 18 July.

– 2000. *The Scottish Nation, 1700–2000*. London: Penguin.

Dewar, Rt. Hon. Donald. 1999. "Diversity Union." Speech delivered as the Lothian European Lecture.

Dickinson, John A., and Brian Young. 1993. *A Short History of Quebec*. 2nd ed. Toronto: Copp Clark Pitman.

Dickson, Malcolm. 1993. "Questioning the Scottish Question." In Anthony Black, ed., *The Question of the Constitution of Scotland*. Dundee: University of Dundee.

– 1994. "Should Auld Acquaintance Be Forgot? A Comparison of the Scots and English Scotland." *Scottish Affairs* 7: 112–34.

– 1996. "Scottish Political Culture: Is Scotland Different?" *Strathclyde Papers on Government and Politics*, no. 108.

Dion, Léon. 1998. "Defence of French, Defence of a Society." *Inroads* 7: 167–75.

Dion, Stéphane. 1998a. "Maintaining National Unity in Plurinational Context: Notes for an Address by the Honourable Stéphane Dion at the London School of Economics." 19 May.

– 1998b. "My Praxis of Federalism: Notes for an Address by the Honourable Stéphane Dion at the Institute of Intergovernmental Relations, Queen's University, Kingston." 28 May.

– 1999. Plenary address to the Triennial Conference of the Nordic Association of Canadian Studies.

Directeur général des élections du Québec. 1980a. *Référendum Non*. Québec.

– 1980b. *Référendum Oui*. Québec.

Dominion Bond Rating Service (DBRS). 1999. *Press Release*. 28 May. Toronto.

Donnachie, Ian, and Christopher Whatley, eds. 1992. *The Manufacture of Scottish History*. Edinburgh: Polygon.

Donneur, André. 1975. "La solution territoriale au problème du multilinguisme." In Jean-Guy Savard and Richard Vigneault, eds., *Les États multilingues: Problèmes et solutions*. Québec: Presses de l'Université Laval.

Dowds, Lizanne, and Ken Young. 1996. "National Identity." In R. Jowell et al., eds., *British Social Attitudes: The 13th Report*. Aldershot: Dartmouth.

Drouilly, Pierre. 1994. "L'élection federale du 25 octobre 1993 au Quebec: Une analyse des resultats." In D. Monière, ed., *L'année politique au Quebec 1993*. Montréal: Fides.

– 1997a. "La polarisation linguistique du vote: Une constante de l'histoire electorale du Quebec." *Bulletin d'histoire politique* 4: 20–41.

– 1997b. "Le referendum du 30 octobre 1995: Une analyse des resultats." In Robert Boily, ed., *L'année politique au Quebec 1995–1996*. Montréal: Fides.

Dryzek, John S. 1996. "Political Inclusion and the Dynamics of Democratization." *American Political Science Review* 90: 475–87.

Dufour, Christian. 1989. *Le défis québécois*. Montréal: L'Hexagone.

Dumont, Fernand. 1998. "French, a Language in Exile." *Inroads* 7: 155–66.

Duncan, A.A.M. 1970. *The Nation of Scots and the Declaration of Arbroath*. London: The Historical Association.

Dunn, Christopher. 1998. *Identity Crises: A Social Critique of Postmodernity*. Minneapolis: University of Minnesota Press.

Dupont, Louis. 1995. "Americanité in Quebec in the 1980s: Political and Cultural Considerations of an Emerging Discours." *American Review of Canadian Studies* 25: 27–52.

Easton, David. 1990. *The Analysis of Political Structure*. New York: Routledge.

Eatwell, Roger. 1997. *European Political Cultures: Conflict or Convergence*. London: Routledge.

Edwards, Wesley. 1998. "Fixing the Terms of Statelessness – Again." *Scottish Affairs* 23: 27–40.

Ekos Research Associates. 1998. *From Trudeau to Mulroney to Chrétien: Trust and Judgement*. Ottawa.

Elections Canada. 1999. *Serving Democracy: A Strategic Plan 1999–2002*.

Elkins, David J., and Richard E.B. Simeon. 1979. "A Cause in Search of Its Effect, or What Does Political Culture Explain?" *Comparative Politics* 11: 127–45.

Environics. 1996–99. *Focus Canada Reports*.

Equality Party. 1994. *Policy White Booklet*. Montreal.

Erikson, Erik. 1974. *Dimensions of a New Identity*. New York: Norton.

Eurobarometer. 2005. *Eurobarometer 64: Public Opinion of the European Union*. Directorate General Press and Communication.

Europinion. 1995. *European Continuous Tracking Surveys*. Brussels. December.
– 1996. *European Continuous Tracking Surveys*. Brussels. November.
– 1997. *European Continuous Tracking Surveys*. Brussels. November.
Evans, Geoffry, and Pippa Norris, eds. 1999. *Critical Elections: British Parties and Voters in Long-Term Perspective*. London: Sage.
Ewing, Margaret. 2002. Address to the Annual Conference of the SNP. 25 September.
Ewing, Winnie. 2002. Address to the Annual Conference of the SNP. 28 September.
Federal-Provincial Conference of First Ministers on the Constitution. 1980. "Opening Statement by Mr. Rene Levesque, Premier of Quebec." Ottawa.
Federation des Groupes Ethniques du Québec. 1996. *Identité – Intégration des allophones du Quebec*. Montréal: Echos ethniques.
Finlay, Richard. 1994a. "Controlling the Past: Scottish Historiography and Scottish Identity in the 19th and 20th Centuries." *Scottish Affairs* 9: 127–42.
– 1994b. *Independent and Free: The Origins of the Scottish National Party*. Edinburgh: John Donald.
– 1997. "Heroes, Myths and Anniversaries in Modern Scotland" *Scottish Affairs* 18: 108–25.
Fishbein, Martin, and Ajzen, Icek. 1975. *Belief, Attitude, Intention and Behaviour: An Introduction to Theory and Research*. London: Addison-Wesley.
Fisher, Samuel, and Richard Vengroff. 1995. "The 1994 Quebec Provincial Elections: Party Realignment, Independence Referendum, or More of the Same." *Québec Studies* 19: 1–15.
Forbes, H.D. 1974. "Two Approaches to the Psychology of Nationalism." *Canadian Review of Studies Nationalism* 2: 172–81.
– 1987. "Hartz-Horowitz at Twenty: Nationalism, Toryism and Socialism in Canada and the United States." *Canadian Journal of Political Science* 20: 287–315.
Forrester, Duncan. 1993. "The Church of Scotland and Public Policy." *Scottish Affairs* 4: 67–81.
Fossum, John Erik. 1999. "The Politics of Identity and Citizenship in Canada." Unpublished paper for the Nordic Association of Canadian Studies Triennial Conference.
Foster, Charles R. 1982. "Political Culture and Regional Ethnic Minorities." *Journal of Politics* 44: 560–69.

Franklin, Daniel, and Michael Braun. 1995. *Political Culture and Constitutionalism: A Comparative Approach*. London: ME Sharpe.
Frégault, G. 1956. *Canadian Society in the French Regime*. Ottawa: Canadian Historical Association.
Freud, Sigmund. 1922. *Group Psychology and the Analysis of the Ego*. London: International Psychoanalytic Press.
Frost, Stanley Brice. 1984. *McGill University: For the Advancement of Learning*. Vol. 2, *1895–1971*. Montreal and Kingston: McGill-Queen's University Press.
Gagnon, Alain-G. 1993. *Quebec: State and Society*. 2nd ed. Scarborough: Nelson.
The Gazette (Montreal). Various issues.
Geertz, Clifford. 1963. *Old Societies and New States: The Quest for Modernity in Asia and Africa*. New York: Collier-Macmillan.
Gellner, Ernest. 1964. *Thought and Change*. London: Weidenfeld and Nicolson.
– 1983. *Nations and Nationalism*. Oxford: Blackwell.
Gellner, Ernest, and Anthony Smith. 1996. "The Nation: Real or Imagined: The Warwick Debates on Nationalism." *Nations and Nationalism* 2: 357–70.
George, Stephen. 1998. *An Awkward Partner: Britain in the European Community*. 3rd ed. Oxford: Oxford University Press.
Geyer, Felix Ed. 1996. *Alienation, Ethnicity and Postmodernism*. London: Greenwood.
Ghosh, Ratna, Rosaline Zinman, and Abdulaziz Talbani. 1995. "Policies Relating to the Education of Cultural Communities in Quebec." *Canadian Ethnic Studies* 27: 18–31.
Gibbins, John R., ed. 1989. *Contemporary Political Culture: Politics in a Postmodern Age*. London: Sage.
Gibbins, Roger, and Guy Laforest. 1998. *Beyond the Impasse toward Reconciliation*. Montreal: IRPP.
Gibbins, Roger, and Neil Nevitte. 1985. "Canadian Political Ideology: A Comparative Analysis." *Canadian Journal of Political Science* 18: 577–98.
Gidengil, Elisabeth. 1990. "Centres and Peripheries: The Political Culture of Dependency." *Canadian Review of Sociology and Anthropology* 27: 23–48.
Gigantès, Philippe. 1995. *Faut-il se quitter pour vivre heureux?* Saint-Laurent: Éditions RD.

Gignac, Jean-Luc. 1997. "Sur le multiculturalisme et la politique de la différence identitaire: Taylor, Walzer, Kymlicka." *Politique et sociétés* 16: 31–65.

Gingras, François-Pierre, and Neil Nevitte. 1984. "The Evolution of Quebec Nationalism." In Alain G. Gagnon, ed., *Quebec: State and Society*. Toronto: Methuen.

The Globe and Mail (Toronto). Various issues.

Godbout, Jacques, ed. 1991. *La participation politique: Leçons des dernières décennies*. Québec: Institut québécois de recherche sur la culture.

Gosling, Jonathan.1996. "The Business of Community." In Sebastian Kramer and Jane Roberts, eds., *The Politics of Attachment: Towards a Secure Society*. London: Free Association Books.

Gougeon, Gilles. 1994. *A History of Quebec Nationalism*. Trans. Louisa Blair, Robert Chodos, and Jane Ubertino. Toronto: James Lorimer.

Gouvernement du Québec. 1979. *Quebec-Canada: A New Deal: The Quebec Government Proposal for a New Partnership between Equals: Sovereignty-Association*. Québec: Éditeur officiel.

– 1985. *Draft Agreement on the Constitution: Proposals by the Government of Quebec*.

– 1995. *Bill 1: An Act Respecting the Sovereignty of Quebec*.

Government of Canada. 1991. *Shaping Canada's Future Together: Proposals*. Ottawa: Ministry of Suppy and Services.

– Parliament. 1992. *Minutes of Proceedings and Evidence of the Special Joint Committee of the Senate and of the House of Commons on a Renewed Canada*. Ottawa: Minister of Supply and Services.

Government Statistical Service. 2000. *The Source of UK Facts and Figures*. London: Stationery Office.

Grant, George. 1965. *Lament for a Nation*. Toronto: McClelland and Stewart.

Greenfeld, Leah. 1992. *Nationalism: Five Roads to Modernity*. Cambridge, Mass.: Harvard University Press.

Greenfield, Howard, et al. 1998. "Inroads Roundtable: Anglophones in Quebec." *Inroads* 7: 115–34.

Guérin, Daniel, and Richard Nadeau. 1998. "Clivage linguistique et vote économique au Canada." *Canadian Journal of Political Science* 31: 557–72.

Guntzel, Ralph P. 1997. "The Motivational Success of Mainstream Québec Separatist Nationalism: A Reevaluation." *Canadian Review of Studies Nationalism* 24: 43–9.

Gwyn, William. 1995. "Political Culture and Constitutionalism Britain." In Daniel Franklin and Michael Braun, eds., *Political Culture and Constitutionalism: A Comparative Approach*. London: ME Sharpe.
Hague, William. 1998. Speech at Dundee, 7 March.
Hahn, Carole L. 1998. *Becoming Political: Comparative Perspectives on Citizenship Education*. Albany: State University of New York Press.
Hall, S. 1996. "Who Needs Identity?" In S. Hall and P. du Gay, eds., *Questions of Cultural Identity*. London: Sage.
Hall, S., and P. du Gay, eds. 1996. *Questions of Cultural Identity*. London: Sage.
Hall, Stuart. 1992. "New Ethnicities." In J. Donald and A. Rattansi, eds., *"Race," Culture and Difference*. London: Sage.
Halman, Loek, and Neil Nevitte, eds. 1996. *Political Value Change in Western Democracies: Integration, Values, Identification and Participation*. Tilburg: Tilburg University Press.
Hartz, Louis. 1964. *The Founding of New Societies: Studies in the History of the United States, Latin America, South Africa, Canada and Australia*. New York: Harcourt Brace.
Harvie, Christopher. 1981. *No Gods and Precious Few Heroes: Scotland 1914–1980*. Toronto: University of Toronto Press.
– 1992. "Scottish Politics." In Tony Dickson and James H. Treble, eds., *People and Society in Scotland*, vol 3, *1914–1990*. Edinburgh: John Donald.
– 1998. *Scotland and Nationalism: Scottish Society and Politics 1707 to the Present*. 3rd ed. London: Routledge.
Hassan, Gerry. 1998. *The New Scotland: Redesigning the State*. London: Fabian Society.
Hassan, Gerry, and Chris Warhurst, eds. 1999. *A Different Future: A Moderniser's Guide to Scotland*. Edinburgh: Big Issue and Centre for Scottish Public Policy.
Hearn, Jonathan. 1998. "The Social Contract: Re-framing Scottish Nationalism." *Scottish Affairs* 23: 14–26.
– 2000. *Claiming Scotland: National Identity and Liberal Culture*. Edinburgh: Polygon.
Heath, Anthony, and Richard Topf. 1987. "Political Culture." In Roger Jowell, Sharon Witherspoon, and Lindsay Brook, eds., *British Social Attitudes: The 1987 Report*. Aldershot: Gower.
Hechter, Michael. 1975. *Internal Colonialism: The Celtic Fringe in British National Development, 1536–1966*. London: Routledge and Kegan Paul.

– 1982. "Internal Colonialism Revisited." *Cencrastus* 10: 8–11.

– 1987. "Nationalism as Group Solidarity." *Ethnic and Racial Studies* 10: 415–26.

Hegel, G.W.F. 1999. *Political Writings*. Cambridge: Cambridge University Press.

Heintzman, Ralph. 1983. "The Political Culture of Quebec, 1840–1960." *Canadian Journal of Political Science* 16: 3–59.

Henchey, Norman. 1972. "Revolution and Education in Quebec." *Canadian Forum* 52: 66–9.

– 1973. "Quebec Education: The Unfinished Revolution." In Terrance Morrison and Anthony Burton, eds., *Options: Reforms and Alternatives for Canadian Education*. Montreal: Holt, Rinehart and Winston.

Henderson, Ailsa. 1999. "Nationalist Constructions of Identity in Scotland and Quebec." *Scottish Affairs* 29: 121–38.

– 2004. "Regional Political Cultures in Canada." *Canadian Journal of Political Science* 37: 595–615.

Henderson, Keith. 1997. *Staying Canadian: The Struggle against UDI*. Montreal: DC Books.

The Herald (Glasgow). Various issues.

Hetherington, Kevin. 1998. *Expressions of Identity. Space, Performance, Politics*. London: Sage.

Hetherington, Marc J. 1998. "The Political Relevance of Political Trust." *American Political Science Review* 92: 791–808.

Hill, Stephen. 1990. "Britain: The dominant Ideology Thesis after a Decade." In Nicholas Abercrombie, Stephen Hill, and Bryan Turner, eds., *Dominant Ideologies*. London: Unwin Hyman.

Hirschman, Albert O. 1970. *Exit, Voice and Loyalty: Responses to the Decline in Firms, Organisations and States*. Cambridge, Mass.: Harvard University Press.

Hobsbawm, E.J. 1990. *Nations and Nationalism since 1789: Programme, Myth, Reality*. Cambridge: Cambridge University Press.

Hobsbawm, Eric, and Terence Ranger, eds. 1983. *The Invention of Tradition*. Cambridge: Cambridge University Press.

Holmes, Jeremy. 1996. "Attachment Theory: A Secure Base for Policy." In Sebastian Kramer and Jane Roberts, eds., *The Politics of Attachment: Towards a Secure Society*. London: Free Association Books.

Horowitz, Gad. 1966. "Conservatism, Liberalism and Socialism in Canada: An Interpretation." *Canadian Journal of Economics and Political Science* 32: 143–70.

– 1977. "The Myth of the Red Tory." *Canadian Journal of Political and Social Theory* 1: 87–8.
– 1985. "Tories, Socialists and the Demise of Canada." In H.D. Forbes, ed., *Canadian Political Thought*. Toronto: Oxford University Press.
Horowitz, Irving Louis. 1996. "The Strange Career of Alienation: How a Concept Is Transformed without Permission of Its Founders." In Felix Geyer, ed., *Alienation, Ethnicity and Postmodernism*. London: Greenwood.
Ignatieff, Michael. 1993. *Blood and Belonging: Journeys into the New Nationalism*. London: BBC Books.
– 1996. "The Narcissism of Minor Difference." In James Littleton, ed., *Clash of Identities: Media, Manipulation, and Politics of the Self*. Scarborough, Ont.: Prentice-Hall Canada.
Iguarta, José. 1974. "A Change in Climate: The Conquest and the *Marchands* of Montreal." In Canadian Historical Association, *Historical Papers*.
Imbeau, Louis M., and Guy Laforest. 1991/2. "Québec's Distinct Socity and the Sense of Nationhood in Canada." *Québec Studies* 12: 13–26.
The Independent. 1996. 23 September.
Inglehart, Ronald. 1977. *Silent Revolution*. Princeton: Princeton University Press.
– 1988. "The Renaissance of Political Culture." *American Political Science Review* 82: 1203–30.
– 1990. *Culture Shift in Advanced Industrial Society*. Princeton: Princeton University Press.
– 1995. "Changing Values, Economic Development and Political Change." *International Social Science Journal* 145: 379–403.
Inglehart, Ronald, Neil Nevitte, and Miguel BasaZez. 1996.. *The North American Trajectory: Cultural, Economic and Political Ties among the United States, Canada, and Mexico*. New York: Aldine De Gruyter.
Innis, Harold. 1930. *The Fur Trade in Canada*. New Haven: Yale University Press.
Jackson, Robert, and Doreen Jackson. 1998. *Politics in Canada: Culture, Institutions, Behaviour and Public Policy*. 4th ed. Scarborough, Ont.: Prentice-Hall Canada.
Jackman, Robert W., and Ross A. Miller. 1996b. "A Renaissance of Political Culture?" *American Journal of Political Science* 40: 632–59.
– 1996a. "The Poverty of Political Culture." *American Journal of Political Science* 40: 697–716.

Jedrej, M.C., and Mark Nuttall. 1995. "Incomers and Locals: Metaphors and Reality in the Re-population of Rural Scotland." *Scottish Affairs* 10: 112–26.

Jenson, Jane. 1995. "What's in a Name? Nationalist Movements and Public Discourse." In Hank Johnston and Bert Klandermands, eds., *Social Movements and Culture*. London: University College London Press.

– 1999. "De la nation à la citoyenneté" *Le Devoir*, 31 July.

Johnson, Daniel. 1996. "Change and Recognition Can Avoid Another Referendum." Speech delivered to the Canada West Foundation.

– 1997. "To Save Canada, Improve It and Acknowledge Quebec in the Constitution." Speech delivered to the Metropolitan Toronto Board of Trade.

Johnson, William. 1994. *A Canadian Myth: Quebec, between Canada and the Illusion of Utopia*. Montreal: Robert Davies.

Johnston, Michael, and Roger Jowell. 1999. "Social Capital and the Social Fabric." In Roger Jowell, John Curtice, Alison Park, and Katarina Thomson, eds., *British Social Attitudes, the 16th Report: Who Shares New Labour Values?* Aldershot: Ashgate.

Joly, Jacques, and Michel Dorval. 1993. *Sondage sur l'opinion publique québécois à l'égard des relations raciales et culturelles*. Québec: MinistPre des communautés culturelles et de l'immigration.

Jowell, Roger, John Curtice, Alison Park, and Katarina Thomson, eds. 1999. *British Social Attitudes, the 16th report: Who Shares New Labour Values?* Aldershot: Ashgate.

Jowell, Roger, and Richard Topf. 1988. "Trust in the Establishment." In R. Jowell, S. Witherspoon, and L. Brook, eds. *British Social Attitudes: The 5th Report*. Brookfield: Gower Publishing.

– 1988/89. "Trust the Establishment." In R. Jowell, S. Witherspoon, and L. Brook, eds., *British Social Attitudes: The Fifth Report*. Aldershot: Gower.

Jowell, Roger, et al. 1997. *British Social Attitudes, the 14th Report: The End of Conservative Values?* Aldershot: Ashgate.

Karmis, Dimitrios, and Alain-G. Gagnon. 1996. "Fédéralisme et identités collectives au Canada et en Belgiuqe: Des itinéraires différents, une fragmentations similaire." *Canadian Journal of Political Science* 29: 435–68.

Kavanagh, Dennis. 1972. *Political Culture*. Basingstoke: Macmillan.

– 1989. "Political Culture in Great Britain: The Decline of the Civic Culture." In Gabriel Almond and Sidney Verba, eds., *The Civic Culture Revisited*. London: Sage.

Keating, Michael. 1995a. "Canada and Quebec: Two Nationalisms in the Global Age." *Scottish Affairs* 11: 14–30.
– 1995b. "Quebec, Scotland, Catalonia: In Search of Semi Sovereignty." *Inroads* 4: 96–107.
– 1996a. *Nations against the State*, London: Macmillan.
– 1996b. "Scotland in the UK: A Dissolving Union?" *Nationalism and Ethnic Politics* 2: 232–57,
– 1997. "The Invention of Regions: Political Restructuring and Territorial Government in Western Europe." *Environment and Planning C: Government and Policy* 15: 383–98.
– 1999. "Regions and International Affairs: Motives, Opportunities and Strategies." *Regional and Federal Studies* 9: 1–16.
Keating, Michael, and David Bleiman. 1979. *Labour and Scottish Nationalism*. London: Macmillan.
Kedourie, Elie. 1994. *Nationalism*. 4th ed. London: Hutchinson.
Kellas, James.1989. *The Scottish Political System*. 4th ed. Cambridge: Cambridge University Press.
Kendrick, S.W. 1989. "Scotland, Social Change and Politics." In D. McCrone, S.W. Kendrick, and P. Straw, eds., *The Making of Scotland*. Edinburgh: Edinburgh University Press.
Kernohan, R.D. 1992. "A Breathing Space in Scotland." *Contemporary Review* 260: 281–6.
– 1994. "The Political Scene in Scotland." *Contemporary Review* 264: 33–7.
King, Maurice, and Janet Hicks. 1994. *The Future of Quebec: Essential Issues*. Huntingdon: Southwest Quebec Publishing.
Kohn, Hans. 1967. *The Idea of Nationalism*. New York: Collier.
Kramer, Sebastian, and Jane Roberts, eds. 1996. *The Politics of Attachment: Towards a Secure Society*. London: Free Association Books.
Kristeva, Julia. 1993. *Nations without Nationalism*. New York: Columbia University Press.
Kymlicka, Will. 1995. *Multicultural Citizenship*. Oxford: Oxford University Press.
Labour Party. 1992a. *It's Time to Get Britain Working Again*.
– 1992b. *It's Time to Get Scotland Moving Again*.
– 1999. Party website at www.labour.org.uk.
Lachapelle, Guy. 1999. "L'américanité des Québécois ou l'émergence d'une identité supranationale." In Michel Seymour, ed., *Nationalité, citoyenneté et solidarité*. Montréal: Liber.

Laclau, Ernesto, ed. 1994. *The Making of Political Identities*. London: Verso.

Laforest, Guy. 1993. "Liberalisme et nationalisme au Canada." In *De la prudence: Textes politiques, 1994–1995*. Montréal: Boréal.

– 1995. *De l'urgence: Textes politiques, 1994–1995*. Montréal: Boréal.

– 1998. "The Need for Dialogue and How to Achieve It." In Guy Laforest and Roger Gibbins, eds., *Beyond the Impasse: Towards Reconciliation*. Montreal: IRPP.

Laforest, Guy, and Roger Gibbins, eds. 1998. *Beyond the Impasse: Towards Reconciliation*. Montreal: IRPP.

Lane, Ruth. 1992. "Political Cutlure: Residual Category of General Theory?" *Comparative Political Studies* 25: 362–87.

Langman, Lauren, and Valerie Scatamburlo. 1996. "The Self Strikes Back: Identity Politics in the Postmodern Age." In Felix Geyer, ed., *Alienation, Ethnicity and Postmodernism*. London: Greenwood.

Laponce, Jean A. 1987. *Languages and Their Territories*. Toronto: University of Toronto Press.

Latouche, Daniel. 1998. "Projecting a Canada-Quebec Partnership on the International Stage: Some Logical Speculations." In Guy Laforest and Roger Gibbins, eds., *Beyond the Impasse: Towards Reconciliation*. Montreal: IRPP.

Lazardsfeld, P, B. Berelson, and H. Gaudet. 1968. *The People's Choice*. 2nd ed. New York: Columbia University Press.

LeDuc, Lawrence. 1998. "The Canadian Federal Election of 1997." *Electoral Studies* 17: 132–7.

Le Duc, Lawrence, and Jon H. Pammett. 1995. "Referendum Voting: Attitudes and Behaviour in the 1992 Constitutional Referendum." *Canadian Journal of Political Science* 28: 5–33.

Legault, Josée. 1992. *L'invention d'une minorité: Les Anglo-Québécois*. Québec: Boréal.

Léger, Jean-Marc, and Marcel Léger. 1990. *Le Québec en question: Une centaine de sondages reflétant le profil des Québécois et Québécoises d'aujourd'hui*. Montréal: Les éditions Quebecor.

Létourneau, Jocelyn. 1997. "Le temps du lieu raconté: Essai sur quelques chronologies récentes relatives à l'histoire du Québec." *International Journal of Canadian Studies* 15: 153–65.

– 1999. "Assumons l'identité québécoise dans sa complexité." *Le Devoir*, 7 August.

Levine, Marc, Louis Balthazar, and Kenneth McRoberts. 1989. "Symposium: Nationalism in Quebec: Past, Present and Future." *Quebec Studies* 8: 119–29.

Levy, Roger. 1990. *Scottish Nationalism at the Crossroads*. Edinburgh: Scottish Academic Press.

Liberal Party of Canada. n.d.. *Philospby, History and Structure*.

– 1997. *Securing Our Future Together: Preparing Canada for the 21st Century*. Ottawa.

Lipset, Seymour Martin. 1968. *Revolution and Counterrevolution*. New York: Basic Books.

– 1986. "Historical Traditions and National Characteristics: A Comparative Analysis of Canada and the United States." *Canadian Journal of Sociology* 11: 113–55.

– 1990. *Continental Divide: The Values and Institutions of the United States and Canada*. New York: Routledge.

Lipset, Seymour Martin, and Stein Rokkan. 1967. "Cleavage Structures, Party Systems and Voter Alignments: An Introduction." In Seymour Lipset and Stein Rokkan, eds., *Party Systems and Voter Alignments: Cross-National Perspectives*. London: Collier-Macmillan.

Littleton, James, ed. 1996. *Clash of Identities: Media, Manipulation and Politics of the Self*. Scarborough, Ont.: Prentice-Hall Canada.

Lynch, Michael. 1992. *Scotland: A New History*. London: Pimlico.

Lynch, Peter. 1996. "The Scottish Constitutional Convention." *Scottish Affairs* 15: 1–31.

– 1998. "Third Party Politics in a Four Party System: The Liberal Democrats in Scotland." *Scottish Affairs* 22: 16–32.

Lyon, Peter. 1983. "Is There an Anglo-Canadian Political Culture?" *Bulletin of Canadian Studies* 6: 95–108.

Macartney, Allan. 1997. *Scotland on the Move*. Edinburgh. SNP.

MacCormick, Neil. 1994. "What Place for Nationalism the Modern World?" In J.L. MacQueen, ed., *In Search of New Constitutions*. Edinburgh: Edinburgh University Press.

– 1998. "The English Constitution, the British State and the Scottish Anomaly." *Scottish Affairs,* Special Issue on Understanding Constitutional Change,129–45.

– ed., 1970. *The Scottish Debate: Essays in Scottish Nationalism*. Oxford: Oxford University Press.

MacInnes, John. 1992. "The Press in Scotland." *Scottish Affairs* 1: 137–49.

– 1998. "The Myth of the Macho Scotsman: Attitudes to Gender, Work and the Family in the UK, Ireland and Europe." *Scottish Affairs* 23: 108–24.

Maclure, Jocelyn. 2000. *Récits identitaires: Le Québec à l'épreuve du pluralisme*. Montréal: Québec Amérique.

– 2003. *Quebec Identity: The Challenge of Pluralism*. Montreal and Kingston: McGill-Queen's University Press.

Maclure, Jocelyn, and Alain-G. Gagnon. 2001. *Repères en mutation: Identité et citoyenneté dans le Québec contemporain*. Montréal: Québec Amérique.

MacMillan, C. Michael. 1990. "Explaining Support for Language Rights: A Comment on 'Political Culture and the Problem of Double Standards.'" *Canadian Journal of Political Science* 23: 531–6.

Macmillan, Joyce. 1999. "Remind Me Who I Am Again." *New Statesman*, 5 July, 30.

Macwhirter, Iain. 1992. "The Disaster That Never Was – the Failure of Scottish Opposition after the 1992 General Election." *Scottish Affairs* 1: 3–8.

– 1993. "The Road to Nowhere: Scotland in Westminster, Parliamentary Session 1992/93." *Scottish Affairs* 4: 11–121.

– 1998. "Will Scottish Parliament Slip into Obscurity? No Chance." *Scotland on Sunday*, 18 January.

Mahler, Gregory S. 1995. "Canada: Two Nations, One State?" In Daniel P. Franklin and Michael J. Baun, eds., *Political Culture and Constitutionalism: A Comparative Approach*. Armonk, NY: M.E. Sharpe.

Marr, Andrew. 1992. "Labour Dilemmas: English Nationalists and Silent Scots." *Scottish Affairs* 1: 9–13.

– 1995. *Ruling Britannia: The Failure and Future of British Democracy*. London: Michael Joseph.

Marsh, Alan. 1977. *Protest and Political Consciousness*. London: Sage.

Marshall, Peter. 1993. "North America's Other Eighteenth Century Constitution." In Thomas J. Barron, Owen Dudley Edwards, and Patricia J. Storey, eds., *Constitutions and National Identity: Proceedings of the Conference on "The Makings of Constitutions and the Development of National Identity" Held in Honour of Professor George Shepperson at the University of Edinburgh, 3–6 July 1987*. Edinburgh: Quadriga.

Martin, Ged. 1993. "The Case against Canadian Confederation 1864–67." In Thomas J. Barron, Owen Dudley Edwards, and Patricia J. Storey, eds., *Constitutions and National Identity: Proceedings of the Conference on "The Makings of Constitutions and the Development of National Identity" Held in Honour of Professor George Shepperson at the University of Edinburgh, 3–6 July 1987*. Edinburgh: Quadriga.

Martin, Pierre. 1994. "Générations poliques, rationalité économique et appui à la souveraineté au Québec." *Canadian Journal of Political Science* 27: 345–59.

– 1998. "Identity, Reference Groups and Values: Dispositions and Choice on the Question of Sovereignty Quebec." Unpublished paper presented at the Annual Meeting of the American Political Sciences Association.

Maslow, Abraham H.. 1968. *Towards a Psychology of Being*. New York: Van Nostrand Reinhold.

Mason, R.A.. 1985. "Scotching the Brut: The Early History of Britain." *History Today* 35: 26–31.

McAllister, Laura. 1998. "The Perils of Community as a Construct for the Political Ideology of Welsh Nationalism." *Government and Opposition* 33: 497–517.

McAndrew, Marie, and Patricia Lamarre. 1996. "The Integration of Ethnic Minority Students Fifteen Years after Bill 101: Linguistic and Cultural Issues Confronting Quebec's French Language Schools." *Canadian Ethnic Studies* 28: 40–63.

McArthur, Colin. 1993. "Scottish Culture: A Reply to David McCrone." *Scottish Affairs* 4: 95–106.

McCann, Lawrence D., ed. 1987. *Heartland and Hinterland: A Geography of Canada*. Scarborough: Prentice Hall.

McConnell, Allan, and Robert Pyper. 1994. "A Committee Again: The First Year of the Revived Select Committee on Scottish Affairs." *Scottish Affairs* 7: 15–31.

McCormick, James, and Graham Leicester. 1998. *Three Nations: Social Exclusion in Scotland*. Edinburgh: Scottish Council Foundation.

McCrone, David. 1984. "Explaining Nationalism: The Scottish Experience." *Ethnic and Racial Studies* 7: 129–37.

– 1992. *Understanding Scotland: The Sociology of a Stateless Nation*. London: Routledge.

– 1993. "Opinion Polls in Scotland July 1991-April 1993." *Scottish Affairs* 4: 125–34.

– 1994a. "Editorial: Who Do We Think We Are?" *Scottish Affairs* 6: 1–4.

– 1994b. "Opinion Polls in Scotland May 1993-June 1994." *Scottish Affairs* 8: 125–35.

– 1995. "Opinion Polls in Scotland July 1994-June 1995." *Scottish Affairs* 12: 141–50.

– 1996. "Opinion Polls in Scotland July 1995-June 1996." *Scottish Affairs* 16: 136–45.
– 1998. *The Sociology of Nationalism: Tomorrow's Ancestors*. London: Routledge.
McCrone, David, and Richard Kiely. 2000. "Nationalism and Citizenship." *Sociology* 34: 19–34.
McCrone, David, and Bethan Lewis. 1999. "The Scottish and Welsh Referendum Campaigns." In Bridget Taylor and Katarina Thomson, eds., *Scotland and Wales: Nations Again?* Cardiff: University of Wales Press.
McCrone, David, Angela Morris, and Richard Kiely. 1995. *Scotland – the Brand: The Making of Scottish Heritage*. Edinburgh: Edinburgh University Press.
McCrone, David, Robert Stewart, Richard Kiely, and Frank Bechhofer. 1998. "Who Are We? Problematising National Identity." *Sociological Review* 46: 629–52.
McEwen, Nicola. 2006. *Nationalism and the State: Welfare and Identity in Scotland and Quebec*. Bern: Peter Lang.
McKenzie, Robert, and Alan Silver. 1967. "The Delicate Experiment: Industrialism, Conservatism, and Working-Class Tories in England." In Seymour Lipset and Stein Rokkan, eds., *Party Systems and Voter Alignments: Cross-National Perspectives*. London: Collier-Macmillan.
McKim, Robert, and Jeff McMahan, eds. 1997. *The Morality of Nationalism*. Oxford: Oxford University Press.
McLeod Arnopoulos, Sheila, and Dominique Clift. 1984. *The English Fact in Quebec*. 2nd ed. Montreal and Kingston: McGill-Queen's University Press.
McLetchie, David. 2003. Address to the spring conference of the Scottish Conservative and Unionist Party.
McRae, K.D. 1978. "Louis Hartz's Concept of the Fragment Society and Its Applications to Canada." *Canadian Studies* 5: 17–30.
McRae, Kenneth. 1964. "The Structure of Canadian History." In Louis Hartz, ed., *The Founding of New Societies*. New York: Harcourt Brace and World.
McRoberts, Kenneth. 1984. "The Sources of Neo-Nationalism in Quebec." *Ethnic and Racial Studies* 7: 19–54.
– 1988. *Quebec: Social Change and Political Crisis*. Toronto: McClelland & Stewart.
– 1993. *Quebec: Social Change and Political Crisis*. 3rd ed. Toronto: McClelland and Stewart.

– 1997. *Misconceiving Canada*. Toronto: Oxford University Press.

Mead, Margaret. 1964. *Continuities in Cultural Evolution*. New Haven: Yale University Press.

Meadwell, Hudson. 1989. "Cultural and Instrumental Approaches to Ethnic Nationalism." *Ethnic and Racial Studies* 12: 309–28.

Melucci, Alberto. 1989. *Nomads of the Present: Social Movements and Individual Needs in Contemporary Society*. London: Hutchinson Radius.

– 1995. "The Process of Collective Identity." In Hank Johnston and Bert Klandermans, eds., *Social Movements and Culture*. London: University College London Press.

Mendelsohn, Matthew. 1999. "Measuring National Identity and Patterns of Attachment: The Case of Quebec." Unpublished paper presented at the "Ethnicity and Culture: The Reciprocal Influences Conference," Georgia, USA.

– 2002. "Measuring National Identity and Patterns of Attachment: The Case of Quebec and Nationalist Mobilization." *Nationalism and Ethnic Politics* 8: 72–94.

Menzies, Robert. 1942. *The Forgotten People*. Robertson and Mullens.

Michael, Mike. 1996. *Constructing Identity*. London: Sage.

Milbrath, Lester W. 1965. *Political Participation: How and Why Do People Get Involved in Politics*. Chicago: Rand McNally.

Mill, John Stuart. 1992. *On Liberty*. New York: Legal Classics Library.

Miller, Jim. 1996. "Language Attitudes and Scottish Inferiority." *Scottish Affairs* 15: 128–33.

Miller, W.L. 1983. "The Denationalisation of British Politics: The Re-emergence of the Periphery." *West European Politics* 6: 103–29.

Miller, William, Annis May Timpson, and Michael Lessnoff. 1996. *Political Culture in Contemporary Britain: People and Politicians, Principles and Practice*. Oxford: Clarendon.

Mitchell, James. 1990. *Conservatives and the Union*. Edinburgh: Edinburgh University Press.

– 1996. *Strategies for Self-Government: The Campaigns for a Scottish Parliament*. Edinburgh: Polygon.

– 2004. *Governing Scotland: The Invention of Administrative Devolution*. New York: Palgrave Macmillan.

– 2006. "Evolution and Devolution: Citizenship, Institutions and Public Policy." *Publius* 36: 153–68.

Moghaddam, Fathali, Donald Taylor, Peggy Tchoryk Pelletier, and Marc Chepanek. 1994. "The Warped Looking Glass: How Minorities

Perceive Themselves, Believe They Are Perceived, and Are Actually Perceived by Majority Group Members in Quebec, Canada." *Canadian Ethnic Studies* 26: 112–23.

Moise, Léna Celine, and Richard Y. Bourhis. 1994. "Language et ethnicité: Communication interculturelle Montréal, 1977–1991" *Canadian Ethnic Studies* 26: 86–107.

Moreno, Luis. 1988. "Scotland and Catalonia: The Path to Home Rule." In D. McCrone and A. Brown, eds., *The Scottish Government Yearbook*. Edinburgh: The Unit for the Study of Government in Scotland.

– 2006. "Scotland, Catalonia, Europeanization and the Moreno Question." *Scottish Affairs* 54: 1–21.

Morton, Graeme. 1999. *Unionist Nationalism: Governing Urban Scotland, 1830–1860*. East Linton: Tuckwell.

Mowlam, Mo. 1996. "The Political Context." In Sebastian Kramer and Jane Roberts, eds., *The Politics of Attachment: Towards a Secure Society*. London: Free Association Books.

Nadeau, Richard, and Christopher Fleury. 1994. "Gains linguistiques anticipés et appui à la souveraineté du Québec." *Canadian Journal of Political Science*: 35–50.

Nairn, Tom. 1977. *The Break-up of Britain*. London: Verso.

– 1988. *Enchanted Glass: Britain and Its Monarchy*. London: Radius.

Nemni, Max. 1994. *The Politics of Secession in Quebec: The Case of the Bélanger-Campeau Commission*. Québec: Université Laval.

Nesbitt-Larking, Paul. 1998a. "The Americanization of Canadian Political Culture." Unpublished paper presented at the British Association of Canadian Studies Annual Conference.

– 1998b. "Canadian Political Culture: The Problem of Americanization." In Mark Charlton and Paul Barker, eds., *Crosscurrents: Contemporary Political Issues*. 3rd ed. Toronto: ITP Nelson.

Nevitte, Neil. 1995. "The Dynamics of Canadian Political Culture(s)." In Robert Krause and R.H. Wagenberg, eds., *Introductory Readings in Canadian Government and Politics*. 2nd ed. Toronto: Copp Clark.

– 1996. *The Decline of Deference*. Peterborough: Broadview.

Nevitte, Neil, André Blais, Elisabeth Gidengil, and Richard Nadeau. 2000. *Unsteady State: The 1997 Canadian Federal Election*. Toronto: Oxford University Press.

Nevitte, Neil, and Roger Gibbins. 1990. *New Elites in Old States: Ideologies in the Anglo-American Democracies*. Toronto: Oxford University Press.

Newman, Saul. 1989. "The Ethnic Dilemma: The Rise of Ethno Regional Political Parties in Scotland, Belgium and Quebec." PhD thesis, Princeton University.

Nicholson, George. 1996. "Place and Local Identity." In Sebastian Kramer and Jane Roberts, eds., *The Politics of Attachment: Towards a Secure Society*, London: Free Association Books.

Norris, Pippa. 1995. *Electoral Change Britain since 1945*. Oxford: Blackwell.

Nunavut Implementation Commission. 1995. *Footprints in New Snow*. Iqaluit.

Office of National Statistics. 1999. *Regional Trends 34*. London: Stationery Office.

Office of the Commission of Official Languages. 1974–97. Annual reports.

Ouellet, Fernand. 1966. *Histoire économique et sociale du Québec, 1760–1850*. Montréal: Fides.

Ouseley, Sir Herman. 1998. "Will the New Scotland Be a Fortress of Intolerance and Racism or a Country at Ease with Its Ethnic Diversity." *Scotland on Sunday*, 8 February.

Pammett, Jon H. 1997. "The Voters Decide." In Alan Frizzell and Jon H. Pammett, eds., *The Canadian General Election of 1997*. Toronto: Dundurn.

Pammett, Jon H., and Michael S. Whittington, eds. 1976. *The Foundations of Political Culture: Political Socialization in Canada*. Toronto: Macmillan.

Parizeau, Jacques. 1991. "Business Relations between a Sovereign Quebec and the United States." Speech delivered to the New York Forum on International Business, 26 February.

– 1995a. *Votre OUI sera celui de la confiance et de la fierté*. Speech delivered on 29 October.

– 1995b. Speech delivered on 30 October.

– 1997. "Who's Afraid of Sovereignty Association?" Speech delivered to the Empire Club of Canada and the Canadian Club of Toronto.

Parry, Geraint. 1969. *Political Elites*. London: Allen & Unwin.

– ed. 1972. *Participation in Politics*. Manchester: Manchester University Press.

Parry, Geraint, George Moyser, and Neil Day. 1992. *Political Participation and Democracy in Britain*. Cambridge: Cambridge University Press.

Parry, Richard. 1995. "Review: Daring to Be Unionist." *Scottish Affairs* 12: 101–4.

Parsons, Talcott. 1969. *Politics and Social Structure*. New York: Free Press

Parti libérale du Québec (PLQ). n.d. *La philosophie libérale*. Montréal.

– 1980. *A New Canadian Federation*. Montréal.

– 1994. *Agir pour le Québec*. Québec.

– 1997. *Reconnaissance et interdépendance*. Québec.

– 1998a. *Garantir l'avenir: Propositions adoptées*. Québec.

– 1998b. *Liberal Values and the Modern-Day Quebec*.

– 1998c. *Mémoire du Parti libérale du Québec à la commission des institutions*. Québec.

– 2001. *A Project for Quebec: Affirmation, Autonomy and Leadership*. Montreal.

– 2007. *Le Programme du Parti libérale du Québec*.

Parti Québécois (PQ). 1987. *Québec: Parti Québécois*. Quebec: Parti Québécois.

– 1990. *La Souveraineté: Pourquoi? Comment?* Service de communications du PQ.

– 1993. *Report of the PQ Task Force on the Status of the English-Speaking Community in a Sovereign Quebec*. Montreal.

– 1994a. *A Challenging Project for Quebec: Summary of the PQ Platform*. Montreal.

– 1994b. *Des idées pour mon pays: Programme du parti québécois*. Québec.

– 1998. *Le Plan à du gouvernement de Jean Chrétien et de Stéphane Dion: Intimidation et ingérence*. Québec.

– 1999. *Travailler pour la souveraineté: Pourqoui maintenant*? Québec.

Pateman, Carole. 1989. "The Civic Culture: A Philosophic Critique." In Gabriel Almond and Sidney Verba, eds., *The Civic Culture Revisited*. London: Sage.

Paterson, Lindsay. 1993. "Democracy and the Curriculum in Scotland." *Edinburgh Review* 90: 21–8.

– 1994a. *The Autonomy of Modern Scotland*. Edinburgh: Edinburgh University Press.

– 1994b. "How Distinctive Is Scottish Higher Education?" *Scottish Affairs* 7: 86–92.

The Patriot for Scotland. Various issues.

Pattie, Charles, David Denver, James Mitchell, and Hugh Bochel. 1998. "The 1997 Scottish Referendum: An Analysis of the Results" *Scottish Affairs* 22: 1–15.

Payne, Peter L. 1996. "The Economy." In T.J. Devine and R.J. Finlay, eds., *Scotland in the Twentieth Century*. Edinburgh: Edinburgh University Press.

Peacock, Anthony A.. 1998. "Socialism as Nationalism: Why the Alleged Americanization of Canadian Political Culture Is a Fraud." In Mark Charlton and Paul Barker, eds., *Crosscurrents: Contemporary Political Issues.* 3rd ed. Toronto: ITP Nelson.

Peele, G. 1983. "The State and Civil Liberties." In Henry Drucker et al., eds., *Developments in British Politics.* London: Macmillan.

Pelletier, Gérard. 1988. "Quebec: Different but in Step with North America." *Daedalus* 177: 265–82.

Pelletier, Réjean. 1989. *Partis politiques et société québécoise: De Duplessis à Bourassa 1944–1970.* Québec: Amérique.

– 1997. "Postmaterialism and the Crisis of Parties in Quebec: Party Workers between New Social Movements Activists and Party Supporters." *Quebec Studies* 24: 74–93.

Pelletier, Réjean, and Daniel Guérin. 1996. "Postmatialisme et clivages partisans au Québec: Les partis sont-ils différents?" *Canadian Journal of Political Science* 9: 71–109.

Penrose, Jan. 1993. "Reification in the Name of Change: The Impact of Nationalism on Social Constructions of Nation, People and Place in Scotland and the United Kingdom." In Peter Jackson and Jan Penrose, eds., *Constructions of Race, Place and Nation.* London: University College London.

Périn, Robert. 1993. "Clerics and the Constitution: The Quebec Church and Minority Rights in Canada." In Thomas J. Barron, Owen Dudley Edwards, and Patricia J. Storey, eds., *Constitutions and National Identity: Proceedings of the Conference on "The Makings of Constitutions and the Development of National Identity" Held in Honour of Professor George Shepperson at the University of Edinburgh, 3–6 July 1987.* Edinburgh: Quadriga.

Pfaff, William. 1996. "The Politics of Exclusion." In James Littleton, ed., *Clash of Identities: Media, Manipulation, and Politics of the Self.* Scarborough, Ont.: Prentice-Hall Canada.

Pinard, Maurice, and Richard Hamilton. 1986. "Motivational Dimensions in the Quebec Independence Movement: A Test of a New Model." *Research Social Movements, Conflicts and Change* 9:

Piroth, Scott. 1998. "Individual Values and Popular Support for an Independent Quebec." Unpublished paper presented at the American Political Science Association Annual Meeting.

Pittock, Murray. *The Invention of Scotland.* New York: Routledge, 1991.

Plamenatz, J. 1976. "Two types of Nationalism." In E. Kamenka, ed., *Nationalism: The Nature and Evolution of an Idea*. London: Edward Arnold.

Pomeyrols, Catherine. 1997. *Les intellectuels québécois: Formation et engagements 1919–1939*. Paris: L'Harmattan.

Porter, John A. 1965. *The Vertical Mosaic: An Analysis of Social Class and Power in Canada*. Toronto: University of Toronto Press.

Portes, Alejandro. 1998. "Social Capital: Its Origins and Applications in Modern Sociology." *Annual Review of Sociology* 24: 1–24.

Portes, Alejandro, and Landolt, Patricia. 1996. "The Downside of Social Capital." *The American Prospect* 26: 18–21.

Preece, Rod. 1977. "The Myth of the Red Tory." *Canadian Journal of Political and Social Theory* 1: 3–28.

– 1978. "Liberal-Conservatism and Feudalism Canadian Politics: A Response to Christian." *Canadian Journal of Political and Social Theory* 2: 135–41.

La Presse. Various issues.

Preston, Richard. 1985. "Regionalism and National Identity: Canada." In Reginald Berry and James Acheson, eds., *Regionalism and National Identity*. Christchurch: University of Canterbury.

Product. 2000. Issue 2.

Putnam, Robert. 1995a. "Bowling Alone: America's Declining Social Capital." *Journal of Democracy* 6: 65–78.

– 1995b. "Tuning In, Tuning Out: The Strange Disappearance of Social Capital in America." *PS* 28: 664–83.

– 1996. "The Strange Disappearance of Civic America." *The American Prospect* 24: 34–48.

Putnam, Robert, with R. Leonardi and R. Nanetti. 1993. *Making Democracy Work: Civic Traditions in Modern Italy*. Princeton: Princeton University Press.

Pye, Lucian. 1965. "Introduction: Political Culture and Political Development." In Lucian Pye and Sidney Verba, eds., *Political Culture and Political Development*. Princeton: Princeton University Press.

Pye, Lucian, and Sidney Verba, eds. 1965. *Political Culture and Political Development*. Princeton: Princeton University Press.

Ramet, Sabrina Petra. 1996. "Nationalism and the 'Idiocy' of the Countryside: The Case of Serbia." *Ethnic and Racial Studies* 19: 70–85.

Rawkins, Phillip. 1984. "The Role of the State in the Transformation of the Nationalist Movements of the 1960s: Comparing Wales and Quebec." *Ethnic and Racial Studies* 7: 86–105.

Rebick, Judy. 1996. "Bridging Identity: A Creative Response to Identity Politics." In James Littleton, ed., *Clash of Identities: Media, Manipulation, and Politics of the Self*: Scarborough, Ont.: Prentice-Hall Canada.

Reform Party. 1998. A *Fresh Start for Canadians: A 6 Point Plan to Build a Brighter Future Together.*

– 1999. *The Blue Book: Principles and Policies of the Reform Party of Canada*. Calgary.

Reid, George. 1995. "Oh to Be in Britain?" 10th Donaldson lecture, 22 September.

Reisinger, William M. 1995. "The Renaissance of a Rubric: Political Culture as Concept and Theory." *International Journal of Public Opinion Research* 7: 328–52..

Renan, Ernest. 1882. *Qu'est-ce qu'une nation?* Paris: Calmann-Levy.

Richard, Anthony H.. 1984. "Ethnic Nationalism and Postindustrialism." *Ethnic and Racial Studies* 7: 4–18.

Richler, Mordecai. 1991. *Oh Canada! Oh Québec! Requiem for a Divided Country*. Toronto: Penguin.

Richmond, Anthony H.. 1984. "After the Referenda: The Future of Ethnic Nationalism in Britain and Canada: Editorial Introduction." *Ethnic and Racial Studies* 7: 1–3.

Robinson, W. Peter, ed.. 1996. *Social Groups and Identities: Developing the Legacy of Henri Tajfel.* Oxford: Butterworth Heinemann.

Robitaille, Antoine. 1999. Plenary Address to the Triennial Conference of the Nordic Association of Canadian Studies, August.

Rocher, François, and Daniel Salée. 1997. "Liberalisme et tensions identitaires: Éléments de reflexion sur le désarroi des sociétés modernes." *Politiques et sociétés* 16: 3–30.

Rose, Richard. 1965. "England: A Traditionally Modern Political Culture." In Lucian Pye and Sidney Verba, eds., *Political Culture and Political Development*. Princeton: Princeton University Press.

Rose, Richard, and I. McAllister. 1986. *Voters Begin to Choose*. London: Sage.

– 1990. *The Loyalties of Voters*. London: Sage.

Rosie, George. 2000. "Who's Got Their Snout in the Trough." *Sunday Herald Seven Days*, 12 March, 1, 5.

Rothwell, Hayley. 1998. "Bordering on Conflict." *Edinburgh Student*, 19 November, 8.

Rousseau, Roger. 1985. "Regionalism and National Identity: Canada and New Zealand." In Reginald Berry and James Acheson, eds.,

Regionalism and National Identity. Christchurch: University of Christchurch.

Roy, Jean-Louis. 1987. "Nationalism in Quebec in the 1980s: After Failure, the Challenge of Relevance." In Michael D. Behiels, ed., *Quebec since 1945: Selected Readings*. Toronto: Copp Clark Pitman.

Royal Commission of Inquiry on Constitutional Problems. 1956. *Final Report*. Québec.

Royle, Trevor. 1999. "Are You a True Brit?" *Sunday Herald Seven Days*, 26 September, 2.

Rudin, Ronald. 1985. *The Forgotten Quebecers: A History of English-Speaking Quebec 1759–1980*. Québec: Institut québécois de recherche sur la culture.

– 1997. *Making History in Twentieth-Century Quebec*. Toronto: University of Toronto Press.

Russell, Peter H. 1993. *Constitutional Odyssey: Can Canadians Become a Sovereign People*? 2nd ed. Toronto: University of Toronto Press.

Rustin, Michael. 1996. "Attachment Context." In Sebastian Kramer and Jane Roberts, eds., *The Politics of Attachment: Towards a Secure Society*. London: Free Association Books.

Saggar, Shamit. 1998. *The General Election 1997: Ethnic Minorities and Electoral Politics*. London: Commission for Racial Equality.

Said, Edward W. 1995. *Orientalism*. London: Penguin.

Salée, Daniel. 1997. "Quebec Sovereignty and the Challenge of Linguistic and Ethnocultural Minorities: Identity, Difference and the Politics of Ressentiment." *Québec Studies* 24: 6–23.

Salmond, Alex. 1995a. *Address to the Annual Conference*. Edinburgh: SNP.

– 1995b. *The Making of the Foundations*. Williamson Memorial Lecture. Edinburgh: SNP.

– 1996. *Address to the Annual Conference*. 27 September. Edinburgh: SNP.

– 1997. *Address to the Annual Conference*. 26 September. Edinburgh: SNP.

– 1998a. "The New Scotland: Politics, Identity, Culture and the Future of Scotland." Speech, 31 May.

– 1998b. *Address to the Annual Conference*. 29 September. Edinburgh: SNP.

Samuel, Raphael. 1989. *Patriotism: The Making and Unmaking of British National Identity*. London: Routledge and Kegan Paul.

Sarra-Bournet, Michel. 1999a. "History and the Construction of National Identities: The Case of the Reform of the Curriculum in Quebec." Unpublished paper presented at the Organization of American Historians Annual Meeting.

– 1999b. "Repackaging Collective Memory: National History and the Challenge of Diversity." Unpublished paper presented at the New York State Political Science Association Annual Conference.

Sarup, Madan. 1996. *Identity, Culture and the Postmodern World.* Edinburgh: Edinburgh University Press.

Savage, Robert L. 1981. "Looking for Political Subcultures: A Critique of the Rummage-Sale Approach." *Western Political Quarterly* 34: 331–6.

Schacht, Richard. 1996. "Alienation Redux: From Here to Postmodernity." In Felix Geyer, ed., *Alienation, Ethnicity and Postmodernism.* London: Greenwood.

Schiller, Nina Glick. 1996. "Power/Identity/Resistance." *Identities* 2: 321–3.

Schudson, Michael. 1994. "Culture and the Integration of National Societies." *International Social Science Journal* 139: 63–83.

Scotland on Sunday. Various issues.

The Scotsman (Edinburgh). Various issues.

Scott, Alan. 1990. *Ideology and New Social Movements.* London: Unwin Hyman.

Scott, Paul H. 1991. *Towards Independence: Essays on Scotland.* Edinburgh: Polygon.

– 1993. *Scotland: A Concise Cultural History*. Edinburgh: Mainstream.

Scottish Conservative and Unionist Association (SCUA). 1979. *The Conservative Manifesto for Scotland.* Edinburgh.

– 1992. *The Best Future for Scotland.* Edinburgh.

– 1997. *Fighting for Scotland: The Scottish Conservative and Unionist Manifesto 1997.* Edinburgh.

Scottish Conservative and Unionist Party (SCUP). 1999. *Scotland First.* Edinburgh.

– 2003. *Time to Do Something about It.* Edinburgh.

Scottish Constitutional Commission. 1994. *Further Steps: Towards a Scheme for Scotland's Parliament.* Edinburgh: COSLA.

Scottish Constitutional Convention. 1990. *Towards Scotland's Parliament.* Edinburgh: COSLA.

– 1995. *Scotland's Parliament, Scotland's Right.* Edinburgh.

Scottish Council for Voluntary Organisations. 1997. *A Guide to the Voluntary Sector in Scotland.* Edinburgh.

– 1999. *Newsletter*, issue 38. Edinburgh.

Scottish Executive. 1999. *Report of the Commission on Local Government and the Scottish Parliament: The Scottish Executive's Response.* Edinburgh.

Scottish Labour Party. 1992. *It's Time to Get Scotland Moving Again. Labour's Election Manifesto April 1992*. Glasgow.
– 1998. A *Lifetime of Opportunity*. Glasgow: SLP, 1998.
– 2003. *On Your Side*. Glasgow.
Scottish Liberal Democrats. 1997. *Make the Difference*. Edinburgh.
– 1999. *Raising the Standard*. Edinburgh.
Scottish National Party (SNP). 1983. *Choose Scotland: The Challenge of Independence*. Edinburgh.
– 1987. *Play the Scottish Card*. Edinburgh.
– 1992. *Independence in Europe: Make It Happen Now*. Edinburgh.
– 1997a. *Forscythed*. Edinburgh. Leaflet.
– 1997b. *Yes We Can Win the Best for Scotland*. Edinburgh.
– 1999. *Compassion, Enterprise, Democracy*. Edinburgh.
– 2001. *Heart of the Manifesto*. Edinburgh.
– Parliamentary Group. 1998. *Who Benefits from Britain? An Analysis of Spending within the UK with a Particular Focus on the Home Counties and London*. Edinburgh.
– Research Dept. 1995. *Citizens not Subjects*. Edinburgh.
– 1996. *Scotland's Budget Surplus within the UK 1979/80–1993/94*. Edinburgh.
Scottish Office. 1999. "The European Social Fund." Available at www.scotland.gov.uk.
– 2000. "New Zone to Boost Employment Glasgow." 9 March news release.
– Education and Industry Department. 1998. *Gaelic Scotland Factsheet*. Edinburgh.
Scottish Watch. 1993. *The Struggle for Scotland*.
– 1994. *The New Scottish Clearances*.
Scowen, Reed. 1991. *A Different Vision: The English in Quebec in the 1990s*. Don Mills: Maxwell Macmillan.
Seawright, David. 1996. "The Scottish Unionist Party: What's in a Name?" *Scottish Affairs* 14: 90–102.
– 1998. "Scottish Unionism: An East-West Divide?" *Scottish Affairs* 23: 54–72.
Séguin, M. 1970. *La nation "canadienne" et l'agriculture. 1760–1850*. Trois-RiviPres: Boréal Express.
Séguin, Rhéal. 2007. "Charest to Play up Québec's Nation Status." *Globe and Mail*. 19 February.
Seton-Watson, Hugh. 1977. *Nations and States: An Enquiry into the Origins of Nations and the Politics of Nationalism*. London: Methuen.

Seymour, Michel. 1999a. *Nationalité, citoyenneté et solidarité*. Montréal: Liber.

– 1999b. *La nation en question: Essai*. Montréal: L'Hexagone.

Shafir, Gershon, and Yoav Peled. 1998. "Citizenship and Stratification in an Ethnic Democracy." *Ethnic and Racial Studies* 21: 408–27.

Shils, Edward. 1982. *The Constitution of Society*. Chicago: University of Chicago Press.

Silver, Arthur. 1997. *The French Canadian Idea of Confederation*. 2nd ed. Toronto: University of Toronto Press.

Simeon, Richard, and Donald Blake. 1980. "Regional Preferences: Citizen's Views of Public Policy." In David Elkins and Richard Simeon, eds., *Small Worlds: Provinces and Parties in Canadian Political Life*. Toronto: Methuen.

Simeon, Richard, and David J. Elkins. 1974. "Provincial Political Cultures in Canada." *Canadian Journal of Political Science* 7: 397–437.

– 1980. "Provincial Political Cultures in Canada." In David Elkins and Richard Simeon, eds., *Small Worlds: Provinces and Parties in Canadian Political Life*. Toronto: Methuen.

Sinclair, Douglas. 1997. "Local Government and a Scottish Parliament." *Scottish Affairs* 19: 14–21.

Smith, Anthony D. 1971. *Theories of Nationalism*. London: Duckworth.

– 1981. *The Ethnic Revival*. Cambridge: Cambridge University Press.

– 1986. *The Ethnic Origins of Nations*. Oxford: B. Blackwell.

– 1988. "The Myth of the 'Modern Nation' and the Myths of Nations." *Ethnic and Racial Studies*. 11: 1–26.

– 1991. *National Identity*. London: Penguin.

– 1992a. "Chosen Peoples: Why Ethnic Groups Survive." *Ethnic and Racial Studies* 15: 436–56.

– 1992b. "Nationalism and the Historians." *International Journal of Comparative Sociology* 33: 58–81.

Smith, Donald, ed.. 1998. *Beyond Two Solititudes*. Halifax: Fernwood.

Smith, Leslie, ed. 1984. *The Making of Britain: The Dark Ages*. London: Macmillan.

Smith, M.G. 1985. "Race and Ethnic Relations as Matters of Rational Choice." *Ethnic and Racial Studies* 8: 484–99.

Smith, Maurice. 1994. *Paper Lions: The Scottish Press and National Identity*. Edinburgh: Polygon.

– 1995. "The Scottish Press." *Scottish Affairs* 10: 1–5.

Smout, T.C. 1986. *A Century of the Scottish People 1830–1950*. New Haven: Yale University Press.

– 1994. "Perspectives on the Scottish Identity." *Scottish Affairs* 6: 101–13.

Sniderman, Paul M., Joseph F. Fletcher, Peter H. Russell, and Philip E. Tetlock. 1989. "Political Cutlure and the Problem of Double Standards: Mass and Elite Attitudes toward Language Rights in the Canadian Charter of Rights and Freedoms." *Canadian Journal of Political Science* 22: 259–84.

Soldatos, Panayotis. 1979. *Nationalisme et intégration dans le contexte canadien.* Montréal: Université de Montréal.

Special Joint Committee of the Senate and the House of Commons on a Renewed Canada. 1991. *Submissions to the Commission.* Ottawa: Minister of Supply and Services.

– 1992. *A Renewed Canada: The Report of the Special Joint Committee of the Senate and the House of Commons.* Ottawa: Queen's Printer.

Statistics Canada. [1986?]. *Census '86: Montreal.* Ottawa: Minister of Supply and Services.

– 1999. *Census '96.* Ottawa: Minister of Supply and Services.

– 2000. *International Trade.* Available at www.statcan.ca.

Stein, Michael. 1978. "Le bill 22 et la population non-francophone au Québec: Les attitudes du groupe minoritaire face à la législation de la langue." *Canadian Review of Studies in Nationalism* 5: 163–87.

Stevenson, Garth. 1998. "Between a Rock and a Hard Place: Anglophones in Quebec's National Assembly." *Inroads* 7: 135–45.

Strathclyde Commission. 1998. *Made in Scotland: A Consultation Paper for Reform of the Scottish Conservative and Unionist Party.* Edinburgh.

Street, John. 1994. "Review Article: Political Culture – from Civic Culture to Mass Culture." *British Journal of Political Science* 24: 94–114.

Studlar, Donley T., and Ian McAllister. 1988. "Nationalism in Scotland and Wales: A Post-industrial phenomenon?" *Ethnic and Racial Studies* 11: 48–62.

Surlin, Stuart H. 1995. "TV, Values, and Culture in U.S.-Canadian Borderland Cities: A Shared Perspective." *Canadian Journal of Communications* 16:431–9.

Surridge, Paula, Lindsay Paternson, Alice Brown, and David McCrone. 1998. "The Scottish Electorate and the Scottish Parliament." *Scottish Affairs,* Special Issue on Understanding Constitutional Change, 38–60.

Swinney, John. 2002. Address to the Annual Conference of the SNP.

Synnott, Anthony, and David Howes. 1998. "Canada's Visible Minorities: Identity and Representation." In V. Amit-Talai and C. Knowles, eds., *Resituating Identities: The Politics of Race, Culture and Ethnicity*. Peterborough: Broadview Press.

Tajfel, H., ed. 1982. *Social Identity and Intergroup Relations*. Cambridge: Cambridge University Press.

Tajfel, H., and J.C. Turner. 1979. "An Integrative Theory of Intergroup Conflict." In W.G. Austin and S. Worchel, eds., *The Social Psychology of Intergroup Relations*. Monterey: Brooks/Cole.

Talman, James J. 1959. *Basic Documents in Canadian History*. Princeton: Van Nostrand.

Talmon, J.L.. 1981. *The Myth of the Nation and the Vision of Revolution: The Origins of Ideological Polarisation in the Twentieth Century*. London: Secker & Warburg.

Tarrow, Sidney. 1996. "Making Social Science Work across Space and Time: A Critical Reflection on Robert Putnam's *Making Democracy Work*." *American Political Science Review* 90: 389–97.

– 1998. *Power Movement: Social Movements and Contentious Politics*. 2nd ed. Cambridge: Cambridge University Press.

Task Force on Canadian Unity. 1979. *A Future Together: Observations and Recommendations*. Ottawa: Ministry of Supply and Services.

Taylor, Bridget, and Katarina Thomson, eds. 1999. *Scotland and Wales: Nations Again?* Cardiff: University of Wales Press.

Taylor, Charles. 1989. *Sources of the Self: The Making of the Modern Identity*. Cambridge: Cambridge University Press.

– 1991. "Shared and Divergent Values." In Ronald L. Watts and Douglas M. Brown, eds., *Options for a New Canada*. Toronto: University of Toronto Press.

– 1992. *Multiculturalism and "the Politics of Recognition": An Essay*. Princeton: Princeton University Press.

– 1995. *Philosophical Arguments*. Cambridge: Harvard University Press.

– 1997. "Nationalism and Modernity." In Robert McKim and Jeff McMahan, eds., *The Morality of Nationalism*. Oxford: Oxford University Press.

– 1999. "De la nation culturelle à la nation politique." *Le Devoir*, 19 June.

Taylor, Donald M., and Ronald J. Sigal. 1982. "Defining 'Québécois': The Role of Ethnic Heritage, Language and Political Orientation." *Canadian Ethnic Studies* 14: 59–70.

Taylor, Ian. 1996. "Is There an Alternative to the Gobal Society." In Sebastian Kramer and Jane Roberts, eds., *The Politics of Attachment: Towards a Secure Society*. London: Free Association Books.

Teghtsoonian, Katherine Anne. 1988. *Institutional Structure and Government Policy: Responding to Regionalism in Quebec, Scotland and Wales*. PhD thesis, Stanford University. Ann Arbor: University Microfilms International.

Tetley, William. 1982. "The English and Language Legislation: A Personal History." In Gary Caldwell and Éric Waddell, eds., *The English of Quebec from Majority to Minority Status*. Quebec: Institut québécois de recherche sur la culture.

Thomson, J.M. 1995. "Scots Law, National Identity and the European Union." *Scottish Affairs* 10: 25–34.

Tierney, Stephen. 2004. *Constitutional Law and National Pluralism*. Oxford: Oxford University Press.

Tocqueville, Alexis de. 1945. *Democracy in America*. New York: Vintage.

Touraine, Alain. 1995. "Beyond Social Movements?" In Stanford M. Lyman, ed., *Social Movements: Critiques, Concepts, Case-Studies*. New York: New York University Press.

Trent, John E. 1979. "La réforme constitutionnelle au Canada: Sa raison d'être, sa forme et se défis." In Panayotis Soldatos, ed., *Nationalisme et intégration dans le contexte canadien*. Montréal: Université de Montréal.

– 1984. "The Quebec Cauldron: A Recent Account." In Alain G. Gagnon, ed., *Quebec: State and Society*. Toronto: Methuen.

– 1997. "Perspectives on Canadian Politics: Accomplishments, Challenges, Prospects." *Zeitschrift fur Kanada-Studien* 17: 22–37.

– 1998. "Neither Integration nor Disintegration: Agenda for the Renewal of the Canadian Federation." Unpublished paper presented at the International Political Science Association Round Table on "Integration and Disintegration"

Trent, John E., Robert Young, and Guy Lachapelle, eds. 1996. *Québec-Canada: What Is the Path Ahead?* Ottawa: University of Ottawa Press.

Trevor-Roper, Hugh. 1983. "The Invention of Tradition: The Highland Tradition of Scotland." In Eric Hobsbawm and Terence Ranger, eds., *The Invention of Tradition*. Cambridge: Cambridge University Press.

Triandafyllidou, Anna. 1998. "National Identity and the 'Other.'" *Ethnic and Racial Studies* 21: 593–612.

Trudeau, Pierre Elliott. 1956. "La province de Québec au moment de la grève." In *La grève de l'Amiante*. Montréal: Éditions du jour.
– 1958. "Some Obstacles to Democracy in Quebec." *Canadian Journal of Economics and Political Science* 24: 297–311.
– 1968. *Federalism and the French Canadians*. Toronto: Macmillan.
– 1978. *A Time for Action*. Ottawa: Minister of Supply and Services.
Truman, T. 1977. "A Scale for Measuring a Tory Streak in Canada and the United States." *Canadian Journal of Political Science* 10: 597–614.
Tucker, Robert C. 1973. "Culture, Political Culture and Communist Society." *Political Science Quarterly* 88: 173–90.
Tullock, G. 1970. *Private Wants, Public Means*. New York: Basic Books.
Tully, James. 1994. "The Crisis of Identification: The Case of Canada." *Political Studies* 42: 77–96.
Turgeon, Laurier, Jocelyn Létourneau, and Khadiyatoulah Fall. 1997. *Les espaces de l'identité*. Sainte-Foy: Les Presses de l'Université Laval.
Turner, Bryan S. 1990. "Conclusion: Peroration on Ideology." In Nicholas Abercrombie, Stephen Hill, and Bryan Turner, eds., *Dominant Ideologies*. London: Unwin Hyman.
Turner, Frederick C.. 1995. "Public Opinion and Electoral Behaviour." *International Social Science Journal* 146: 515–24.
Vachon, Robert, and Jacques Langlais, eds. 1979. *Qui est québécois*. Montreal: Éditions Fides.
Van Der Veer, Peter. 1998. "Cultural Politics and the State." *Cultural Dynamics* 10: 281–86.
Venne, Michel, ed.. 2000. *Penser la nation québécoise*. Montréal: Québec Amérique.
Verba, Sidney. 1965. "Comparative Political Culture." In Lucien Pye and Sidney Verba, eds., *Political Culture and Political Development*. Princeton: Princeton University Press.
– 1996. "The Citizen as Respondent: Sample Surveys and American Democracy." *American Political Science Review* 90: 1–7.
– 1997. "The Civic Culture and Beyond: Citizens, Subjects and Survey Research in Comparative Politics." In Hans Daalder, ed., *Comparative European Politics: The Story of a Profession*. London: Pinter.
Verba, Sidney, and Norman Nie. 1972. *Participation in America: Political Democracy and Social Equality*. New York: Harper Row.
Verba, Sidney, Norman H. Nie, and Jae-On Kim. 1978. *Participation and Political Equality: A Seven-Nation Comparison*. New York: Cambridge University Press.

Volunteer Development Scotland. 1998. *Volunteering Matters in Scotland*. Stirling.

Waite, P.B. 1980. "Survivance: Climate, Culture and Quebec." Great-West Life Annual Lecture Series 3, Centre of Canadian Studies, Edinburgh.

Walzer, Michael. 1992. "The New Tribalism: Notes on a Difficult Problem." *Dissent* 39: 164–8.

Webb, Keith. 1977. *The Growth of Nationalism in Scotland*. Harmondsworth: Penguin.

Weber, Max. 1958. *The Protestant Ethic and the Spirit of Capitalism*. New York: Scribner's Press.

Weinfeld, Morton. 1996. "Social Identity in the 1990s." In James Littleton, ed., *Clash of Identities: Media, Manipulation, and Politics of the Self*. Scarborough, Ont.: Prentice-Hall Canada.

Weinstein, Jeremy M. 1999. "Abandoning the Polity: Political Parties and Social Capital in American Politics." Unpublished paper presented at the American Political Science Association Annual Conference.

Welch, Stephen. 1993. *The Concept of Political Culture*. New York: St Martin's Press.

Wells, Paul. 1999. "Identity Doesn't Follow Political Border." *National Post*, 7 April.

Westle, Bettina. 1993. "Changing Aspects of National Identity Germany." In Dirk Berg Scholosser and Ralf Rytlenski, eds., *Political Culture in Germany*. London: Macmillan.

Wetherell, Margaret. 1996a. "Group Conflict and the Social Psychology of Racism." In Margaret Wetherell, ed., *Identities, Groups and Social Issues*. London: Sage.

– ed. 1996b. *Identities, Groups and Social Issues*. London: Sage.

Whitaker, Reg. 1996. "Sovereign Division: Quebec Nationalism between Liberalism and Ethnicity." In James Littleton, ed., *Clash of Identities: Media, Manipulation, and Politics of the Self*. Scarborough, Ont.: Prentice-Hall Canada.

White, Stephen. 1979. *Political Culture and Soviet Politics*. London: Macmillan.

– 1984. "Political Culture in Communist States: Some Problems of Theory and Method." *Comparative Politics* 16: 351–65.

Whitefield, Stephen, and Geoffrey Evans. 1999. "Political Culture versus Rational Choice: Explaining Responses to Transition in the Czech Republic and Slovakia." *British Journal of Political Science* 29: 129–55.

Whittington, Michael S., and Richard J. Van Loon. 1996. *Canadian Government and Politics: Institutions and Processes*. Toronto: McGraw-Hill Ryerson.

Wildavsky, Aaron. 1987. "Choosing Preferences by Constructing Institutions: A Cultural Theory of Preference Formation." *American Political Science Review* 81: 3–21.

Wilson, Andrew. 1999. "Finding the Fast-Track to Independence." *Sunday Times* Lecture, SNP Conference.

Wilson, John. 1974. "Canadian Political Cultures: Towards a Redefinition of the Nature of the Canadian Political System." *Canadian Journal of Political Science* 10: 597–614.

Wilson, Richard. 1992. *Compliance Ideologies: Rethinking Political Culture*. New York: Cambridge University Press.

Wiseman, Nelson. 1988. "A Note on 'Hartz-Horowitz at Twenty': The Case of French Canada." *Canadian Journal of Political Science* 21: 795–806.

Wood, Brennon. 1998. "Stuart Hall's Cultural Studies and the Problem of Hegemony." *British Journal of Sociology* 49: 399–414.

Wood, Richard L. 1997. "Social Capital and Political Culture: God Meets Politics in the Inner City." *American Behavioral Scientist* 40: 595–605.

Woshinsky, Oliver H. 1995. *Culture and Politics: An Introduction to Mass and Elite Political Behavior*. Englewood Cliffs: Prentice Hall.

Wright, James D. 1976. *The Dissent of the Governed: Alienation and Democracy in America*. London: Academic Press.

Young, Robert A. 1999. *The Struggle for Quebec: From Referendum to Referendum?*
Montreal and Kingston: McGill-Queen's University Press.

– 2006. "A Theory of Ethnic Conflict." Paper presented to the European Public Choice Society, Turku, 20 April.

Yuval Davis, Nira. 1997. *Gender and Nation*. London: Sage.

Zapotochny, Joe, ed. 1999. *Scott's Canadian Sourcebook*. Don Mills: Southam.

Zirakzadeh, Cyrus Ernesto. 1997. *Social Movements in Politics: A Comparative Study*. London: Longman.

Index